The Ambition of an Aspie

Best regards
Jay Serdula

"His coach told him to dig down deep, right down to his toes, and pull courage all the way up," she said. "And [his sister], Claire, kept telling him how proud she was of him."

Marilyn Korzekwa M.D., [Swim Master, Solo Swims of Ontario] said this encouragement made Serdula pump faster, but his stroke would eventually fall apart, as it will with exhausted swimmers. But Serdula wasn't giving up. In the last 200 metres, where Serdula struggled the most, Korzekwa said something that pushed Serdula all the way to shore.

"I said 'Do you want me to pull you out of the water?' and he just took off like a bullet!" said Korzekwa.

—[*Kingston This Week, August 1, 2008, used with permission*]

The Ambition of an Aspie

A stroke by stroke account of
one man's swim across Lake Ontario

by Jay Serdula

Kingston, Ontario, Canada

Copyright © 2009 Jay Serdula
All rights reserved.
No part of this publication may be reproduced without the
written consent of the author.

ISBN 978-0-9864839-0-5

A portion of the proceeds from the sale of this book
will be donated to the following:
(www.aspergers.ca) and (www.kerrysplace.org)
– that support people with Asperger's Syndrome;
the Kingston Y Penguins Aquatic Club
– a swimming club for children with physical disabilities
and their able-bodied siblings, coached by marathon swimmer
and Swim Master Vicki Keith: (www.penguinscanfly.ca);
and
Solo Swims of Ontario, Inc.: (soloswims.com/sso.htm).

Design and Layout, Dennis Saunders

Printed and bound in Canada by;
Allan Graphics
170 Binnington Court,
Kingston, Ontario, K7M 8N1

Dedication

To my parents, Kenneth and Ann Serdula, and
my sister, Claire Serdula, for their ongoing love and
support through every swim stroke and each word of this book.
Without their encouragement, my dreams would never have come true.

Contents

Dedication i
Editor's Note vii
Foreword by Vicki Keith.. viii
Foreword by Glenn Rampton... ix
Map.. x
Timeline xi
Preface.. xiii
Acknowledgements xv
Introduction xxiii
List of Characters xxix

Part One – Asperger's Syndrome 1

Chapter 1 – A Synopsis of Asperger's Syndrome 2

Part Two – Becoming an Athlete.................................... 21

Chapter 2 – The Cross-Country Running Team 22
Chapter 3 – Cross-Country Running:
             The Importance of Training 25
Chapter 4 – Gatineau.. 27
Chapter 5 – My First Marathon.. 30
Chapter 6 – Moving to Kingston.. 35
Chapter 7 – The Polar Bear Plunge 38
Chapter 8 – Navs Reunion 2005 41
Chapter 9 – Pushing My Limits 44
Chapter 10 – Navs Reunion 2006 47
Chapter 11 – A Sabbatical From Running 49

Part Three – Training for a Dream.................................. 53

Chapter 12 – The Dream Desire... 54
Chapter 13 – Hypothermia? 59
Chapter 14 – A Risky Adventure 63
Chapter 15 – Embarking on a Training Regime......................... 67
Chapter 16 – How Safe is Safe?... 72
Chapter 17 – Plunges and Open-Water Swimming 2007........... 78
Chapter 18 – Spring 2007 83
Chapter 19 – My First Night Swim 94

Chapter 20	–	Navs Reunion 2007	96
Chapter 21	–	Camp Iawah	99
Chapter 22	–	Chippego Lake	104
Chapter 23	–	Swim for the Cure	112
Chapter 24	–	Starting an Organizational Committee	115
Chapter 25	–	Fall 2007	117
Chapter 26	–	Navy Bay Swim 2007	121
Chapter 27	–	Heartbreaking News	126
Chapter 28	–	Speed Intervals	131
Chapter 29	–	Return to the Gatineau	138
Chapter 30	–	Spring 2008	141
Chapter 31	–	Meeting Pam	151
Chapter 32	–	The Trial Swim	158
Chapter 33	–	Tapering My Training	167
Chapter 34	–	Renting the Boats	170
Chapter 35	–	John C.'s "Discouraging" Opinion	173

Part Four – Crossing Lake Ontario 179

Chapter 36	–	Crossing Lake Ontario – The First Day	180
Chapter 37	–	Crossing Lake Ontario – The Second Day	187
Chapter 38	–	Treatment	197

Part Five – After a Dream Comes True 201

Chapter 39	–	St. Michael's Hospital	202
Chapter 40	–	Recovery	206
Chapter 41	–	What Next?	210

Conclusions 214
Highlights 220
Frequently Asked Questions 225
References 233

Appendices

Appendix A	–	Outline of a Typical Talk Given by Jay	235
Appendix B	–	Excerpt from *Hitchhiking Through Asperger Syndrome* by Lise Pyles	245
Appendix C	–	Infallible IQ Test	246
Appendix D	–	Injuries	247
Appendix E	–	Letter to Aspergers Society of Ontario	252

Appendix F	– Letter to Special Olympics Kingston	254
Appendix G	– Letter to Lois	257
Appendix H	– Ben Wronged Me Three Separate Times	262
Appendix I	– HELP!!	266
Appendix J	– I had a Dream!	269
Appendix K	– The Half-Ironman	271
Appendix L	– Hypothermia	
	– Recognition of Signs and Symptoms	276
Appendix M	– List of Questions (for Rescuer)	277
Appendix N	– Training History	278
Appendix O	– Speed Interval Times	298
Appendix P	– The Big Day	303
Appendix Q	– Swim Master's Report	309

List of Tables

Table 5-1   Marathon training schedule 30
Table 18-1 List of smaller lakes..83
Table 22-1 List of boats and crew for marathon swim at
            Chippego Lake..105
Table 30-1 Lap times for 16-kilometre time trial in Dog Lake.....146
Table 36-1 Crew members..181
Table 37-1 Schedule of kayakers 190
Table 40-1 Treadmill test 209

List of Figures

Figure 16-1 Poster advertising need for volunteer paddlers 77
Figure 31-1 Excerpt from e-mail message from Pam 155

Editor's Note

Q. How did the keyboard get across Lake Ontario?
A. It followed the swimmer every stroke of the way.
—*Chris Cavan*

I was introduced to Jay through a mutual friend, Val Hamilton, in February 2009. Jay was writing a book about his amazing swim across Lake Ontario and needed an editor. I met Jay in person for the first time in March 2009 and we immersed ourselves in the detailed task of editing this book in October. We had one more face-to-face meeting in October, but we've built most of our strong working relationship through the exchange of many phone calls and emails. We've "stroked" through the manuscript line by line, page by page over eight intense weeks. As I edited, my first priority was to ensure that Jay's voice and his intense focus on details – a salient feature of his Asperger's – shines through in the story. Consequently, I used different parameters to edit his manuscript for clarity, coherence, correctness and consistency of communication in order to allow Jay's unique voice to be heard. The way the book is written provides a valuable window into understanding how an Aspie's mind works. I was very conscious as I edited to keep the integrity of this perspective.

Getting to know Jay through interactions and by working so closely with his manuscript has been a very rewarding experience for me. I have great admiration for Jay's tenacity and commitment to his goals. We have compared writing and editing this book to the incredible feat of his swim across Lake Ontario. Although we were warm and dry doing the editing, it was often taxing and required a lot of stamina from both of us. We each had to be totally committed to reaching our goal on time. We have had to push ourselves to the limit during the final weeks as we pored over the text to bring readers our best effort to tell his story in his own words and still meet the tight deadlines.

Jay Serdula is a remarkable person. He is an exceptional role model for young people, especially those who live with Asperger's Syndrome. I hope that you are inspired as you read this awe-inspiring story of Jay's courage and dedication to fulfilling his dream.

Chris Cavan
November 2009

Foreword by Vicki Keith

You've been in the water for hours. The sun is setting and you are about to face Lake Ontario in the frigid, inky darkness. Your arms don't feel like they can go around another cycle, but something deep inside of you keeps pushing. Giving up is not a component of who you are. Failure is not an option you are willing to accept, so you continue to plod forward. Crew members' voices echo through the pitch black murkiness that envelops you, as they encourage you forward. You are beyond exhaustion, but still you persevere.

This is an experience that every marathon swimmer faces; however Jay Serdula faced additional challenges. A natural runner, Jay took up marathon swimming as a second sport. Although swimming isn't as instinctive to him, he set a goal and endeavoured to accomplish it. Most people would think that someone with Asperger's Syndrome would find organizing, planning and completing a lake swim like this an overwhelming ordeal, but I think the Asperger's was an asset to Jay. His intense focus allowed him to think through the process, identify his needs, ask pertinent questions and then focus completely throughout the many challenges he faced in his 41 hour ordeal.

"The Ambition of an Aspie" is not just an insight into the types of challenges that an ultra marathon athlete faces to overcome the many obstacles and challenges they face to achieve their goal, but also it provides an insight into the unique perceptions and perspectives of someone with Asperger's Syndrome.

Vicki Keith

Foreword by Glenn Rampton

Jay Serdula is one of those rare individuals who is able to learn from great adversity and turn it to advantage. Though significantly challenged with the social and sensory effects of Asperger's Syndrome, Jay's accomplishments in his relatively young life so far include: a Masters degree in Physics/Oceanography; a number of significant athletic achievements, including swimming across Lake Ontario; and being elected to the Board of Directors of Kerry's Place Autism Services. In addition to these accomplishments and his employment as a researcher at the Royal Military College of Canada, he has now found time to write and publish this book: another truly remarkable accomplishment.

This book may be of interest to three quite different audiences:

The topic of Autism Spectrum Disorder in general, and Asperger's Syndrome in particular, have recently received much more profile in the popular media; this book will be of interest to the general public as the story of an individual who has accomplished a lot in a social environment that presents difficulties for him. It will also be of interest to professionals, service providers and parents of individuals with ASD to help them understand how their family members or individuals that they support perceive the world. The third group that may profit from this book will be people with ASD themselves. Individuals with Asperger's Disorder, and other individuals with ASD who can read, will be able to use this book to help them develop strategies for dealing with us "neurotypicals" who must often seem so emotional, inconsistent, and unpredictable. People with ASD may also profit if people around them who read the book gain a greater understanding of Asperger's, and if this new understanding leads to more sensitive and appropriate support.

I feel honored to know Jay Serdula and to have had the opportunity to write a foreword to this book. It is truly a book about someone who is "differently abled".

Glenn Rampton, C.D., Ph.D., C.Psych.
C.E.O. and Clinical Director
Kerry's Place Autism Services

Map of Kingston and Area

1. Fairfield Park
2. Lemoine's Point
3. Everett Point
4. Pleasant Point
5. DuPont
6. Carruthers Point
7. Lake Ontario Park
8. Kingston Psychiatric Hospital
9. Portsmouth Olympic Harbour
10. PUC Dock
11. Murney Tower Museum
12. Cataraqui Canoe Club
13. HMCS Cataraqui
14. Fort Frederick & HMCS Ontario
15. Navy Bay
16. Deadman's Bay
17. Knapp Point

Map Created by Peter James McKenty

Timeline of Jay Serdula's Life

1972	Jay was born
June 1991	Jay completed high school
September 1991	Jay began studies at University of Waterloo: Honours co-op Applied Math; Electrical Engineering Electives
May - August 1995	Jay attended a Navigators summer training programme in Calgary
December 1996	Jay completed undergraduate degree at University of Waterloo
May - August 1997	Jay attended another Navigators summer training programme, this time in Ottawa
July 1998	Jay diagnosed with Asperger's Syndrome
July 1999	Jay ran first marathon in Calgary Jay moved to Kingston; began working as civilian research assistant at Royal Military College
September 2000	Jay began a Masters degree in Physics/Oceanography at the Royal Military College
January 2003	Jay completed Masters degree at RMC
July 2006	Jay commits to swimming across Lake Ontario
August 2006	Jay's first long training swim from HMCS Cataraqui to Wolfe Island (5.25 km)
November 2006	Jay joins Kingston Masters Aquatic Club
March 2007	Jay first learned about Kerry's Place Autism Services
March 29, 2007	Jay takes his first plunge of the season
June 2007	Jay gives first speech for Extend-a-Family through Kerry's Place Autism Services

June 23, 2007	Jay's first attempt at point-to-point swim
July 7, 2007	Jay's second attempt at point-to-point swim
July 13-14, 2007	Jay attempts 24-hour swim at Camp Iawah; aborted after 14 hours
July 21-22, 2007	Jay attempts 24-hour swim at Chippego Lake; ended after 19 hours
July 28, 2007	Jay participates in the annual 13 km Swim for the Cure
August 2007	Swim Master Vicki Keith informs Jay of unwritten guideline: 16 km trial swim should be completed in 6 hours
September 22, 2007	Jay's third attempt at point-to-point swim
December 2007	Jay completes first independent set of speed intervals, as suggested by Swim Master Vicki Keith; continues with one set every 2-3 weeks
February 2008	putting off crossing until 2009 is considered due to organizational difficulties; Jay increases speed interval training to once per week
May 2008	Pam agrees to be Jay's swim coach
June 1, 2008	Jay's first training session with Pam
June 22, 2008	Jay's trial swim
July 6, 2008	Jay's fourth attempt at point-to-point swim
July 28-30, 2008	Jay completes his swim across Lake Ontario
August 1, 2008	Jay is discharged from St. Michael's hospital
March 2009	Jay elected to Board of Directors - Kerry's Place Autism Services

Preface

Q. What did the water say to the boat?
A. Nothing. It just waved.
—source unknown

My name is Jay Serdula. This book is an autobiographical account of the events leading up to my swim across Lake Ontario, the swim itself and an account of what happened after my swim. Although I hope that most readers will gain more insight about Asperger's Syndrome as a result of reading this autobiography, the reader should be advised that this book was not written with the intent of providing an overview of Asperger's Syndrome. Therefore, this book is not the most authoritative source for someone who is solely interested in the nature of Asperger's Syndrome and nothing else. Other than the Introduction, Chapter 1, the Frequently Asked Questions section, Appendix A and Appendix B, Asperger's Syndrome is only occasionally mentioned in this book. Nonetheless, Asperger's Syndrome is reflected in the style of the writer.

This book can be divided into five parts:

Part I (Chapter 1) gives a short but detailed overview of Asperger's Syndomre
Part II (Chapters 2-11) describes my life before the idea to swim across Lake Ontario entered my mind
Part III (Chapters 12-35) describes my training to swim across Lake Ontario plus all the events leading up to the swim.
Part IV (Chapters 36-38) describes the actual crossing of Lake Ontario and the treatment that followed immediately afterwards.
Part V (Chapters 39-41) describes the events following the swim across Lake Ontario.

This book is written in chronological order for the most part. Some stories, however, had to be told out of order so that stories of a similar nature could be grouped together. Several chapters stand very well on their own. Which chapter or chapters the reader chooses to read will depend on the reader's interests.

This book is suitable for: those who have already decided they want to swim across Lake Ontario and want some pointers on how to train and/or prepare; those who can't see themselves ever swimming across Lake Ontario but are interested to read the account of someone who has done it; and other people who have completed a similar crossing and would like to read the account of someone else who has done it.

This is, however, not the ideal book for people who are unsure about whether or not they want to swim across Lake Ontario and are hoping to find the information required to make that decision. My case of Asperger's Syndrome enables me to pursue a goal with unwavering focus, but also requires me to filter out all other distractions. Reading this book might give readers the false impression that they must train as diligently as I did in order to be successful. If readers become discouraged when they learn how much time and dedication I invested in this project, please rest assured that my case of Asperger's Syndrome gave me the ability to block out distractions. Once I had my mind set on swimming across Lake Ontario, I would allow *nothing short of death* to stand in the way of achieving my dream.

One final note is in order: What worked for me may not necessarily work for the average person. Conversely, what works for the average person may not have worked for me.

Jay Serdula
October 2009

Acknowledgements

First Race Horse: Don't you remember me?
Second Race Horse: The pace is familiar but I don't remember the mane.
—source unknown

Marathon running is an individual sport whereas marathon swimming is a team sport. I could not have achieved my dream desire of swimming across Lake Ontario alone.

I am very grateful to everyone who contributed to the success of my swim and the publication of this book. I would like to thank the following people, organizations and businesses:

★ Marathon swimmer and Swim Master Vicki Keith, for her constant encouragement, regular advice, faithful and timely replies to my all my email messages and verification of some of the details and terminology in this book. She deserves part of the credit for the success of my swim as I counted on her coaching wisdom: I heeded her sage words of caution and advice because they were always encouraging.

★ Marilyn Korzekwa, for going way over and above her duties to me as my Swim Master. I especially appreciated her swimming the last five hours with me; monitoring my physical condition at all times during the swim; travelling to Kingston to supervise my trial swim; and verifying some of the details and terminology in this book.

★ Pam Haldane, for acting as my coach, encouraging me throughout the crossing, and providing four days of coaching – making a special trip to Kingston on three of the days.

★ John Commerford, for his repeated advice, expertise, and encouragement during the two-year training process, and for taking the photographs on the front and back covers of this book.

★ Kerry's Place Autism Services, for overseeing the event, ensuring an adequate supply of food for me and the crew, arranging transportation for the Swim Master and swim coach to Niagara-on-the-Lake before the swim, and from Toronto back to their homes after the swim.

★ Christine Johnson, for co-ordinating the swim and looking after the boat requirements.

★ Solo Swims of Ontario, Inc., for ensuring the safety of all lake crossings including mine.

★ Jenna Lambert, for inspiring me by her remarkable swim across Lake Ontario.

★ Dr. Brent Lewis, my supervisor, and my employer, the Royal Military College, for allowing me time off work to complete the swim in addition to the flexibility in my working hours during my two years of training for the swim.

★ Don Fulford, John Steer, Doug Moon and Marjorie Adam, for coaching the cross-country running and cross-country ski teams while I was in high school, for accompanying me while running or skiing and, most of all, for encouraging me to take the steps which eventually brought my level of physical activity to where it is now.

★ Long-time friends Karen Jutzi and Peter Wong, for having unwavering faith in my ambition right from the start and for immediately agreeing to be part of the support crew.

★ My parents, Kenneth and Ann Serdula, for accompanying me on my training swims; coming to Kingston to watch my trial swim; driving me from Kingston to Niagara-on-the-Lake; and driving me from Toronto to Deep River and then back to Kingston so I wouldn't have to go on the bus alone. I would like to thank them most of all for keeping vigil over me during my night in the hospital until I woke up five hours after touching land.

★ Claire Serdula for being my big sister, for being concerned for me and for flying all the way from Calgary and leaving her young family behind to watch my swim.

- ★ Pat Probert, for bringing some of my land crew in his boat from Marilyn Bell Park to the flotilla to encourage me, including my sister and mother, who remained with the flotilla after Pat left.

- ★ Eric Weiner, for maintaining my website.

- ★ Eden Cantkier, for recertifying her NLS specifically for my swim – even before I was officially sanctioned by SSO to undertake the crossing.

- ★ Andra Jones, the assistant Swim Master, for her support before and during the crossing.

- ★ Charlene Wilhelm, the nurse during the crossing.

- ★ The people who were part of the support crew, for taking two entire days out of their busy schedules and compromising their sleep in order to look out for my safety, steer me in the right direction and ensure that I was well fed during the 41 hours it took me to cross Lake Ontario.

- ★ The crew members and spectators for filling in many of the details mentioned in this book since I was not able to obtain the details myself.

- ★ Peter Snell, for his willingness to talk to me in great detail about my training and swim across Lake Ontario and for all the invaluable insight and advice he gave me during the rides to and from work. I really appreciate his constant support and encouragement of my dream from the first day I informed him of my desire to swim across Lake Ontario.

- ★ Chris Cavan for editing this manuscript.

- ★ Sharon Jessop-Joyce for assisting with the editing of this manuscript.

- ★ Ann Serdula, Marilyn Korzekwa, Karen Jackson, and Sharon Jessop-Joyce, for giving the book a thorough review and finding obvious errors prior to the submission of the book to Chris Cavan for professional editing.

- ★ Karen Jutzi, Jason Wamboldt, John Perreault, Ann Serdula, and Peter Snell, for taking the photographs shown in book.

- ★ John Perreault, for taking the portrait on the back cover of this book

- ★ Peter James McKenty, for creating the map used in this book

- ★ Ron Abarbanel, for encouraging me to get a diagnosis after earlier attempts had failed when I was younger.

- ★ Progress Fitness Centre, for providing me with the complimentary use of their facilities while I trained for the crossing of Lake Ontario.

- ★ Trish Hawkes and Andrew Jones, for coaching me at the Kingston Masters Aquatic Club during my training regime.

- ★ The more than one hundred people who accompanied me in a canoe or kayak or who swam beside me during my training swims. Special mention goes to:
  - ★ John Commerford, who paddled beside me during my training swim at night in Lake Ontario.
  - ★ Jens Frandsen, who put his life at risk when he paddled beside me in rough water at the end of September. Despite capsizing the kayak, Jens still agreed to paddle beside me again the following year.
  - ★ Sara Hay, who despite never having been in a canoe before, paddled beside me for 6 hours during my 19-hour swim at Chippego Lake and again in Lake Ontario in 4-foot waves.
  - ★ Mike Bird and Alex Mundy, who managed to keep a canoe near me for three hours in four-foot waves.
  - ★ Sara Lavigne, who was vigilant in case I went into hypothermia when I crossed Wolfe Lake and offered me a spare sweatshirt when I absent-mindedly thought I could ride back in the canoe wearing only a Speedo.
  - ★ The RMC sea cadets, who paddled beside me four times during their six-week stay and, if I had asked, would undoubtedly have done so more often.
  - ★ Ashley Kayla Sagan, eight years old at the time and the youngest of all my paddling volunteers, who canoed beside me with her father, Greg Sagan.

- ★ Richard Cadman, his wife Laurie Ross, and his children Robert and Sarah, for opening up their home to me and allowing me to swim in Dog Lake during my training swims; for providing shower facilities; and for preparing meals for me and my paddling volunteers after my swim.

- ★ Catriona Jackson, for accompanying me on my speed intervals and walking me through the Total Immersion drills.

- ★ Thomas Peters, for shuttling the volunteer paddlers back and forth during my point-to-point swims.

- ★ Ewen and Sharon Mackenzie, for giving me permission to start my point-to-point training swims from their property and letting me store my kayak at their house the night before the training swim.

- ★ Ken and Jean Crawford, for the use of their cottage during the weekend of my 19-hour swim at Chippego Lake.

- ★ Joan and Earl Shaw, for hosting all of the paddling volunteers.

- ★ Heather Shaw, for overseeing the meals and transportation for all the helpers for my 19-hour swim in Chippego Lake.

- ★ Camp Iawah, for giving me permission to do a training swim in Wolfe Lake and providing canoes, paddles, lifejackets and other safety equipment.

- ★ Emily Garrett and Emily Filipcic, for assisting in the coordination of the marathon swim at Camp Iawah.

- ★ Everyone who helped with the trial swim, including:
  - ★ Kristine Mattson, my co-worker, and her husband Collin Mosier, for providing the use of a powerboat for the trial swim.
  - ★ Alicia Walton, John Commerford, Marilyn Korzekwa, Shannon Nudds, and Ann Serdula, for paddling beside me during the trial swim.
  - ★ Kenneth Serdula, for driving the power boat occupants back to the marina after the breakdown of the powerboat.
  - ★ Loyalist Cove Marina in Bath, for the use of their shower and other facilities and for rescuing the stranded powerboat.

- ★ All the spectators who were present at Loyalist Cove Marina before and after the trial swim in order to show their support.

★ My coworkers, especially Kim Sampson, Kristine Mattson and Michelle Boudreau, for caring about my safety, including cautioning me about cold-water swimming.

★ Everyone on the organizational committee. Special mention goes to:
  - ★ Jess Foran, for heading the media and promotions subcommittee.
  - ★ Oliver Holmes and Megan Carrigan, for heading the fundraising subcommittee.
  - ★ Louise Frink, for heading the volunteer recruitment subcommittee.
  - ★ Susan Sampson, for heading the hospitality subcommittee that reserved Marilyn Bell Park and organized the Fun Day.
  - ★ John Commerford, for assuming role of coordinating the swim until he was unable to do so because of unfortunate circumstances beyond his control.

★ Everyone who helped organize and host the Fun Day at Marilyn Bell Park.

★ Susan Sampson, my cousin, and her husband Cortney Sampson, for hosting a reunion for all the relatives the night before the swim and for making a pasta supper.

★ All the spectators and supporters who drove along the rough road to Vicki Keith Point at the tip of Leslie Street Spit to keep vigil for six hours while waiting for me to finish my swim – especially my father, Kenneth Serdula, who held an armful of blankets for several hours.

★ Ileen Kennedy, for repeatedly sending food to me while I was in the hospital to help replenish lost nutrients during the swim.

★ Special Olympics Kingston, for letting me attend two of their monthly meetings and taking the time to discuss my requirements for boats for the crossing as well as volunteer-paddlers for the training sessions.

- ★ All the sponsors – individual sponsors, as well as corporate sponsors.

- ★ Bay Port Yachting Club, for selling the Zodiacs at a discount price.

- ★ Frontenac Outfitters, for supplying canoes and kayaks that people used to paddle beside me during my early-season training swims.

- ★ Precious Lady Charters, for renting the boats *Precious Lady* and *Formula One* to us which were used for the crossing.

If I have inadvertently forgotten any person, organization or business, please accept my gratitude.

Introduction

"Physical fitness is a journey – not a destination."
—source unknown

    I learned to swim when I was seven. That was considered a late age, given that I lived within walking distance of a river and I grew up in a small town where everyone knew everyone else. Even though no one ridiculed me for not being able to swim, everyone got involved in the same activities (in this case, swimming lessons) and those who couldn't swim felt left out. Interestingly, not much changed with my swimming during the entire time period between my first triathlon, which was in 1990, and the day before I set the goal to swim across Lake Ontario: I could swim, could get from point A to point B, and could tread water without using my hands. However, I'd swim only in triathlons or for enjoyment; I hardly did any pool swimming but would simply wait until the river warmed up and then swim only in the summer. As soon as I set the goal, I became obsessed with thoughts of swimming and immediately started preparing mentally, although it took some time for my actions to follow. At this time, my longest swim without touching bottom was about three kilometres.

    I used to have a tendency to want to do the least amount of work possible. For example, when I was in grade school, I blindly assumed that everyone had to go to university. A number of years later, my mother, who had grown up in a family of ten, told me that only she and two of her siblings had attended university. I immediately decided when I heard this news that I wouldn't go to university but would become either a postman or a farmer, because those jobs don't require a university education.

    I used to be afraid to try new things. For example, every day throughout the summer, children my age would go to the beach and line up to go down the slide. I'd be afraid to do so and, once in a while, I'd feel disappointed with myself for not having tried the slide. Now I push the opposite extreme and am on the lookout for challenges.

    Not always was I as physically active as I am now; becoming physically active was a gradual process and resulted largely from encouragement from my parents, my sister, and my coaches from the high school cross-country running and cross-country skiing team. Many times, I told myself – and others – that it felt great to be in shape. After I had been physically active for a few years through cross-country

The Ambition of an Aspie

skiing, cross-country running and cycling (plus being able to swim well enough to complete a triathlon), I was happy with my life but I had no idea what I was missing - until I decided that I wanted to swim across Lake Ontario. I knew for some time that my swimming had potential for improvement – lots of potential for improvement – but I had never had an incentive to improve my swimming.

When I was in grade twelve, my parents showed me the movie Rain Man and, immediately afterwards told me that I had a lot of the same characteristics as the main character (but to a much lesser degree) and therefore I might be autistic. This was my first time hearing the term "autistic" and I had almost completed university before I heard the term "Asperger's Syndrome". I thought people would view autism as a handicap and would look down on me. Therefore, I tried not to let people know that I was autistic and I thought my best chance was to bluff my way through situations (i.e. hide the fact that I might be autistic). With any luck, I'd be able to appear "normal" and hide my handicap long enough for people to accept me.[1] Perhaps this was a carryover from grade school when classmates would take advantage of me.

> *"Autistic children are often tormented and rejected by their classmates simply because they are different and stand out from the crowd. Thus, in the playground or on the way to school one can often see an autistic child at the centre of a jeering horde of little urchins. The child himself may be hitting out in blind fury or crying helplessly. In either case he is defenceless."*
> —Hans Asperger ([1944] 1981) [Attwood, 2007, pg. 95]

When I first found out that I had Asperger's Syndrome, that knowledge didn't change my life in any noticeable way. I had already completed university and found a job and learned how to make friends. I had learned to cope with my differences and make changes accordingly. Interestingly, in order to get diagnosed I had to know the name of the syndrome or disorder that I have. When I contacted the Royal Ottawa Hospital, the receptionist basically said, "Tell me what your diagnosis is and I'll try to find you a psychiatrist who is a specialist in that area."

---

[1] A generation ago, before Asperger's Syndrome had a name, trying to appear normal was considered the "best" thing to do. See http://community.livejournal.com/ask_an_aspie/877.html (June 20, 2008 posting).

Occasionally, I would tell someone that I have Asperger's Syndrome but only after I felt that I could trust the other person and only after I had known that person long enough to feel comfortable; seldom would I tell someone on the first day of meeting him/her and never within the first five minutes. The tables turned when I decided that Asperger's Syndrome would be the designated charity for my swim; I had to tell people that I have Asperger's Syndrome in order to use my swim to raise awareness about and fundraise for Asperger's Syndrome.

In grade six, I asked for a set of weights for my birthday, and then I started to lift weights regularly. I wanted to be able to defend myself physically if someone tried to beat me up. If I were more muscular and athletic, I reasoned, people would be less likely to pick on me in the first place. In high school, I went to the weight room almost every day after school. In grade eleven, this routine gradually got displaced by cross-country running and cross-country skiing.

In grade eight, in the boys' change room after phys. ed. class, one of my classmates picked up my pencil case and threw it to someone else who threw it to another person. Each time, I tried to reach for the pencil case and the others enjoyed watching my reaction. It's safe to assume that only two or three people decided to bully me in this way and the rest of them went along with the game for fear of standing out. This tormenting went on for a few minutes when, luckily for me, but unfortunately for the others, the teacher came in and firmly said, "Give him the pencil case." This was not the only time that my classmates ganged up on me by throwing one of my belongings back and forth. Nonetheless, what I went through in grade school was a walk in the park compared to what others have gone through, in particular the son of Lise Pyles. For a brief overview of some of the things that Lise Pyles's son went through, see Appendix B.

My classmates would often pick on me because I was different. Even in the best case scenario, if some classmates had a sincere desire to help me and resolved to stick by me no matter what, they might think that I was choosing to break the rules. They wouldn't realize that I am, by nature, slower than the average person at picking up social cues.

For the last several years, I have been working at a steady job. I can support myself financially and have a vast network of friends. I am past the initial handicaps that come with Asperger's Syndrome. Looking back at those years makes me want to help make the childhood years more bearable for younger people living with Asperger's Syndrome. I feel for children who are going through what

I went through as a child. I feel not only for the children but for the adults as well who may be struggling to maintain friends or find a job.

If I could only give one piece of advice to someone with Asperger's Syndrome, it would be: "Get good at something - ideally physical activity." This is poor motivation if you're doing it strictly on my advice since it will take time for the results to show and you might become discouraged. It is much more motivating if an Aspie focuses on physical activity as a means of getting or staying in shape. The subsequent recognition by classmates and friends is reward enough when the Aspie becomes an accomplished athlete or a model of fitness and good health.

Aspies tend to "dwell" on things. This can be good as well as bad for me. It is bad in that I fixate on things that don't really matter, but can be good because I can persevere. When I was eighteen months old, I worked on jigsaw puzzles with remarkable perseverance. My sister, who is two years older than I am, would not touch the puzzles at the time. My father concluded then and there that I was capable of accomplishing anything if I put my mind to it. His biggest concern was that I might put my mind on the wrong thing. My father concluded that I could even rob a bank if I put my mind to it.

A lot of my friends can put in a full day at work, eat supper, and then finish their income tax in the remainder of the evening. I have not found this to be the case; I have to look through all my receipts (I keep them all in the same place), let my thoughts settle for a while and then remind myself exactly what I'm supposed to do. It gets easier each year, but marginally so. It takes me two or three days to attain the focus required to complete my income tax. Until I'm really focused, I have to take many breaks. Once I have my focus, I can stay focused for several hours without a break.

It takes me longer than the average person to get my mind in the right gear, but once my mind is focused on the task, I am capable of great accomplishments. In general, Aspies are less likely to succeed than non-Aspies on a two hour project (such as completing their income tax) but more likely to succeed on a two year project (such as swimming across Lake Ontario) because, once they are focused, they are able to retain their focus and make that project their whole lives.

When I was in grade five, my family purchased a VIC 20 (yes, I am old enough to remember when this was the typical household computer). These were the days when computers were hooked up to the TV screen and everything was saved on cassette tapes; diskettes were not common and disk drives were more expensive than the computer itself. We subscribed to a once-a-month magazine which contained the code for several computer programs. More than once, when my father was watching TV, I asked if I could program on the computer. A few days later, I finished typing in the program (I didn't do it all at once). When I finished the program, it didn't work so I quit (i.e. I thought it was too much of a bother to find my errors). My father gently put pressure on me to verify that I had entered the code correctly. At the time, I thought my father was being unreasonable and it seemed that, once I undertook the task of entering the code into the computer, I wasn't allowed to do anything else until the program worked. I overlooked the fact that he had made a compromise (at my request) to give up a TV program. I failed to see my father's point of view even after he said calmly, "I won't let you program on the computer when I'm watching TV (if you're going to quit that easily)." In hindsight, the sensible thing to do would have been to work my schedule around my father's schedule. Quitting an undertaking is one thing but asking others to go out of their way to help you and then quitting is something else. This could very well be an example which helped "train" me not to undertake a project unless I was sure I could follow through.

If I had quit my dream desire of swimming across Lake Ontario because I went into hypothermia (or even near-hypothermia) on one of my training swims, or because I came close to drowning and couldn't make it to shore without floatational assistance, or my supporters and I all agreed that it was best to discontinue this undertaking, my volunteers would have understood. But if I had quit because it was too much work or required too much training time, a lot of my paddling volunteers, who had graciously volunteered their time to paddle beside me while I swam, would have felt cheated. This form of accountability helped me, without knowing it, make a resolution to do everything within my power to make my dream happen – which meant giving it 100 percent of maximum.

At University of Waterloo, I found one term so stressful that, instead of going on a work term the following term, I took the summer off to attend the Navigators summer program in Calgary. There, I delivered flyers for twelve hours a week plus mowed someone's lawn once a week. I found that summer a lot less stressful than any school term or work term I had done. I was not anxious to go back to university and, when I did go back, I told one of my friends, whose opinion I trusted, that I was thinking about quitting university and getting a job in the physical labour force.

He replied, "If you're truly convinced that you belong in the physical labour force, then quit. But don't quit university just because it's too difficult. If you do, you'll want to quit a job in the physical labour force as soon as it gets difficult."

I got over my feelings and did complete the degree.

I enjoyed open-water swimming even before my first triathlon; otherwise, I wouldn't have kept doing triathlons. Even though swimming in a pool is faster than swimming in open water (except when there is a current flowing in the right direction) and the pool is safer and more controlled, I find that I have more freedom in open-water. I still enjoy pool swimming, just not as much as open-water swimming. For this reason, foregoing a training swim in the summer "because I didn't feel like it" was seldom an issue.

List of Characters, Organizations and Other Terms

Access Bar – an energy bar produced solely by Melaleuca, designed to inhibit the production of adenosine and therefore help increase one's tolerance to cold water

Al – loaner of canoe

Alex – volunteer paddler

Alicia – volunteer paddler, kayaker on trial swim

Amy – Colorado '96 Navs participant

Andra – part-time employee of KPAS, assistant Swim Master

Andrew – KMAC coach

Ann Serdula – Jay's mother, kayaker on trial swim

Artillery Park – see Royal Artillery Park

Ashley – volunteer paddler

ASO – Asperger's Society of Ontario

Aspie – a person with Asperger's Syndrome

Ben – Colorado '96 Navs participant, Ottawa '97 Navs participant

Bill – volunteer for Special Olympics

Brandon L. and Cynthia – loaner of canoe

Brandon S. – volunteer paddler

Brent – Jay's supervisor

Catriona – co-worker, swimmer and volunteer paddler; accompanied Jay on many of his speed interval sets in the pool

Chantal – Ottawa '97 Navs participant, Gunnar's wife

Charlene – nurse on crossing

Christine (Chris) Johnson – Executive Regional Director for KPAS, Jay's swim co-ordinator

Chris – motorboat driver encountered on night swim

Chris Shaw – Heather Shaw's husband

Claire – Jay's sister

Colleen K. – volunteer paddler, member of organizational committee

Colleen Shields – Swim Master

Dave D. – United Way representative for RMC

Dave K. – volunteer paddler

Debbie – organizer of the annual Swim for the Cure

Dog Lake – a shallow lake located near Battersea, created when the Rideau Canal system was built

Earl – Heather Shaw's father-in-law, host for Jay's marathon swim at Chippego Lake

Eden – pacer on crossing, lifeguard on crossing, currently employed as a Program Supervisor for the Ministry of Children and Youth Services, former employee of KPAS

Emily F. – volunteer paddler, Camp Iawah summer staff worker

Emily G. – volunteer paddler, Camp Iawah summer staff worker, in charge of boathouse at Camp Iawah

Eric – webmaster

Ewen – Sharon's husband, Jay's friend, at whose home Jay commenced some of his point-to-point swims

Formula One – a 33 foot cigar boat with twin gas motors, used as the evacuation boat for Jay's crossing

Frank Kennedy – Jay's uncle, Ileen Kennedy's husband

Frontenac Outfitters – one of Canada's largest on-the-water canoe-and-kayak retail store, located 10 kilometres north of Sydenham and 30 kilometres north of Kingston[2]

Mr. Fulford – Jay's high school cross-country running coach

Gatineau Park – a national park in Quebec popular for cross-country skiing, named after a city on the Quebec shore of Ottawa

---

[2] www.frontenac-outfitters.com

List of Characters, Organizations and Other Terms

Gatineau Loppet – an annual cross-country ski race[3] held in Gatineau Park, formerly known as the Gatineau 55 followed by the Keskinada Loppet

George – volunteer paddler

Gord – zodiac driver on crossing

Greg – volunteer paddler

Gunnar – Ottawa '97 Navs participant, Colorado '96 Navs participant, Chantal's husband

Guy – volunteer paddler

Heather Shaw – volunteer paddler, Chris Shaw's wife, co-ordinator for attempted 24-hour swim in Chippego Lake

HMCS Cataraqui – Her Majesty Canadian Ship, located on the Cataraqui River

HMCS Ontario – Her Majesty Canadian Ship, located on Lake Ontario on the RMC peninsula

Camp Iawah – a year-long camp which holds week-long camps for youth throughout the summer, acronym for "In All Ways Acknowledge Him"

Ileen Kennedy – Jay's aunt, Frank Kennedy's wife

Jacquie – volunteer paddler

James – co-worker

Jason – volunteer paddler

Jane – volunteer paddler, kayaker on swim across Navy Bay

Jean – swimmer, assistant coach; accompanied Jay on some of his speed interval sets in the pool

Jenna Lambert – marathon swimmer whose successful crossing of Lake Ontario inspired Jay to undertake the crossing

Jennifer – co-worker

Jens – volunteer paddler, Jay's former roommate from University of Waterloo

---

[3] http://www.gatineauloppet.com

Jess – volunteer paddler, head of media/promotions subcommittee

Joan – Heather Shaw's mother-in-law, hostess for Jay's marathon swim at Chippego Lake

Jo Ann – Jay's volunteer paddler for the Swim for the Cure

Joe – professor at RMC, repeated source of advice

John C. – volunteer paddler, kayaker on trial swim, Jay's original swim co-ordinator

John P. – zodiac driver on crossing, Ottawa '97 Navs participant

Karen – pacer on crossing, Colorado '96 Navs participant, Ottawa' 97 Navs participant

Kathy – department head of RMC Chemical Engineering Department

Kelly – volunteer paddler

Ken Franklin – Jay's Christian mentor, youth leader

Kenneth Serdula – Jay's father

Keskinada Loppet – former name for the Gatineau Loppet

Kingston Velo Club – a club of cyclists who meet once or twice a week during the summer months for long-distance bicycle rides in the greater Kingston area[4]

KMCSC – Kingston Military Community Sports Centre (a.k.a. base gym), located across the street from the Royal Military College

KPAS – Kerry's Place Autism Services

Kim – co-worker

KMAC – Kingston Masters Aquatic Club

Kristine – co-worker, volunteer paddler and provider of the motorboat for the trial swim

Leslie Street Spit – an artificial piece of land which protrudes out from the Eastern gap entrance to Toronto Harbour

Lois – volunteer paddler, educational assistant

---

[4] www.kvc.ca

List of Characters, Organizations and Other Terms

Louise – volunteer paddler, head of volunteer-recruitment sub-committee, coach for Special Olympics swim team

Luke – Jens's brother, Jay's volunteer paddler for the Swim for the Cure

Marc – Claire's friend, athlete, and noticeably fast cross-country skier

Margot – executive director of ASO

Marilyn – Jay's Swim Master, kayaker on trial swim, kayaker on crossing, secretary for SSO, and Medical Doctor

Marilyn Bell Park – the park in Toronto which is the planned finish site for the majority of the swims across Lake Ontario

Marsha Abarbanel – Ron Abarbanel's wife, University of Waterloo Navs staff member, Calgary '95 Navs staff member, Ottawa '97 Navs staff member

Megan – KPAS summer student, head of the fundraising subcommittee

Michael – volunteer paddler, Camp Iawah summer staff worker

Michelle – co-worker

Mike Bird – volunteer paddler

Mount Martin – a mountain, actually a hill, but the highest one in the vicinity, on the Quebec shore of the Ottawa River across from Deep River

Nate – volunteer paddler

Navigators – an interdenominational Christian club at various universities across Canada

Navs – abbreviation for Navigators

Nicola – friend from Calgary, source of advice

NLS – National Lifeguard Service

Oliver – volunteer paddler, volunteer for Special Olympics, original head of the fundraising subcommittee

Pam – Jay's swim coach

Pat – owner of Margaritaville boat

Peter Snell – neighbour, gives Jay a ride to work during winter months, a good conversationalist plus source of advice

Peter V. – Camp Iawah employee

Peter Wong – volunteer paddler, kayaker on crossing, Ottawa' 97 Navs participant

Phil – co-worker

Precious Lady – a 68 foot boat with twin diesel motors, used as the lead boat for Jay's crossing

Progress Fitness Centre – a privately owned fitness centre in Kingston

PUC[5] dock – a dock located on Lake Ontario at the water purification plant, a common landmark for open-water swims

Rej – co-worker

Richard C. – triathlon coach, resident on Dog Lake

RMC – Royal Military College

Rob – volunteer paddler, kayaker on crossing

Ron Abarbanel – Marsha Abarbanel's husband, University of Waterloo Navs staff member, Calgary '95 Navs staff member, Ottawa '97 Navs staff member

Royal Artillery Park – the building containing the only municipal indoor swimming pool in Kingston

SAIT – Southern Alberta Institute of Technology

Sara H. – volunteer paddler

Sara L. – volunteer paddler, Camp Iawah summer staff worker

Shannon – volunteer paddler, kayaker on trial swim

Sharon – Ewen's wife, Jay's friend, at whose home Jay commenced some of his point-to-point swims

Solo Swims of Ontario[6] – a volunteer-driven organization which oversees and ensures the safety of marathon swims across lakes where the distance swum exceeds ten miles

Special Olympics – an organization that provides sport training and competition for people with intellectual disabilities

---

[5] PUC stands for Public Utilities Commission
[6] http://soloswims.com/sso.htm

List of Characters, Organizations and Other Terms

SSO – Solo Swims of Ontario, Inc.

Steve L. – the team leader for the team of Directors at Camp Iawah

Steve S. – volunteer paddler

Swim for the Cure[7] – an annual fundraiser for breast cancer, in which participants swim 13 kilometres in the Severn River from Swift Rapids to Big Chute, either individually or as a relay

Summerfest – a four-day arts, entertainment and sporting festival in Deep River that happens bi-annually on the August long weekend

Susan – Jay's cousin, head of the hospitality subcommittee

Thomas – volunteer paddler, provider of shuttle service for other volunteer paddlers on my point-to-point swims

Tim – volunteer paddler

Tracy – volunteer paddler

Trish – KMAC coach

Vicki Keith – marathon swimmer, Swim Master, and long time source of advice and encouragement

Vicki Keith Point – the tip of Leslie Street Spit

Youth Group – a Christian-oriented group that meets for bible study, prayer, and games once a week

---

[7] www.swimforthecure.ca

Part One

Asperger's Syndrome

Chapter 1

A Synopsis of Asperger's Syndrome: Features of Aspergers with Personal Anecdotes and Comments

"I'm a bit of an abstract figure that people can project their fantasies on; it's pretty much what we all are, otherwise we wouldn't be stars, and people wouldn't be interested. But people project things on you that have nothing to do with what you really are, or they see a little something and then exaggerate it. And you can't really control that."

—Salma Hayek

Overview of Chapter

This chapter is an overview of my own life.[8] In this chapter, I note the general features of Asperger's Syndrome. The comments and examples, however, concern specific manifestations for my particular case of Asperger's. Each person who has Asperger's has unique perspectives and distinctly different ways of coping with the Syndrome. Some of the characteristics I mention in this chapter may be applicable to anyone, but they are more pronounced/prevalent in Aspies like me.

Intelligence, Asperger's and Autism

Asperger's Syndrome lies at the upper end of the autism spectrum. Although similar to high-functioning autism, it is *not* the same. By definition, people with Asperger's Syndrome have average to above-average intelligence [*Pyles, 2002*] and do not have delayed onset of language, as people with Autism tend to do. A comprehensive summary of Asperger's Syndrome is given in several books, including *Hitchhiking through Asperger Syndrome* by Lise Pyles. Instead of condensing her descriptions, or anyone else's, I will refer the reader to a few sources. I will describe Asperger's Syndrome according to what I know about it, based on knowledge mostly obtained through my personal experience.

---

[8] An alternate overview is given in the section on How Asperger's Syndrome affects me in Appendix A.

The Social Realm

If people with Asperger's Syndrome have at least average intelligence, where does the problem lie? The diagnostic criteria for the syndrome state that Asperger's includes deficits in social comprehension, behaviour and communication. In practical terms, this includes following rules, and reading and understanding non-verbal communication signals, such as other people's vocal inflections and facial expressions. In the social realm, grey areas are ubiquitous. Misperceptions and unusual reactions occur because following a certain social rule may be mandatory in one setting but totally inappropriate in another setting. When trying too hard to obey one rule, the Aspie will often break another rule. The fact of the matter is that most Aspies are completely capable of learning social rules, etiquette, and picking up on social cues; it just takes longer for Aspies than for average people.

The best way to learn right from wrong is by example. If the people around me (be they classmates, teachers, co-workers, etc.) are patient with me, I will learn the rules eventually and then these people are even more likely to accept me into their circle of friends. On the contrary, if they give up on me and conclude that I'm incapable of learning the rules or else conclude that teaching me the rules is more hassle than it is worth, they won't want to spend time with me. The net result is that I will be socially isolated and may instead associate with other people who don't know how to behave. I may learn bad habits from them and may be even less likely to be accepted into a circle of friends. This can result in a Catch-22 situation or a vicious cycle that traps Aspies in negative social interactions.

The Problem is Recognizing the Problem

People with Asperger's Syndrome often don't understand or value social conventions and therefore have problems dealing with other people, including peers and authority figures, such as teachers and doctors. However, the problems seem to "disappear" as soon as the other people make an attempt to deal with a problem. For example, a doctor begins an appointment with an Aspie thinking *This person has a problem. I will find out what the problem is and do what I can to help him or her fix it*, then there is no problem – or so it seems – because the Aspie's communication is much smoother when the Aspie is prepared for the encounter, it takes place one-to-one, rather than in a group, and the doctor has the Aspie's best interests in mind. It's only when the Aspie is forced to interact with people without this kind of consideration that problems manifest themselves. This leaves the person with Asperger's Syndrome caught in a conundrum.

> *"The really frustrating thing is that our kids often don't display their social deficits in the doctor's office. As wrong-footed as our kids are among their peers, they frequently are able to hold wonderful conversations with doctors, who often find our kids charming. It's almost funny (or it would be if it weren't an expensive time-waster) that many inexperienced doctors reject a diagnosis of Asperger's Syndrome because the child is too sociable and talkative. In my mind's eye, I picture a doctor saying, 'He seems fine to me' and then I picture the doctor's own young son spending a few minutes with the patient, tugging at his daddy's sleeve and whispering, 'What's up with that kid?' Our kids can be quite sociable, just ineptly so. It's just one reason why you should make sure that any doctor who sees your child really understands Asperger's Syndrome."* [Pyles, 2002, pg. 37]

Some people, apparently even psychiatrists, think that people with Asperger's Syndrome find it difficult or impossible to make friends – and subsequently draw the conclusion that someone who has friends does not have Asperger's Syndrome. Nothing could be further from the truth. (See http://community.livejournal.com/ask_an_aspie/2715.html (entry from July 29, 2008) for a counter-example.)

Difficulty Discerning When People Are Joking

I have difficulty reading facial expressions so, in order to discern when people are joking, I tend to rely on the context at large. In general, people know their friends and acquaintances well enough to discern whether they are joking or serious. I don't catch onto such cues as quickly as the average person.

In a grade ten geography class, the teacher gave us an "Infallible IQ Test". (See Appendix C.) I had blindly assumed that the "test" would count towards our mark and I couldn't get any of the questions except the first one. I thought I'd be in trouble but I had hope because:

a. the teacher had a smile on his face;
b. Noah's ark is spelled 'ark' not 'arc'; and

c. the title said "infallible"; I thought this meant that the test was 'impossible to fail'.
I concluded that maybe there weren't any answers.

The Need to Be Left Alone

Sometimes I don't want to talk and want to be left alone. This is true for all introverts, since introverts often get their energy from being alone. However, once I start talking, it's difficult to get me to stop. Talking about myself and having someone to listen to me unload my thoughts helps me to recharge my batteries – but only if I've had ample time to first think about what I want to say.

I tend to "get in the driver's seat" by telling jokes. I have worn people out with my jokes so I try not to tell too many jokes at once. The general rule I make is to tell a maximum of one joke per person per day[9] with the exception that, no more than once a week, I'm allowed to tell two jokes if they're short and go together. For example:

Q. Why did the strawberry call 911?
A. It was in a jam.

Q. Why did the cucumber call 911?
A. It was in a pickle.

Whenever there are three people in a room, more often than not it is the other two people who dominate the conversation. I have trouble understanding the conversation so it takes me longer to learn the assumptions on which the conversation is based. When there are only two people in the room, the other person has to make sure I follow most of the implicit assumptions.

Many times, I have been in a room full of people without taking part in the conversation. People start asking me questions or making comments and I feel forced to participate. They think that they're being considerate by including me in the conversation. I feel like they're forcing me to be part of the conversation when I'd prefer to have space. For obvious reasons, I would find it awkward to ask, "Do I have to hide my face in order to get my space?" Hiding my face would make me seem antisocial. Those around me might not realize that I'm

---

[9] The guideline to set a maximum of one joke per person per day is suitable for Peter Snell, whom I associate with for fifteen minutes a day every day while he drives me to work but not suitable for people like my sister whom I see all day every day for one week but only once or twice per year.

content to relax. In the lunch room where I work, there is a large group of people who are younger than I. They almost never talk to me, not even to say "Hello", unless I speak to them first. But they will listen if I talk to them. This is actually what I want. Because I often have people around me, I don't have a habit of being antisocial. I started telling jokes to these people in the lunch room but limited myself to one joke per day.

While at the University of Waterloo, I went home about once every four months. I always go to church and it seemed that each time I went, there was a new person at the service. Conversations like the one below would often take place after church:

"Where are you going to school?"
"University of Waterloo."
"What are you taking?"
"Applied math."
"And you're just home for the weekend?"
"I'm on co-op at Waterloo so I alternate between four months of school and four months of work."
"Where have some of your work terms been?"

All of the above-mentioned questions had specific answers but, nonetheless, I'd think, "The sooner this person stops asking me questions, the better." I didn't want to tell them this, for the following reasons that include, but are not limited to:

- I didn't want to imply that I don't ever want them to ask me questions.
- When situations like this happen too many times, I get overwhelmed.
- I don't bother asking the other person any questions because I am face-blind. This means I can meet people a number of times and not remember their features, a common and frustrating challenge for Aspies. Therefore, I will not likely remember that person the next time we meet at church.

What really drains my energy is when I am "cross-examined", i.e., when two or more people ask me questions and their frames of reference are very different. I have a very difficult time following conversations that involve more than one other person. When a number of people ask different questions that I'm expected to answer, I have trouble figuring out their points of view. I often answer one person's question from a completely different angle than the listeners were expecting. They think I'm off on a tangent and this gives them the opportunity to ask even more questions than they would otherwise have thought to ask. I feel like I'm in a pinball machine of questions so I get very confused, exhausted and just want to be alone.

While I was unemployed, I often went to Toronto for a week to stay with my aunt and uncle. It was 1997-98 during the high-tech boom and I thought I would have a better chance at finding a good job in a larger city. My relatives had a friend my age who came over for supper every Wednesday. Every time this friend came over, he and my aunt and uncle would ask me questions about how my job search was going. This drained my energy faster than a double dose of questions asked by any one of them individually. It was so difficult for me to be in the middle of this confusion that I resorted to going out for supper on Wednesdays.

Explanations Require Energy

With my case of Asperger's Syndrome, I process my thoughts differently than most neurotypicals. It's often difficult for me to explain my reasons – and for other people to understand my explanations – simply because I'm different. This doesn't necessarily mean that one method is right and the other method is wrong, but it does mean I have to translate my terms into other people's terms, which takes time and effort. We all have our own reasons for doing something. Often, explaining my reasons is more hassle than it's worth. On many occasions, I'm tempted to give in and do things another person's way because that is less of a disturbance than explaining why I am doing things my way. Therefore, I'd prefer to do things a certain way without explaining why.

Bullies Under the Radar

"Another act of bullying is to torment the child with Asperger's syndrome (ensuring that a teacher does not detect the provocation) and enjoy the benefits of the child's reaction. Children with Asperger's syndrome can be impulsive in their response to such goading without thinking of the consequences to themselves. Other young children in the same situation would delay their response so as not to be 'caught', or would recognize how to respond without getting into trouble. When the child with Asperger's syndrome retaliates with anger to this provocation, perhaps causing damage or injury, the covert 'operative' appears to be the innocent victim, and receives compensation from the supervising adult.

Covert bullying, because of the havoc that often ensues, can also be used to avoid a class activity or examination. When I was examining the circumstances regarding several disruptive classroom incidents involving a child with Asperger's syndrome, I was told by the child's classmates that they encouraged his emotional outbursts. Since the teacher would then be preoccupied with taking the child to the school principal for punishment, they could successfully avoid having to do a class test or exam." [Attwood, 2007, pp. 97-98]

Good Role Models Are Essential

Here are two examples that explain why Asperger's Syndrome children need good role models growing up:

Children and young adults who have Asperger's should not be sent to schools for children who have problems with behaviour. A young boy who had Asperger's was sent to a school like this where there were programs for students with behavioral issues. This did him more harm than good because he learned bad habits from the other students. Also, he was frequently beaten up because the students in this school had more difficulties with anger management and got into more fights. The student's mother was eventually forced to home-school her son, despite being a single parent. [*Pyles, 2002*]

The other thing not to do is to give a child with Asperger's poor role modeling. In phys. ed. class, one of my classmates used to run quickly towards the wall, put one foot against the wall in order to jump higher, and then hang from the rim of the basketball net. As soon as he came down, I did the same thing. My classmate asked me, "Jay, how come you do everything I do?"

When I was in grade ten, my parents had guests for supper, my mother served a variety of foods including beets that were generously covered in beet sauce. I was a picky eater who didn't like sauces, so I wiped the sauce off the beets onto the plate as best I could, leaving a large pool of red sauce on my plate. When I was finished, one of the guests commented, "You can fingerpaint, Jay."

My sister immediately admonished, "Don't give him ideas!"

In summary, do not expose an Aspie to bad examples.

The Need for Structure

When I took swimming lessons, we did drown-proofing for part of the class, and we always did it on the same side of the pool. One day, there was another swimming class in the pool and they were swimming lengths on that side of the pool so my instructor asked us to do drown-proofing on the other side. I told her that I couldn't do drown-proofing on that side.

My instructor said to the instructor of the other class: "Jim, he says he can't do drown-proofing on that side."

Jim replied, "OK, we'll just sneak by."

The instructors consented to my need for consistency and the structure of doing the same activity on the same side of the pool.

When I first started working at the Royal Military College, my job was ideal. Not only did it involve applying math to real-world issues, but the structure was laid out.

My supervisor would say, "Do this – and show me when you're done."

Then he'd say, "Now, do this."

I had previously held jobs that were either too demanding and/or where my supervisor gave me nothing to do. This job was neither. When I began a Master's degree for the same supervisor, I took some courses. My supervisor didn't give me any research work to do, telling me to concentrate on my course work. As soon as the courses were completed, my supervisor and I were back to the previous routine of him telling me what to do. I didn't have to do any plan management; he did the overseeing.

Eventually, my supervisor said, "These results look great. This is what I want to see. You're now ready to start writing your thesis."

For days, I was saddled with the question of "Where do I begin?"

I had lots of time and lots of work to do, but without structure, I didn't know how to allocate my time. This is analogous to getting a weekly allowance versus being given a large sum of money up front.

When I'm told to "Learn this software package.", that instruction is too vague. I don't know where to begin, and I don't know how to determine whether I am making progress. Even if I am making progress, I have no way of measuring how much progress I am making. On the contrary, when I'm given a specific instruction, such as "Write a program that accomplishes x or y task.", it is much easier to measure my level of progress. For this reason, I'm hesitant to give a project or assignment too much focus in case I end up wasting energy that could have been used somewhere else.

One time, my supervisor gave me an assignment that I quickly subdivided into three smaller assignments. When I am first learning something on a new project, my mind needs to "process" the new ideas for a while. I am able to work on other things while my mind is doing this processing, but most of my attention is taken up by thinking. Therefore, when I hit a "bottleneck" and have to take time to absorb the facts as well as discern how to proceed, I might be able to focus on one of the two other smaller assignments. If I could not break the original larger assignment down into different parts, then, every time I had to "take a break" to let my thoughts unwind, I would feel that I was wasting company time and would want to make the break as short as possible. By breaking the larger task into smaller parts, I knew I was still working towards the goal.

When training for my swim across Lake Ontario, I knew as a marathon runner, how to increase my stamina: swim for two hours; wait a few days to make sure I hadn't overtrained, that I was not hurting and that there were no other negative repercussions; and then swim for three hours, increase this to four hours, and so on. That way, I knew even before I completed the two-hour swim, what my next training session would be. By proceeding like this, I could easily discern whether or not I was "making progress" and therefore knew whether I simply needed to continue with my plan, or alter my course of action.

What enabled me to work toward the goal of swimming Lake Ontario so diligently were the following combined factors:
- The instructions – swim across Lake Ontario – were simple, which meant that it was easy to keep my eye on the target and decide what actions needed to be taken.
- The training process was complicated; if the process were simple, anyone could achieve the goal. I had the task of breaking the training down into smaller parts so I could reach my goal in the time I had before key swims. Vicki Keith and Marilyn, my Swim Master, among others, gave me advice along the way to keep my training on schedule.

Obsessive-Compulsive Traits

The sidewalk from my parents' driveway to the doorstep originally contained ten concrete stones. When my father widened the garden that was located between the sidewalk and the house, he moved the sidewalk further from the house and added three more stones so that the six steps closest to the doorstep formed a two by three grid. Every time I walked from the driveway to the doorstep, I had to step on all thirteen concrete stones with both feet. When walking on any sidewalk, if I stepped on a crack with my left foot, I had to make sure I stepped on a crack with my right foot "to even it out".

Living in a Dream World

My tendency to dwell on things is so great that, many times, I have caught myself in a dream world when I'm supposed to be focusing on something else, such as paying attention in class. Often, I dwell on situations that happened years ago. For example, while in class I caught myself thinking about an incident which took place several years ago at a chess club: a member who was watching the game asked my opponent sternly, "Why didn't you take the Pawn with your Queen Pawn?".

He followed this comment with the very adamant suggestion, "Think, Jeffrey!"

Taking Things Literally

When I was in grade five or six, my sister agreed to type her classmate's essay in exchange for a fee. Claire told my mother and father that if he didn't pay, she would take him to court. (I'm quite sure she was joking.)

I thought "court" meant "tennis court", so I asked, "What is "court"?"

At a later date, when I asked "What is "court"?" my mother replied, "Do you really not know what "court" is, or are you just pretending not to know?"

Apparently my mother didn't believe me the first time. I told her that I really didn't know. She explained the meaning of "court" and I didn't understand her explanation. At the time, it seemed to me that I had forgotten my mother's answer and I figured there was no point asking again.

In grade eight, I attended Youth Group once a week. One week, we held kangaroo court. It wasn't until then that I really understood the meaning of the word "court".

Fear of the Unknown/Literal Interpretations

As I mentioned in the introduction, I was afraid to try new things as a child, even something as simple as going down the children's slide at a local beach. When I was eight years old, I had just learned how to swim and wanted to take swimming lessons. I signed up for the "beginner" level that was the next level after "pre-beginner". My classmate's older sister attended one class with us. The instructor asked the older sister to crawl on the bottom. I remember that the older sister didn't seem very happy about doing this. This incident stayed with me as I progressed through the lower levels of the classes. At one point, I looked ahead to the requirements for passing the higher-level tests. One of the requirements was "100 metres of front crawl". I thought "front crawl" meant "crawl on the bottom of the pool". I dreaded going into that level and didn't even want to think about it.

During the process of training for my swim, I tried crawling on the bottom of the shallow end of the pool on my hands and knees. I could kneel down on the bottom but couldn't get my head and hands to stay at the bottom. If I relaxed my body, my feet would fall towards the bottom of the pool, but my head would stay about three inches above the surface of the water, presumably because of the air in my lungs. I could almost float, i.e., keep my face out of the water without moving, by tilting my head back. SSO will not allow swimmers to use any kind of flotation device when swimming across a Great Lake. In the days prior to my crossing, I even wondered if I could feasibly take a nap during the crossing. I wasn't sure I could sink my body even if I tried. The reader might argue that I could indeed sink my body if I put lead in my pockets. However, then it wouldn't be my body that was sinking; it would be the lead that was sinking and my body would be going along for a free ride!

The Need for Clear Rules and Following Them Rigidly

I follow rules rigidly, but only if they're stated clearly. For example, at Youth Group, I heard one of the other members call Ken Franklin "Ken Flanklin". Then I started calling him "Ken Flanklin" as well. Some time later, the pastor moved and was replaced by a new pastor, Earle Hawley. I deliberately showed up for bible study almost an hour late and declared that the reason I was late was because the previous pastor had always been late. Pastor Hawley replied that his name is Earle with an 'e', and if you wanted to pronounce the 'e' on the end, it becomes "early". He went on to say that he likes to start things on time. After that, I kept saying, "Early Hawley".

Richard T. commented, "He says that instead of 'Ken Flanklin'."

After this went on for several months, Richard said to me, "Jay, I'll bet you can't go without saying that…" Richard paused for about five seconds and then said, "…for a year."

I made it a rule to say to Richard once every two months, "Richard, as you noticed, I haven't said his name for x number of months." I also pointed this out to Pastor Hawley.

After undertaking the bet not to say "Early Hawley" for a year, I was back to saying "Ken Flanklin". I told this to my mother and my mother replied that she was going to get Richard to make a bet with me regarding saying "Ken Flanklin". Once I start something, it is very difficult for me to stop it unless there is a bet or firm instruction involved.

This is another example of how I follow rules very rigidly. When my eldest niece was born, my sister and brother-in-law deemed it ultra-important not to swear since they didn't want their daughter to learn bad words. They made it a rule that any time that they, or any visitors, said a swear word, they had to put a loonie in the swear jar. This money would be used for my niece's university education.

When I came to visit, my brother-in-law said to me, "Because you don't swear, we have to trap you in another way."

Then he told me that I had to put a loonie in the "bad habit jar", as I called it, every time I mentioned a particular subject. This topic may have been worthy of discussion at one time, but it should have been put to rest a long time ago. I can't tell you what that subject was or else my sister will charge me a loonie when she reads this!

My parents had to give me very specific instructions. When I was four years old or younger, i.e. too young to remember, if my father said, "Jay, stop jumping on the blue couch," thirty seconds later I would start jumping on the yellow chair. Any child will, to a certain extent, try to push the limits of rules. My parents learned quickly how specific they had to be with their rules and instructions. They also had to follow up carefully and pay extra attention to make sure that what they said had registered with me.

Teachers often misunderstood me and thought that I was choosing not to follow the rules or was incapable of learning the rules. Teachers deal with many more children than a parent does. A teacher only sees a student for a fraction of the day and only for ten months of the year; therefore, they don't have as much time to learn how any particular child "adapts". Whenever there was a fight at school, I would get into trouble but the other people were less likely to be reprimanded or punished. If the teachers had no way of knowing who started the fight, they often assumed that I was "the bad guy" because I wouldn't follow the rules. They didn't realize that their rules hadn't been stated clearly and they often did not understand my Asperger's Syndrome. Therefore, from the teacher's point of view, I was the one more likely to have started the fight. My "solution" was to surrender before a fight broke out. Some classmates probably knew this and took advantage of it, thinking, "If I want to have my way with Jay, I don't have to be strong enough to beat him up and I don't have to even try to fight; all I have to do is threaten to fight."

Capable of Working Wonders When Motivated

Like everyone, I know that something needs to be done but won't want to work on it because "I'm too tired" or "I just don't feel like it". However, I can work wonders "when I'm motivated".

On a Friday evening, I was on a Waterloo co-op work term. My sister, who was taking courses for a Masters degree, telephoned me to ask for help with a math problem. She asked me if I had the time and I told her I was about to go to bed. She explained the problem to me and I told her I'd work on it for a while. I worked on it for more than an hour until it was done. My sister was very grateful for my help.

In 1993, at the University of Waterloo during final exams, I was on campus studying when I felt tired mid-afternoon, so I decided to go back to my room for a nap. En route, I wanted to check something at the tutorial centre. There I met another classmate, Monica, who solicited my help and then we talked for a long time. When Monica and I finished talking, I had barely enough time to get back to residence for supper. I was living in residence and there was a fixed time period for supper. Just before we parted, Monica and I agreed to meet back on campus after supper. We continued studying until late at night. All this while, I had never taken the nap that I had originally planned to take.

A People Pleaser

Often, when I want to do something and people suggest I do it a different way or want to know why I am doing something a certain way, explaining the reasons for my approach often takes more energy than it is worth. What's more, I often can't tell whether other people are asking only out of interest or are demanding an explanation. If it is the latter, I feel that I can't proceed until I deal with their questions. Furthermore, I feel that I can't "shake people loose" until they understand my answers to their questions. It feels like I have to engage

in these explanations before I can move on to doing the task because I can't multi-task very well. Often, I'll "give in" and do things another way for this very reason. My options, in order of preference, are:
Option #1: Do things my way, with no explanation.
Option #2: Do things other people's ways, with no explanation.
Option #3: Do things my way and explain to other people why I am doing it my way.

If I delay plans for a number of commitments in favour of beginning a larger project like swimming across Lake Ontario, and people question me, I can feel defensive. If I can't show noticeable progress on the project, it might look like I was only making excuses and might eventually have to give up on the project. People might think I would have been better off not to undertake the larger project in the first place. Therefore, I can't invest too many resources, e.g., time, money and/or mental energy into something unless I can see myself completing it and ensuring that my other commitments aren't going to suffer. This makes it hard for me to commit to a big project and to tell many people once I've made the decision to go ahead with it. Once I have made up my mind, feel confident about reaching that goal and focus all my time and energy on that dream, then it is much more difficult to dissuade me from taking on the project. I found that once I was committed to swimming across Lake Ontario, nobody wanted to stand in the way of undertaking this worthy achievement.

Any unanswered question is an albatross around my neck. For example, when people repeatedly offer me sweet things to eat to the point where their offer becomes pressure, or ask me to explain why I choose not to eat sugar, I often feel like ignoring their questions. I have done this sometimes, but I often feel compelled to respond. The reason I avoid sugar is because sweet things combined with mental stress give me headaches. This has happened to me too many times to be disputed. People have told me to eliminate mental stress from my life, but this is impossible. They've also suggested that I find the "threshold" below which I can eat sugar. This solution won't work because the threshold is highly variable and dependent on many factors, including fluctuating levels of stress. It's far better, in my opinion, to avoid sugar altogether whenever there is any doubt. My motto is the following: Don't mess around with a solution that works. I can, however, eat sugar when I'm doing a lot of physical activity because I burn it off. I may also be able to eat some sweets when I'm in a completely relaxed environment, but these situations vary and can change quickly. If I do accept something sweet, people who know me will then question me and say, "I thought you didn't eat sugar?" This can be very frustrating! In general, so many factors affect a decision that it's quite common for me to make one decision at one time and a seemingly contradictory decision at a different time when a few factors have changed. People ask me to explain the inconsistencies, but unless I'm feeling very energetic and positive, I often find it easier just to give in than explain my reasons for doing or not doing something.

How to Say No

I have had some unpleasant experiences with people when I have said no. I've come to understand that it's not because I say no that people react poorly, but it's the way that I say no. This is because I don't have the people skills to say no in a more polite way. Therefore, if the other person won't take 'no' for an answer quickly, I have three choices:
1. I say no in a rude way.
2. I give in to what the other person wants.
3. I leave and avoid having contact with that person or people.

Handling Disagreement

With my case of Asperger's Syndrome, I often have a difficult time handling disagreements or differences of opinion in a conversation. The following incident is an example of this. I told one of my friends who is not an athlete that Vicki Keith had said that everyone swims more slowly in open water. This friend argued that I should be faster in open water since I didn't have to turn around every 25 metres. I'd believe Vicki any day over my friend. I didn't have the people skills to terminate the discussion in a polite way. It's possible that this friend was only joking, but unless I rudely discontinued the conversation, I was forced to listen to his incorrect viewpoint and waste energy trying to explain my viewpoint.

One issue I need to work on is discontinuing discussions on controversial topics. The discussion might be worth pursuing if the other person's viewpoint directly affects me, but that was not the case in the above-mentioned conversation. I know that people do not go on forever with their points of view, but I find it very uncomfortable to feel trapped when they are disagreeing with me. I prefer to disengage from the conversation and I know that I will likely not change my mind and will probably continue with my preferred approach no matter how many arguments the people make. All that results from the discussion is that it wastes people's time and drains my energy while I try to explain my point of view or why I do things my way. I can't control what other people say or do, but I can control how I respond. For example, I could say, "As soon as you finish your argument, I will likely continue to do things the way I see fit."

The week before the Gatineau Loppet in February, 2007, I was talking about the race with a friend. He kept harassing me to try to win the race. He asked me how much the registration fee cost and then told me that I shouldn't pay a sum of money like that unless I intended to win. Some people enter a race hoping to win, while others enter a race for the enjoyment. There is nothing wrong with either decision. If you do it to win, you'll be motivated to train and perform better, but you are also much more likely to be disappointed if you don't win. The conversation about the Gatineau race took place during a two-hour car ride the winter after I decided I wanted to swim across Lake Ontario. I didn't want to anger my friend, especially since I might have to depend on him to paddle beside me during my training swims. In the early stages of planning for my crossing, I thought there would be a shortage of paddlers. It was impossible to walk away from that conversation because I was trapped in the car. We continued to disagree for several minutes until we finally talked about something else. I walked away from the discussion with an unchanged viewpoint except for the conclusion that my friend is arrogant. I guess that he also had an unchanged viewpoint and I didn't dare ask him. He did paddle beside me once the following summer. If I had my life to live over again, I would have changed the subject much sooner.

I have learned a number of important things about myself over the years. I know I have difficulties handling differences of opinion. Everything is fine as long as the conversation is going smoothly, but I collapse whenever there is disagreement. I know that this is true to some extent for most people, but I think it is more true for people with Asperger's Syndrome.

Reading People's Reactions Correctly and Responding Appropriately

I thought that the most difficult part of the process of swimming across Lake Ontario would be finding people to paddle beside me on my training swims. One extreme would be to sit back and hope people offer, and only ask the people whom I know really well and whom I know have experience kayaking or canoeing. The other extreme would be to go up to every person I see and ask, "Would you be willing to paddle beside me on one or more of my training swims?" The key is to find a balance between these two extremes.

I have often found myself doing things which, unbeknownst to me, are deemed inappropriate by the average person. When I'm not sure whether something is appropriate, my solution is to tread lightly and then pay extra attention to the other person's reaction before proceeding. This is usually easier said than done and I don't always follow this course of action. In the case of recruiting paddling volunteers, I thought that the way to tread lightly would be to give people lots of advance notice and make it clear to them that I was giving them the option of saying no. In the fall of 2006, when I first started recruiting volunteer paddlers, I thought I would be desperate for volunteer paddlers and therefore I wasn't too quick to take no for an answer. I had asked so many people that I got into pattern of responses that depended on their reasons for saying no. If a person said, "I won't have time," I'd reply with: "Everyone thinks the same thing, but the net result is that no one is willing. All I'm asking you to do is paddle beside me once. Think of what would happen if everyone said no. Suppose I ask fifty people. What's fifty times one and what's fifty times zero?"

If a person said, "I wouldn't know how to help you if you get into trouble," I would reply with: "All I'm asking you to do is keep the canoe or kayak near me and throw me the spare lifejacket when I request it."

I probably annoyed some people with my persistence. Most people who initially said no wouldn't budge from their decision. This didn't really matter by the following summer because more than enough people had volunteered.

When you ask people if they want to attend a function or get-together, the average person can figure out from the intonation of the response about whether or not the other people are interested in attending. I can't discern people's responses to my requests and invitations as easily as the average person. However, I've developed my own surefire method that increases the likelihood that I'll be certain about whether or not other people are interested in doing something with me.

Facial expressions alone are not a foolproof method of figuring out whether people are serious, no matter how well someone is able to read them, because there are people who can make jokes – and even tell lies – with a straight face. For example, when I was using online dating, I met someone at a restaurant for the first time. After we were finished eating, we walked together for a while until our paths separated. Just before we parted, she said with a neutral facial expression and appearing slightly interested, "We should get together again."   She never took the initiative to call me after that. I called her a few times and she either didn't have the time to talk or gave a reason why she couldn't get together. She was only in Kingston for the summer and I didn't have her contact information after she left Kingston. I never heard from her again.

Here is a surefire way of knowing that people enjoyed spending time with you: if they get in touch with you to arrange another meeting or agree to another invitation from you, they prove that they enjoy being with you by actually showing up for another get-together. For example, I have been inviting my Navigators friends to Deep River once a year for a summer reunion. They keep coming back, which clearly indicates that they enjoy the reunions. Similarly, if people paddle beside me on training swims and then show up to do it again, that means they were satisfied with the experience and want to help out again.

In 1991, shortly after I started at the University of Waterloo , I traveled out of town and spent the weekend with a family. As one of them was driving me back to the bus terminal, I said, "I wish I had something to offer you."

He replied, "The best thing you can offer is to promise to come again."

Now I know what he means.

Going into Too Much Detail

Finally, as the reader will discover upon reading the remainder of this book, I have a tendency to go into too much detail, i.e., to talk on and on about myself or a topic that interests me. Other people may not be interested in that particular subject and, even if they are interested, they rarely want to hear that many details. "For example, a child may discuss at length a single topic that is of little interest to others." [*Myles and Simpson, 1998*] I tend to be fastidious about getting all the details correct; I almost always have the urge to make sure I don't leave anything out and I understand that this may be annoying to some people, but I can't help myself from getting into all the nitty-gritty.

The Swim Master's Report (see Appendix Q) says, "He never asked to come out". This is not entirely true because, twice, I said, "Pull me out." Marilyn, my Swim Master, didn't mention that I had asked to come out because I was so easily dissuaded from quitting my swim across Lake Ontario. If I were writing the report, I would be uncomfortable saying what Marilyn said because I would be very picky and concerned about getting all the details right. Marilyn was right to be brief and concise; I would have written a report that was far too detailed. It is better to sacrifice a little bit of accuracy for the sake of brevity.[10]

---

[10] Marilyn could concisely clarify by saying "he never seriously asked to come out".

Part Two

Becoming an Athlete

Chapter 2

The Cross-Country Running Team

"One way to get the most out of life is to look upon it as an adventure."

—William Feather

In May, 1985, when I was in Grade 7, my phys. ed. class played scrub baseball most days. At the beginning of the period, everyone would run one lap around the school and people would pick their position in the order that they finished. I was usually one of the first four finishers. I told my parents this. As I was leaving for school one day, my father called out, "Good-bye to the top runner!"

In Grade 8, my parents forced me to join the cross-country running team. For several days, I came home every day after school to watch Masters of the Universe at 4:00 p.m. We had a VCR but I was adamant on being home so that I could delete all the commercials as I taped each episode. When my parents asked me why I didn't want to go to practice, I lied and told them it was too cold outside. My parents bought me a jogging suit so I wouldn't have the excuse of being too cold running in shorts and a T-shirt. My teacher even gave me a pep talk. He praised me and said, "You're a good runner. I don't know why you don't join the cross-country team."

I thought my parents had encouraged me to join cross-country because of telling them about my running achievements the year before: I regretted having mentioned this to them. I knew they probably just wanted me to get involved in some sports and clubs where I would meet other students, but I didn't want to feel pressured to join the team.

I had done a cross-country ski race every year since I was four years old. The distance of the race increased with age and in the winter of 1986, I raced 3.5 kilometres in 28 minutes. When I finished the race, my mother exclaimed proudly, "Well done, Jay! You cut four minutes off your time from last year! Four minutes is a lot of time."

In Grade 9, my father asked me why I was late getting home from school. I knew he was asking because he cared and was interested in what I did socially. I explained, "I was at cross-country running practice."

My father started asking me questions about the practice and, as is often the case, I felt burdened by the numerous questions coming all at once. I asked, "Would you rather I didn't go to cross-country running?"

My father replied semi-harshly, "No, but I'd prefer you to go into other sports in addition to cross-country running."

Cross-country practice was held every Monday, Wednesday and Friday. On each of these days my father asked me, "Did you go cross-country running today?"

I had made my own decision to join the cross-country running team in Grade 9 and I wondered if I could have avoided this kind of pressure from my father if I had not joined the team in the first place.

One Monday, my knee was bothering me so I preferred not to go to practice. I told Mr. Fulford, the coach. He replied, "Okay, you rest your knee today, and go for a run tomorrow instead." I didn't have the nerve to tell him that I didn't think my knee would be better by the next day.

When my father arrived home, he asked me, as always, "Did you go to cross-country running today?" I told him that my knee was bothering me and he wouldn't buy that. His initial reaction was to think I was trying to find an excuse; I could hardly blame him because I had not been very keen to exercise at all when I was younger.

I attended the first two meets in Grade 9 and then quit, partly because the third meet required us to be at the school at 6:30 a.m., but more because I wasn't motivated to enter the races.

At the cross-country running meeting at the beginning of Grade 10, Mr. Fulford said, "This year, I'm not going to chase anyone to go to practices." After the meeting, some other teammates and I headed to the track. I ran three laps (1200 metres) around the track and then went to the weight room, where I had gone regularly after school in Grade 9. I decided that I'd go back to lifting weights after school and do my run at a different time since there was no coach at the after-school running practices and my weightlifting wouldn't be as productive if I went running first. This ended up being a bad decision because I rarely went running. I attended only one cross-country meet in Grade 10 and then quit.

In the spring of Grade 10 (1988), my sister asked me, "Are you going to join the track and field team?"

I replied, "I don't like missing school."

My mother commented that when I graduated and looked back at my high school days, I would remember the extra-curricular activities better than the time spent in class. I took history that semester and almost failed it. I have trouble multitasking, so when I'm not doing well at something, 9 times out of 10 I either give up on it or limit my focus on other things until I can complete it and get it out of the way. I didn't even consider joining the track and field team but I managed to pass history. History class was an albatross around my neck and I was happy to have it behind me.

Our entire school was shown a video of Terry Fox in the fall of Grade 11. Terry is a Canadian hero who had a dream to run across Canada despite having his right leg amputated above the knee due to cancer. He ran from St. John's, Newfoundland to Thunder Bay where a recurrence of cancer in his lungs forced him to stop his run. I thought to myself, I may never run across Canada but the least I can do is join the cross-country running team and make sure I attend all the meets this year. Inspiration and remorse motivated me to run in all the practices and meets from Grades 11 to 13: Terry Fox's determination inspired me and my remorse over quitting the cross-country running team for two years made me honour my commitment to the team. My team never won any prizes but involvement, enjoyment, and personal satisfaction were what mattered to me.

Chapter 3

Cross-Country Running: The Importance of Training

"If you want to go fast, go alone. If you want to go far, go together."

—*African proverb*

My running regime may have been smooth during the cross-country season in Grade 11, but it could have been smoother after the season ended. During the three-hour ride back from the final meet of the season, only Mr. Fulford and I were in the car so we had a long conversation. He said, "You just ran eight kilometres at race pace. You're ready to run ten kilometres." I kept telling him that I didn't want to. Finally, he gave up and said, "Let me know when you're ready to run ten kilometres."

In May 1989, I ran the MDS Nordion 10K in Ottawa – and fast. I was totally exhausted for the rest of the evening. That was my first time ever running ten kilometres. In hindsight, running ten kilometres casually with Mr. Fulford would have been much easier than running a ten kilometre race. I thought "Running ten kilometres with Mr. Fulford plus running a ten kilometre running race on a later date equals more physical exertion than only running a ten kilometre running race." The main reason I didn't run ten kilometres with Mr. Fulford was that I was afraid of the unknown; I was reluctant to push myself beyond my comfort zone, except in a race. The fact that I was set in my routine of lifting weights every day after school certainly didn't help matters, but I could have easily made time for a ten kilometre run on the weekend.

The Monday after the MDS Nordion 10K, I said to Mr. Fulford, "I'm ready to run ten kilometres with you."

He immediately shot back with another challenge, and asked, "Want to go for a ten mile run with me?"

I said nothing but silently and angrily thought, "You can't satisfy this guy! When I'm ready to run ten miles, he'll probably want me to run even further."[11]

---

[11] I told Mr. Fulford this years later and he told me that he asked me that because he knew I was ready to go further.

In Grade 12, I joined the cross-country team, attended practices when they fit into my schedule and naively expected everything to fall into place. I missed many practices. I felt free when the cross-country season ended and I had no motivation to continue running. It was at least a month before I went for a run. The only running I did regularly was on my paper route: I usually ran most of the route as I delivered the newspapers.

In Grade 13, I made a commitment to attend the practices faithfully before the cross-country running season started, instead of being forced into a training regime by the coaches when I wasn't ready and repeating my poor performance of Grade 12. I enjoyed the practices much more in Grade 13 than in Grade 12, but the problems did not disappear entirely. I still thought my coaches were encroaching on my rights and trying to run my life by pressuring me to go to practices. I resented them and even wrote a letter to one of my coaches expressing my anger. As I look back on cross-country running in high school, I realize how important the influence of coaches like Mr. Fulford was. I know that my tenacity to swim across Lake Ontario was built by these formative experiences. My high-school coaches showed me the importance of physical activity and the necessity of being committed to a training regime. I now realize that building endurance and speed and accomplishing an athletic feat can only happen through a commitment to consistent training and pushing your limits.

Since then, I often go for a run to relieve stress. A friend from university used to tell me that after long nights of studying, he would sometimes consider going for a run but would abandon the idea because he was too tired. My solution to this problem was to take a break and go for a run earlier in the evening to make sure I did it. When someone who is not in shape tries running, it takes time before it becomes more of a benefit than a chore. I know this from experience and from being fit enough to take a break any time I need the stress-relieving benefits of running. Being in shape is what motivates me to stay in shape. I have my high-school coaches to thank for teaching me these important lessons about training and fitness.

Chapter 4

The Gatineau

"Nothing is pleasant that is not spiced with variety."
—*Francis Bacon*

In February 1992, my sister, Claire, participated in the annual 25 kilometre cross-country ski race in Gatineau Park. Later that day, she phoned to tell me about her race and asked me why I hadn't participated – a logical question since I was living in Ottawa. Less than a month before, I had started my first of six co-op jobs: this job was my very first time being hired by a company outside my family. I'd had a very difficult time finding a job – not an uncommon problem for people with Asperger's Syndrome – so I explained to Claire that I wanted to keep my activities to a minimum until I was settled into the job. Claire informed me that she wanted to do the 55 kilometre race in 1993 and I commented that she couldn't possibly plan that far ahead. She explained that every year after she does the Deep River triathlon, she commits to doing it again: otherwise, she wouldn't do it. By doing this a year in advance, she dedicates herself to the race and to training for it all year.

Because I took the co-op program at the University of Waterloo, I alternated between four months of school and four months of work. In the winter of 1992, I was on a work term in Ottawa and, in January 1993, I was back in Waterloo. That year, I didn't even consider coming to Ottawa to do the Gatineau Loppet. Claire registered for it but chose not to do it because she had bronchitis.

In January 1994, I began a work term in Markham. Unlike school terms when most of my weekends were spent studying, my weekends on co-op terms were free. I took advantage of this freedom to participate in the Gatineau 25, largely in response to Claire's invitation to me to participate two years before. My cross-country ski coach from high school seemed surprised that I would travel all the way from Markham to Ottawa just to do a 25 kilometre ski race; he reasoned that if I was going to travel that far, I should do the 55 kilometre ski race.

Claire registered for the 55 kilometre race but switched to the 25 kilometre on the day of the race because she wasn't feeling well. We both did the 25 kilometre race. The temperature was above zero which enabled skiers to glide very well – ideal conditions for ski-skating, but not optimal had it been a classical race. My mother, who had bought a new pair of cross-country skis for ski-skating, went out to meet Claire and skied the last five kilometres or so with her.

I felt fine after I completed the race, even though my training had been sporadic. I knew I could easily have skied another ten kilometres. I told Claire that I wanted to do the 55 kilometre race in 1995. Claire warned me that I would have to be in top shape to ski 55 kilometres. She mentioned that Marc, one of her friends, had finished the 55 kilometre race within one hour of the fastest finisher. However, the first year he participated, he didn't eat enough breakfast, and nearly ran out of energy climbing a really steep hill. He knew there was a check point at the top of the hill so he figured that all he had to do was make it to the top. He did make it, only to find out that the only food available was chocolate-covered peanuts and he has a nut allergy. He would have posted a faster time if he had eaten properly to prepare for his ski race.

In 1995, I participated in the 50 kilometre race[12]. Claire was doing a Masters degree at University of Toronto. She and her boyfriend Ron (now her husband) both did the 25 kilometre race and they gave me a ride to the race. Other than a minor stomach cramp at the 40 kilometre mark and again immediately after I crossed the finish line, everything went fine. I had fulfilled my dream to finish the 50 kilometre race, by which time Claire and Ron had both completed their race.

In 1996, I participated in the 50 kilometre once again and I enjoyed it. Unfortunately, Claire could not participate on account of a figure skating competition.

In 1997, I took a step down and participated in the 25 kilometre classical race[13].

In 1998, I had been unemployed for several months and had put almost everything on hold – including cutting back noticeably on my physical activity – in order to focus on finding a job. It was several years before I participated in the Gatineua Loppet again.

I enjoyed the Gatineau Loppet, but not enough to make it an annual event. It was still an important feature in my life as the following story illustrates: At the beginning of my school term at the University of Waterloo in the Winter of 1995, I joined a small group with the Navigators. We played a "Get-to-know-each-other game" in which five questions were asked. People had to write down their answers on

---

[12] As of that year, the 55km race had been shortened to 50km.
[13] "skating" and "classical" are two different techniques for cross-country skiing.

a piece of paper. The leader then read each set of answers and everyone had to try to guess which person had given those answers. The last question was, "If you could spend one week anywhere in the world, where would it be?" I replied, "Gatineau Park".

Chapter 5

My First Marathon

"There is no such thing as bad weather – just inappropriate clothing."

—*unknown origin*

On the last day of the Calgary '95 Navigators summer-long program, I had completed a ten kilometre run just as Rhona was heading back to the residence where we were staying throughout the program. Rhona commented that I didn't look at all tired and was quite surprised that I could run that far without appearing fatigued. I took that as a compliment, but her comment made me realize that I had been running ten kilometre races on and off for six years and it was time for something more challenging. That was the day I decided I wanted to run a marathon.

In August 1995, about two weeks after the Calgary Navs summer-long program ended, I ran about twenty kilometres with Mr. Fulford. Previously, my longest run had been fifteen kilometres. During the run, Mr. Fulford explained his training regime: do a base run on Mondays, Wednesdays and Fridays, a longer run on Tuesdays and Thursdays, the longest run on Saturdays when you'd really push your endurance, and then rest on Sundays. You'd gradually increase the

Table 5-1 – marathon training schedule

	Monday	Tuesday	Wednesday	Thursday	Friday	Saturday	Sunday
week #1	30 min.	45 min.	30 min.	45 min.	30 min.	60 min.	rest
week #2	30 min.	50 min.	30 min.	50 min.	30 min.	70 min.	rest
week #3	30 min.	55 min.	30 min.	55 min.	30 min.	80 min.	rest
week #4	30 min.	60 min.	30 min.	60 min.	30 min.	90 min.	rest
week #5	30 min.	65 min.	30 min.	65 min.	30 min.	100 min.	rest
week #6	30 min.	70 min.	30 min.	70 min.	30 min.	110 min.	rest
week #7	30 min.	75 min.	30 min.	75 min.	30 min.	120 min.	rest
week #8	30 min.	80 min.	30 min.	80 min.	30 min.	130 min.	rest
week #9	30 min.	85 min.	30 min.	85 min.	30 min.	140 min.	rest
week #10	30 min.	90 min.	30 min.	90 min.	30 min.	**150 min.**	rest
week #11	30 min.	75 min.	30 min.	75 min.	30 min.	120 min.	rest
week #12	30 min.	60 min.	30 min.	60 min.	30 min.	90 min.	rest
week #13	30 min.	60 min.	30 min.	rest	rest	rest	**Marathon!!**

distances of the longer runs, but wouldn't necessarily increase the duration of the base run.

The peak run should be done three weeks before the marathon. After that, you should taper down. Few people run the full distance in training. You should be able to run twice as far as your top-trained distance. Mr. Fulford firmly believed that a runner should focus on the time of the training run[14], not the distance covered. I always prefer to have some idea of how far I am running.

By September 1995, one month later, I was mentally preparing myself to run the Ottawa marathon in May 1996. A quick calculation told me that following Mr. Fulford's training schedule would require me to commence the training regime immediately after the 50 kilometre Gatineau Loppet on February 17th. With the Gatineau Loppet taking place immediately before reading week[15], I stayed in Ottawa for two extra days to ski the Gatineau trails. On Tuesday evening, I took the overnight bus back to Waterloo and headed directly from the bus terminal to my 8:30 a.m. class. I stayed on campus all day and was sick by the time I got home, presumably from not eating enough after all the exercise I had done. This forced me to delay my marathon training until two weeks after the Gatineau Loppet. After running for four consecutive days, my ankle felt strained, as if I had turned it, so I postponed the training – again.

In early March 1996, my roommate Jens, informed me about the annual Around the Bay 30K Road Race[16] in Hamilton, close to where his parents lived. Jens thought it would be held in April, but on March 16th, I went to a local running store and found out that it would be held on March 31st, only two weeks away. Luckily, I was able to register the day before the race at no additional cost.[17] I went right back into training mode and attended the Wednesday evening and Sunday morning workouts[18] both weeks, ending my training with a 17 kilometre run three days before the race.

---

[14] This training schedule assumes a pace of roughly five minutes per kilometre.

[15] At University of Waterloo, students in the engineering and math faculties get only two days off instead of a whole week, on account of the co-op program.

[16] http://www.aroundthebayroadrace.com

[17] Since then, the Around the Bay Road 30K Race has grown significantly. Early-bird registration closes well before the race and the general registration fills up at least a month in advance.

[18] I had learned earlier in the term that the local running store had a group run every Wednesday evening and Sunday morning. I had avoided them until now because their dates didn't jive with Mr. Fulford's training schedule that required Sunday as my rest day. In hindsight, it would have made more sense to slightly alter my training schedule and attend the workouts. Running with others who are the same speed as you or faster is more beneficial than running alone; the whole is greater than the sum of the parts.

The race went well, except that I had to wait for three and a half minutes while the Burlington Canal Lift Bridge went up to let a lake freighter go by[19]. I crossed the finish line feeling like I could have easily run another five kilometres. On another positive note, training for the race put me in a more relaxed mode to study for final exams.

I enjoyed the Calgary '95 Navs program so much that I participated in a two-week Navigators program in Colorado at the beginning of May 1996. This program ended the day before a wedding I planned to attend which was the day before the Ottawa marathon that I had been planning to run which was the day before I started my co-op job. Because of all these complications and the resulting interruptions to my training, I decided not to run the marathon. Nonetheless, the Around the Bay 30K Road Race was a satisfying jump from my previous longest running race which had been ten kilometres.

I completed my undergraduate degree at the University of Waterloo in December 1996. Since there was no need to study, I was able to divide my energies between work and running. In 1997, I participated in another Navigators summer-long training program, this time in Ottawa. I had planned to run a marathon in Montreal in September, one month after the Navs program ended. Unfortunately, the marathon was cancelled. This may have been a blessing in disguise because I hadn't trained very well.

I took stock of the status of my marathon running in the fall of 1997. Without a stable job, I often spent my winters in Deep River where there is so much snow that it's difficult to run. Besides, whenever I'm in Deep River for the winter, I tend to spend more time cross-country skiing than running because I like to cross-country ski. This makes it difficult to train for a spring running marathon. Planning to run a fall marathon involves the risk of wasting your training if the marathon has to be cancelled. Unfortunately, there are no marathons in Ontario in the summer. My sister moved to Calgary in May 1997 and I was elated to discover that there was a marathon in Calgary in early July. I decided to run it the summer of 1998 reasoning that, if for some reason I couldn't run it, I'd have another chance to run a marathon in the fall.

After being unemployed continuously for almost a year, I finally found a job at the end of March 1998. The date for the Calgary Marathon was set for the weekend immediately after my three-month

---

[19] Boats are not normally allowed into port before April 1, which is probably the reason why the race is held in March. The 1996 case was highly unusual and only the second time since the inception of the race in 1894 that the race was disrupted by the lifting of the bridge.

probationary period. I didn't want to risk training to the point where it would disrupt my focus on the job. I decided to play it safe and wait until 1999. This time, I resolved that nothing would stand in my way.

I got let go from that job after the six month assessment, because the company was so small that it depended on short-term (i.e. three-week-long) projects for its money and employees would more often than not start a completely different project as soon as that project was finished[20]. The president pointed out that I would only be stressing myself out trying to repeatedly adapt to a new project every three weeks.

Six weeks later, I landed another contract job that ended on March 31, 1999, after which I was unemployed once again. In June, I got offered a job at the Royal Military College in Kingston. Luckily, my supervisor was going on holidays and would return to work on July 19th, two weeks after the Calgary Marathon. This freed me up to pursue my plan of driving to Calgary for the marathon, visiting friends and relatives along the way, and driving back in time to start my job. Being unemployed isn't pleasant, but it did give me more time to train for the marathon.

As planned, three weeks before the marathon I completed my peak run of two and a half hours, covering an estimated 30 kilometres. A few days later, I embarked on my trip across Canada. I think we Canadians have to traverse the country by car or bus or train at some time in our lifetimes in order to appreciate the breadth of our country. I arrived in Calgary on a Friday. That weekend, Claire and I went hiking in the mountains. The following Monday, which was six days before the race, I ran for 90 minutes. I wore spandex and a windbreaker, but because of the rain, my hands were cold. I decided that, the next time I ran in the rain, I would wear gloves.

The Calgary Marathon started at 7:00 a.m. I set my alarm for 4:30 a.m., trying to get as much sleep as possible, but allowing time for my breakfast food to digest. I didn't get up right away so I was late starting breakfast. I followed the regime suggested in [*Diamond, 1985*]: you eat fruit shortly after you get up and then wait twenty minutes before eating anything else. This put me further behind. It was 5:40 a.m. when I finished eating; the race started in one hour and twenty minutes.

The air temperature was +5°C. There was only a slight drizzle, so I was torn about whether to wear shorts or spandex pants. The strap for my wristwatch broke that morning. I didn't want to run the race without a watch, and I didn't have any pockets for my watch in my

---

[20] He let me go in a nice way and said, "I don't think this is a good fit for you." He agreed to act as a reference and said I was welcome to use their PC to work on my resume.

spandex pants. I ended up wearing shorts. The rain picked up during the race and continued for its entirety. As is often the case, I could feel the strain in my quadriceps which resulted from the combination of running far and running faster than my normally comfortable pace. My triceps seized up roughly half-way through the race. This was the first time I had ever felt triceps pain while running. Shortly afterwards, I could feel the food swishing in my stomach; I had not allowed enough time for the food to digest. By this time, I gave up looking at my watch, which was still tucked away in my pocket. My walking breaks became more frequent. Shortly after the 30 kilometre mark, everything fell apart and the quadriceps pain had become quite intense. I knew that quitting was not an option; I would have to put myself through the agony of training for a marathon all over again. With four kilometers left to go, I grimly resolved to walk the remainder of the race – not caring about anything other than finishing. Within one kilometer of the finish line, Claire appeared to cheer me on and ran beside me, and this motivated me to run to the finish line.

I was shivering when I finished the race and my nipples had become tender and chafed against my shirt. I didn't notice that my shirt was soaked in blood from my bleeding nipples until Claire told me, because my quadriceps were in so much pain. Claire walked with me to the refreshments tent, made sure I put on warm clothes and got me something warm to eat and drink. My quadriceps were so stiff for the next four days that it was too painful to descend stairs facing forwards; I had to go down sets of stairs facing backwards. I left Calgary the day after the marathon so it wasn't pleasant carrying my luggage down the stairs.

While driving, I refrained from using cruise control because it was actually more painful, and therefore less safe, to move my foot from the floor to the brake pedal than from the accelerator to the brake pedal. If I had used cruise control, my leg muscles might have seized up without me knowing – until I needed to brake suddenly and then it would be too late to stop safely. I had to hope that without using cruise control, I would realize when my leg muscles seized up and would have time to guide my leg to the brake pedal with my hands to bring the car to a stop. Fortunately, I did not have to test this theory.

After the race, I told Joe, one of the professors in my department at RMC that it had rained for the entire marathon and I had run it wearing shorts, a T-shirt, and gloves.

Joe replied, "The only worse thing you could have done was run barefoot."

Chapter 6

Moving to Kingston

"You take a chance when you reveal your weaknesses to your friends. But you destroy all your chances by keeping them secret."
—*Ron Abarbanel*

When I finished university in December 1996, I needed a break from the stress of studying and co-op work terms, so I wasn't anxious to jump into a full-time job. I planned to wind down for two or three months while I cross-country skied, played chess, and worked on jigsaw puzzles. However, only two weeks before I finished writing exams, my mother informed me of a job opening at Chalk River Laboratories. It sounded like I was well qualified for the job, so I applied. I couldn't turn down a potential job offer because many university graduates and other well-qualified people were out of work. The contract was only for three months and I simply resolved to postpone taking my break until the contract was completed.

During the summer of 1997, I went to another Navigators summer program – this time in Ottawa. I met Karen, Peter, and John there; I became friends with them and a few others from the program and we still get together for reunions two or three times a year. Navigators is an interdenominational Christian club on campus that is run by people who are mostly Christians. About once every two years, the Navigators host a summer-long training program. The aims of the program are to nurture students in their spiritual journey, to provide opportunities for them to meet other young Christian from across Canada, and to teach them how to look for employment. I attended a summer program in Calgary two years before and enjoyed it so much that I wanted to attend more gatherings. I had jokingly said that I was trying to fail a course during my final term so that I'd have an excuse to return to university in the winter and attend the program.

Ron Abarbanel, a Navs staff member and one of the leaders of both the Calgary '95 summer program and the Ottawa '97 summer program, originally considered rejecting my application to the Calgary '95 summer program. He prayed about it and decided he should at least get to know me. Ron called me in for an interview, described the program to me, and asked me how I thought I could contribute. I told Ron that I could entertain the other participants by telling jokes. Then he asked me if there was anything I thought he should know. I told him that I might be autistic. I had never heard the term "autistic" until my parents showed me the movie *Rain Man* in Grade 12; I still hadn't heard the term "Asperger's Syndrome" at that point.

During the Calgary '95 program, Ron strongly recommended that I get diagnosed. He thought that if I knew the name of my syndrome, I could explain my differences to people and then they'd know better how to adjust their approach when dealing with me. For example, I could tell employers that they would have to spend extra time with me initially but the investment would pay off. I would also need to change. All along, I had thought that people would look down on me if they found out I was autistic; I feared they would be less likely to accept me as a friend and would certainly be unwilling to hire me. Therefore, I thought my best chance was to bluff and make people think I was "normal".

I mentioned Ron's suggestion to my parents who explained that they had tried to get me diagnosed when I was younger, but eventually gave up because each doctor said something different. Ron thought it would be easier to get a diagnosis for me as an adult because my behaviours would be more consistent at this point. For a while, I found it too burdening to act as a mediator; Ron had not met my parents. In 1998, I took Ron's suggestion to heart and began the difficult task of trying to find a psychiatrist who was qualified to give a diagnosis in that area.[21] I was eventually referred to Dr. Paul Dagg, a psychiatrist at the Royal Ottawa Hospital. His first question was why I wanted to get a diagnosis and I replied, "Because Ron Abarbanel told me to." It was several years plus a major accomplishment later before the value of Ron's suggestion was recognized.

∽

It was July, 1999 when I began working at the Royal Military College, two and a half years since I completed my degree at University of Waterloo. I had accepted whatever job I could get and had been unemployed over half of this time. After I moved to Kingston, life seemed like heaven in three ways: I enjoyed my job; my living situation was ideal; and Kingston's location on Lake Ontario and its green space were ideal for triathlon training and exercise in general. Having completed a degree in Applied Math, I wanted a job applying math to real world issues. This job was just that: applying math in the

---

[21] See page xxiv for details

field of oceanography. I found a place to live because I knew the pastor of a local church who had previously pastored in Ottawa and his Youth Group and the Deep River Youth Group often did things together when I was in high school. When I asked him if he knew of anyone looking for a tenant, he suggested a couple from their church who had a spare room in the basement where their son was living. Their son and I got along like brothers. Being next to Lake Ontario made open-water swimming convenient. Kingston also had a running club with many runners my age who ran at the same speed or faster. Once a month, I cycled to Gananoque and back for the lovely view and exercise. County Road 2 has a three-foot-wide paved shoulder and little traffic since most drivers use Highway 401, so it was perfect for cycling.

On December 18th, 1999, the first winter after moving to Kingston, I cycled to Gananoque and back when the temperature was -5°C. There was no snow and I had dry roads to bike on, but I froze my feet. I still had to ride ten kilometres before I got home so I stopped off at work to get a break from the cold by doing a bit of work. When I stepped off my bike, I felt like I was walking on two blocks of ice.

Chapter 7

The Polar Bear Plunge

Q. Why did the nasty kid put ice cubes in his aunt's bed?
A. Because he wanted to make antifreeze.
—*http://www.scatty.com/jokes/riddles/strangeriddles7.html*

    I have known for some time that I can withstand more cold than the average person. It's not uncommon to see me cross-country skiing in the winter in a T-shirt because exercise helps to generate heat. I was a newspaper carrier in high school and almost always ran the entire route. One woman on my route would see me through her window every day and would decide what to wear based on what I was wearing for that day's weather. If I wore a T-shirt, she wore a winter coat. If I wore a sweatshirt, she wore several sweaters and a winter coat. No one knows what she would have worn if she'd seen me wearing a winter coat; she would probably hibernate.

    Deep River, where I grew up, is much colder than Kingston. In Grade 10, I never wore anything over my torso other than a T-shirt and a sweatshirt until December 18th. This was pushing my limit; I was unknowingly trying to see how long it would take me to come down with a cold. (The reason I finally wore a jacket on December 18th is that I finally did catch a cold.)

    When I was in Calgary in March, 2006, I ran around the Glenmore reservoir. The air is drier in Calgary which makes it seem warmer than it would be at the same temperature in Ontario. It was about +5°C when I left my sister's house. I took the bus to my starting point wearing shorts, long underwear, and a long-sleeved shirt. Immediately before the run, I removed my long underwear because it had warmed up. Part way through the run, I removed my shirt. I enjoyed the reactions of the people I met, especially since many of them were wearing winter coats. I said "Hello" or "It's a nice day" to almost everyone I met. One woman told me I was brave. When I passed three girls in their mid- to late-twenties, who were wearing long pants, short-sleeved shirts and jackets tied around their waists, I said, "It's a nice day." One of them replied in a friendly and enthusiastic way, "We thought it was hot, but you've taken it to the extreme." When I passed a woman walking towards me who was wearing a winter coat, I said, "It's a nice day," and she replied, "It's not that nice."

The Polar Bear Plunge

When I found out about the annual polar bear swim at Confederation Basin in Kingston on December 31, 2001, I leapt at the opportunity to participate, largely for the thrill. It cannot be properly classified as a dip because the water was too deep to stand and participants had to swim from one dock to another dock. It was a fundraiser for CASCA (Community Awareness to Stop Child Abuse) which I had never heard of. This swim helped raise awareness and money for CASCA.

I asked my Bible study group for information about how I could find out about the polar bear plunge because most of them had lived in Kingston longer than I had. Most of the group strongly discouraged me from doing the swim. I tried to tell them that my body has a remarkable ability to generate heat, but the following story wouldn't even convince them: On more than one occasion, I've travelled to the bus terminal carrying lots of luggage. Ottawa public transit would only take me within six blocks of the bus terminal and I got extremely overheated in my winter jacket carrying that much luggage for that distance. I would remove my winter jacket as soon as I got to the bus terminal where I could set down my luggage. I got into the habit of walking those six blocks in short sleeves and wouldn't feel cold. In hindsight, I realize that the people at my Bible study group told me not to participate in the polar bear plunge because they care about me.

I asked Joe, one of my professors, for information on how I could find out about the polar bear plunge. Joe warned me about the possibility of dying as he knew someone who had been very fit but died from the shock of entering the frigid water. Joe went on to say that this was no reason not to do it because my chances of dying riding my bicycle to work in the summer were greater than my chances of dying doing the polar plunge. He also cautioned that if one or two people died doing the polar plunge every year, it would be discontinued. About a week later, I asked Joe to sponsor me for the polar bear plunge and he did. Minutes later, Joe said something to my classmate but I was too far away to hear. Then Joe said to me, "We were just saying – you're going to die, Jay."

At the department Christmas party, I told Joe's wife that I would be doing the polar bear plunge and she called me a fool.

Cold water draws heat from the body approximately 23 times as fast as cold air. I predicted that during the polar plunge, I would be in the water for 30 seconds and concluded that this would be equivalent to being outside in the cold for 11.5 minutes. About a month before the polar bear plunge, I went for a walk outside after dark wearing only a bathing suit and running shoes. Someone told me after the fact that I'd either have an ambulance behind me or a police car behind me. I was confident that my neighbours were not likely to see me since it was dark outside and even if someone did call the police, I'd be finished my walk before the police arrived. Besides, what I did was completely legal.

A friend from my running club told me not to strip down to my bathing suit right before I entered the water. She explained that it was better to stand outside in my bathing suit for two or three minutes before entering the water in order to help get my body acclimatized.

The day of the polar bear swim finally arrived. During the swim, I could feel that the water was cold but I wasn't chilled. I was completely comfortable but didn't put my head under.

After the swim, I told Joe to tell his wife that I had enjoyed the swim and planned to do it again the next year.

The next time I saw Joe, I asked him, "Did you tell your wife...?"

He interrupted me and said, "Yes, and she said, 'Okay. There's no stopping him.'"

Then Joe went on to say that, "The first time you do it, it's a mistake. The second time, you mean to do it."

The polar bear swim was held for the last time in Kingston in 2001. The city's insurance company decided not to insure the event anymore because the previous year in New Brunswick, someone was carried underneath the ice and his body wasn't found for four hours.[22] I thought this was an absurd decision because Lake Ontario never freezes before New Year's Day and even if it did, there is no current in that part of the lake strong enough to pull someone under the ice. I was disappointed that this event was discontinued.

Over a week later, Joe told me again that I could have died.

I replied, "But I didn't die."

Joe commented, "Most people who do it don't die - just like most people who walk across Highway 401 don't die."

---

[22] This information was obtained from the Kingston Whig-Standard.

Chapter 8

Navs Reunion 2005

The good guest is almost invisible, enjoying him or herself, communing with fellow guests, and, most of all, enjoying the generous hospitality of the hosts.
—*Emily Post*

    The Navigators, an interdenominational Christian group at several university campuses across Canada, hosts a summer-long training program about once every two years. The daytime is open so that participants can either hold a full-time job or treat looking for work as a full-time job. The evenings consisted of modules with guest speakers. Special events, such as camping, white water rafting, or downhill skiing took place on weekends. The thrust of the program was to give the students spiritual nourishment and also to teach students how to look for a job.
    I attended the Calgary program in 1995 and the Ottawa one held in 1997. The Calgary '95 gang held a reunion at New Years. The reunions, although well-attended, were held for only three years. The Ottawa '97 reunions, on the other hand, were not so well-attended. Out of the 33 participants and staff members, only 12 attended but 8 of us still keep in touch. We have been getting together about two or three times a year for various occasions in addition to the annual reunions: we gathered for John's baptism and a surprise visit to Gunnar and Chantal's after they returned to Canada from being in India for a year.
    I had an idea in 2003, after the reunions had been happening for several years: I wanted to invite the Navs to Deep River for a weekend. I thought we could cross the Ottawa River in a canoe, kayak or my parents' sailboat and hike up Mount Martin, a popular hiking trail on the Quebec shore. Our family used to make that hike regularly when my sister and I were younger, but we got tired of doing it. On the Thanksgiving weekend in 2000, my mother and I hiked there again and that trek became an annual tradition. Thanksgiving weekend is the best weekend for the hike because it's not too hot, snow hasn't yet fallen and mosquito season has ended. I looked forward to showing my Navs friends this beautiful trail.
    By the time I checked with my parents and tried to coordinate dates and travel arrangements to Deep River with my friends, there wasn't a

weekend that was convenient for everyone to do the hike. We decided to plan early for 2004. Despite advanced planning, no one could make it except Karen and me.

※

The 2005 reunion took place in Deep River on the weekend of August 23-25, 2005, attended by Karen, John, Gunnar, Chantal and me. On the Saturday morning after we finished breakfast, I packed snacks, water, and Gatorade for the hiking trip. I carried water and Gatorade in a couple of two-litre pop bottles for refills for my friends and made sure everyone had his/her own water bottle. I am the type of person who likes to be prepared: I prefer to carry unwanted items rather than need something we could have packed for the trip; my backpack is always heavy.

My parents had planned to be home when my guests were there, but unexpectedly had to leave town because of a funeral. This made our Ottawa River crossing more challenging since my father is the only person in the family with a license to operate the sailboat; we had to cross the river in our canoe and the two kayaks. I realized just before we launched that I had forgotten to bring the spray skirts for the kayaks, but John and Gunnar didn't feel it was worth driving back to the house to get them. John and Gunnar each paddled a kayak while Karen, Chantal, and I paddled the canoe. There was a strong cross-wind and, even with Chantal and Karen paddling on the same side and me paddling on the opposite side, the canoe eventually started turning and I had to keep ruddering my paddle to straighten the canoe. I frequently turned the canoe eastward to hit waves head-on. About two-thirds of the way across the river, John announced that the footrests in his kayak were in an uncomfortable position, so he was going to head to the Quebec shore by the shortest route to adjust them. Gunnar stayed with John for safety reasons while the three of us proceeded in our canoe to the starting point of the hiking trail. Suddenly, John capsized. Karen, Chantal and I changed our course so we could get to the Quebec shore as soon as possible to deposit Chantal and the heavy gear and then help John. Once he was safely in our canoe, John explained that the waves kept splashing water into the cockpit of the kayak, and it had become too difficult to control. I regretted that I had forgotten the sprayskirts; they may have prevented John's flip.

John and Gunnar traded kayaks when we reached the Quebec shore, and John capsized the other kayak less than a minute after getting in, his second flip. Luckily, we didn't have to venture too far from shore for the remainder of the journey to the hiking trail. Gunnar and John were faster than the canoe and had to wait at the destination, but they seemed quite happy to have the chance to paddle along the scenic shoreline.

The hike begins with a short walk along a path followed by a stretch along a logging road – both of which are more or less flat – until you get to a trail that contains many more ascents than flat sections. When you get off the logging road and on the trail, it is fairly obvious which direction the trail goes, except for one confusing fork, but I was sure of the route. It took us 52 minutes to hike from the shoreline to the top of the mountain.

The view is spectacular! The entire town of Deep River and several miles of the forested shorelines of the Ottawa River are visible from the top of the mountain. We spent several minutes taking pictures, having a snack, and relaxing. The hike back down the mountain took 46 minutes. My supply of water and Gatorade ran out before the hikers reached the bottom of the summit and my cumbersome backpack had become noticeably lighter without the heavy liquids. Back on the shoreline, sweaty from the hike and pleasantly tired, the five of us had a refreshing swim in the Ottawa River before returning to the Ontario shore.

The river was calmer for our crossing to the Ontario side so it was a much more uneventful than the earlier one had been. Gunnar and I paddled the kayaks while Karen, Chantal, and John paddled the canoe with John in the stern.

After breakfast on Sunday, we went to the beach for a swim. While we were all relaxing in the river, Karen suggested that the following year, she and I should swim across the river with the others accompanying us in some of the boats. I thought this sounded like an interesting idea. After lunch, we left Deep River and headed home. We'd all had a great weekend.

Chapter 9

Pushing my Limits

"Good judgment comes from experience, and experience comes from bad judgment."

—Barry LePatner

    To celebrate its 50th anniversary, Camp Iawah hosted a retreat on the Victoria Day weekend of 2006. Most of the events took place in the dining hall. The people attending the retreat stayed in cabins. On Sunday afternoon, after the retreat had officially ended, I swam across Wolfe Lake as part of my triathlon training. Several people thought I was crazy. Sara L. and Michael, whom I met at that retreat, were going for a leisurely canoe ride and they agreed to paddle the canoe beside me while I swam across the lake.

    Since I wasn't wearing a bathing cap, the top of my head would often get cold so I would often switch to head-up breast stroke. There was a strong wind and one could see the ripples on the surface of the lake. I tried to aim for a point upstream so that the current would bring me to my destination. I knew the current was strong from the previous day when I went canoeing solo: the canoe would have turned in the opposite direction if I hadn't been paddling hard on the other side.

    Except for a five-minute swim at Higley Lake (about one mile north of Charleston Lake) the previous weekend, the swim across Wolfe Lake was my first open-water swim that season. I had done very little swimming all winter. It took me twenty minutes to cross the lake and I thought that was plenty of time in the water for my first swim of the season. I asked to ride back in the canoe. I blindly assumed that I would be fine as soon as I got out of the water. How wrong I was. I had not thought to bring any clothes with me – not even a towel. Luckily, Sara foresaw the impending predicament. She was wearing two sweatshirts, had warned me that it was going to be cold and windy in the middle of the lake and cautioned that the last thing we needed was a case of hypothermia. Sara removed her outer sweatshirt and told me to put it on and then put my lifejacket on top of it. I started to shiver less than five minutes into the canoe ride. I can't help but wonder if Sara wore an extra sweatshirt in anticipation of this happening, a forethought worthy of Sara's caring nature.

I was shivering so much that I didn't even try talking until about half-way across: Sara broke the silence by asking me how I had gotten into doing triathlons. She may have done this to get an idea of how I was feeling or maybe even to verify that I was still conscious. I started to answer the question but cut my answer short because my voice was shaking; talking made my throat feel constricted. When we were several minutes from shore, Sara told Michael to pick up the pace a little and challenged him to make it to the shore in four minutes. Minutes later, it started to rain lightly and Sara told Michael to paddle even faster. Poor Sara had to watch me shiver and probably wondered whether I'd survive the canoe ride. Michael, in the bow, couldn't see me shivering so he didn't understand the seriousness of my situation.

I had never been in a situation like this before and was unsure about how to proceed. I asked Sara for advice on whether to take a hot shower or just relax in the dining hall. Sara told me to get dried off quickly and get some warm clothes on. She told me that she didn't need the sweatshirt back right away so I put my windbreaker on over Sara's sweatshirt and headed back to the dining hall. I had to walk initially because my quadriceps were so tight; after several steps, I was able to run. I knew that as soon as people in the dining hall saw me, they would know I was in a state of potential hypothermia. One friend, who was playing cards with a few others, told me to have a hot shower – and quickly. I stopped shivering while in the shower but resumed shivering as soon as I stepped out of the shower. I had left my sweatpants in the cabin where I was staying and I wondered if I should have someone else get them for me. A friend told me to run there, as fast as I could, so I would generate heat. I followed her instructions as soon as I put on my running shoes. It took less than two minutes to run to the cabin and I did not shiver while running. I later researched hypothermia and found out that, while exercise will generate heat, it will also deplete energy reserves. [*Forgey, 1985*] I put on long underwear, spandex pants, socks, running shoes, a clean T-shirt, sweatshirt, and windbreaker. After I ran back to the dining hall, I had stopped shivering.

When I had sufficiently recovered, I talked to my friend and her husband, who is a doctor, hoping to gain more insight into hypothermia. I knew that hypothermia occurs when one is too cold but the question I wondered was, "How cold?" I wanted to know at what point you are considered to be hypothermic. Internet research yielded the following definition: "Hypothermia is defined as a core temperature of less than 35 degrees Celsius. It is the clinical state of subnormal temperature when the body is unable to generate sufficient heat to efficiently maintain functions."[23] (See Appendix L for definitions of the different levels of hypothermia.) My friend explained that when your body gets really cold, the blood doesn't circulate to your brain properly so you don't know that you're cold, and you won't care or realize that you need to get out of the water.

After the fact, it was suggested that I would have been better off to ride in the canoe across the lake and swim back. This is very true, but I had two reasons for not doing so: I wasn't sure whether I'd make it all the way across the lake and I was considering the possibility of swimming both across the lake and back if my stamina held out. Given the circumstances, I probably would have been better off to swim both ways instead of riding back in the canoe.

The moral of the story is this: avoiding hypothermia means not only knowing when to get out of the water but what you must do when you get out.

---

[23] http://www.freshpatents.com/-dt20090430ptan20090107491.php

Chapter 10

Navs Reunion 2006

"Friendship makes prosperity more shining and lessens adversity by dividing and sharing it."

—Cicero

June 30th, 2006 marked the third annual Navs reunion in Deep River. Amy joined Karen, John, Gunnar, Chantal and me that year. Amy, who had been living in Toronto for a few years and was good friends with Karen, did not attend the Ottawa '97 Navs summer program but had attended the two-week Navs program in Colorado in '96 that Karen, Gunnar, and I had also attended.

Once again, my parents were not present for the reunion since they had driven across Canada and were on their way back. When trying to decide on a weekend to hold the reunion, it was a trade-off between the July long weekend, which meant an extra day to enjoy the town of Deep River and also a backup day to undertake the hike in the event of rain, or later in July when my parents were home and we could ride in the sailboat. Having the reunion too early involved the risk that the Ottawa River might not be warm enough for swimming. A few years before at the beginning of July, I had found the temperature of the Ottawa River okay for practicing my strokes for triathlon training, but too cold to enjoy.

I asked my guests for their preferred date and activities. I made recommendations but the final decision depended on what my guests wanted from the reunion. Chantal said she trusted my judgment. The fact that the Navs are so easy-going makes my job as a host all that more enjoyable.

In 2006, instead of using one canoe and two kayaks to get the people across the Ottawa River, we used two canoes, one of which was borrowed from my friend Mark in Deep River. The river was reasonably calm. Karen had suggested the year before that she and I swim across the river because she enjoys open-water swimming but gets few opportunities to do so other than the annual Kingston triathlon. We took Karen up on her idea, and she, Amy and I swam across the river, a distance of about two kilometres. Gunnar paddled my parents' canoe solo while John and Chantal paddled Mark's canoe. I reached the Quebec shore in 48 minutes, Karen in 53 minutes and Amy in 58 minutes. Then we all rode in the canoes for about half a kilometre to the starting point of the hiking trail.

Gunnar and Chantal took one hour to climb the mountain. Chantal, being five months pregnant, didn't want to walk too fast. We all enjoyed the spectacular view again, ate our picnic lunch, took pictures and then hiked back down. Again this year after our hike, we cooled off in the river with a leisurely swim. Then Karen and I proceeded to swim back to the Ontario side from the base of the hiking trail, so the swim was longer than the earlier swim from the Ontario shore to the Quebec shore. The rest of them canoed back with us. On the return trip, I swam for an hour and 20 minutes and Karen for 1 hour and 26 minutes. I did the "puppy dog" approach, i.e., kept swimming ahead, turning around to meet Karen and then swimming ahead again. I probably swam close to three kilometres.

Amy and I paddled Mark's canoe to the same place where we had launched it – no one ever wants to carry a canoe further than necessary – while Gunnar drove the truck back to my parents' house.

On Monday, Chantal stayed at the house while the rest of us went to the beach to relax. Amy, John, and I took turns paddling my mother's kayak.

Once again, we'd all had a great weekend. Having a Navs reunion was now likely to become an annual event, providing I was in a physical and geographical position to host the reunion and that my parents were agreeable.

Chapter 11

A Sabbatical from Running

"Neither should a ship rely on one small anchor, nor should life rest on a single hope."

—*Epictetus*

In approximately November 2005, I decided that I would take a nineteen month sabbatical from running, starting immediately after the Kingston triathlon in August 2006 and ending with the Around the Bay 30K Road Race in Hamilton in March 2008. I would cut back on running for the entire race season of 2007 plus the winter on either side. Although I run all year round, I tend to do more running during racing season, which runs from mid-March until mid-October.

Running in general, not to mention running races, had been my main focus for almost ten years; it was time to re-think my priorities in terms of long-term plans. If nothing else, my lifestyle was due for a change. I had tentatively planned to maintain long distance cycling, casual open-water swims in the summer, and cross-country skiing. In other words, I would maintain all my other hobbies but significantly cut back on running. A few years ago, I participated in the Gatineau Loppet in both the 53-kilomtre race on Saturday (classical technique) and the 53-kilometre race on Sunday (skating technique). I planned to do the double race in both 2007 and 2008.

I would still run, and try to run at least once every two weeks, with the following changes:
- I wouldn't run more than twice a week.
- I wouldn't run more than 11 kilometres at once.
- I wouldn't do any races except for the Deep River triathlon.
- I wouldn't do any hill training or speed work.

I planned to show my face at the running club once in a while to see my friends and let them know I still existed but I would run casually while the rest of the club did their speed workout.

I had five reasons for taking this sabbatical:
- I wanted to give my knees and my back a rest.
- Taking the sabbatical would hopefully free up more time for other things.
- I would enjoy the races more after taking a break from them.

- I wanted to avoid letting the races dominate my life. (I'm not sure if I will ever get married, but if I do, I will have to be prepared to make many compromises for my wife and will likely have to give up some running races.)
- Most importantly, I wanted to prove to myself that running races wasn't the only way to stay in shape. I might live to be 80, but when I turn 60 my heart might still be good, but knee and back problems might prevent me from running. I have been told that running is not a long-term solution for staying in shape because of the impact it has on the joints.

The idea of taking a sabbatical from running was nothing new. In 1998, after being unemployed for eleven months and finally landing a job, I decided to focus on work and keep other activities to a minimum. All summer, I never ran more than six kilometres except for running the Deep River triathlon and running the 11 kilometres between work and home twice.

After starting at University of Waterloo, I never ran more than six kilometres for nearly two years and I didn't even come home for the Deep River triathlon because it took place during final exams. About a year before the sabbatical, although I still attended the running club and still participated in running races, I didn't do so as often, nor did I take running as seriously. I mentioned my plan of taking a running sabbatical to an acquaintance at the running club who totally agreed with me. He had once pushed the extreme and quit his job to move to a different city based on the belief that moving to that place would help him run faster. It didn't, so he moved back to Kingston and, luckily, he got his job back.

Cutting back on running to reduce injuries was not a new idea for me: I had been forced to take the occasional sabbatical from running. Over the years, I had several injuries that interfered with my running regime, including knee and back injuries and shin splints. (Appendix D explains this in greater detail.) The only difference between this sabbatical and previous sabbaticals was that this sabbatical was planned and completely voluntary. Some people wondered why I would arbitrarily take this sabbatical; others didn't believe I would do so because they thought I was already totally hooked on running and wouldn't be able to give it up.

Conceivably, in ten years, I could be married, have children and own a house. House repairs and spending time with my children would be very time-consuming. If I also had an injury, that would make running difficult. How could I be true to my other commitments while still remaining physically active? I could see a day coming when I would have to eliminate running from my lifestyle and take up less strenuous forms of exercise to remain fit.

I had been participating in triathlons with the same used bicycle for years. That was partly because I didn't see the point in spending large sums of money on an expensive bike just to shave a few minutes off my time when I do triathlons mainly for fun. I commute to work and get around town by bicycle; I wanted a cheap bike for commuting since it was less likely to get stolen. Being an avid cyclist, I had first joined the Kingston Velo Club in 2004. During one of the club rides in 2006, we got talking about the cost of a good used bicycle. I momentarily considered that I might buy one after I began my sabbatical when I might have more time to cycle.

The sabbatical from running was mainly a test to see if I could stay in shape and be happy without relying on running races, or running in general. I thought that I'd maintain a comfortable level of physical activity by doing less than usual, but at a more comfortable pace. If another form of exercise took over, so be it. In retrospect, I should have been able to predict that some other form of activity would take over. What would it be? Competitive cycling? Tennis? Only time would tell.

Part Three
Training for a Dream

Chapter 12

The Dream Desire

"To accomplish great things, we must dream as well as act."
—Anatole France

On July 19, 2006, 15-year-old Jenna Lambert of the Greater Kingston Area, who has cerebral palsy, completed her swim across Lake Ontario. The hardest part of the swim was the feeding times when she had to eat with one hand while treading water with the other hand. This was the first time I had heard of anyone swimming across Lake Ontario (or any of the other great lakes). Within a matter of days of Jenna's successful crossing, I thought to myself, "I want to swim across Lake Ontario."

After making my decision to cross Lake Ontario, I did a lot of thinking about whether or not the swim was actually feasible and started to plan a training schedule to see what the timing might look like. I momentarily thought of doing the swim in 2007 but quickly decided to play it safe and focus on 2008; I was doubtful that one year would be long enough to train. There is a 13 kilometre Swim for the Cure held annually in the Severn River[24]. I resolved to do that swim in 2007 to see how I would handle swimming a distance of that order of magnitude[25] before undertaking something much longer. If I aimed for 2007, I'd be tempted (at the beginning of the summer) to push myself beyond my comfort level. Besides, by aiming for 2008 I could train in open water for the entire summer of 2007 and decide at the end of the season whether I thought I'd be ready for summer 2008; if I didn't think I'd be ready, I would still have the option of aiming for summer 2009. Another advantage is that I had an entire year to focus mainly on the training – and make sure it was something I really wanted to do – before I needed to get serious about the organizational aspect or get other people heavily involved in the organizing.

The furthest I had ever swum without touching land or using floatation was approximately three kilometers when I swam across the Ottawa River with Karen three weeks earlier.[26] Karen has more faith

---
[24] www.swimforthecure.ca
[25] My experience taking part in the 2007 Swim for the Cure is described in Chapter 23.
[26] See Chapter 10 for a description of this swim.

in my athletic capabilities than I have in myself; no one has more faith in me than Karen does. Therefore, Karen was one of the first people I informed of my dream desire. I asked Karen, "Do you think I can swim across Lake Ontario?"

Karen immediately replied, "Yes."

I'm glad she said yes because, if she didn't believe I could do it, no one would. Karen later expanded on her answer by saying that she knew I would not try it unless I adequately prepared for it and was confident that I could do it. Peter Wong, a mutual friend, also expressed his faith that I could complete the crossing and he said that he'd accompany me in his kayak.

∽

Vicki Keith, a Swim Master and marathon swimmer, is well known in the greater Kingston area for her swimming accomplishments. Vicki had been Jenna's coach and Vicki once swam across all five great lakes within a two-month period. Several people whom I informed of my ambition told me to talk to Vicki Keith. One friend whose opinion I trust said, "Don't do it based on your own knowledge. Talk to people who have done it like Vicki Keith."

As soon as I touched base with Vicki, she directed me to the website for Solo Swims of Ontario (SSO), a non-profit volunteer-driven organization. Vicki said that she would be unable to coach me because she coaches thirty young people and wouldn't have the time. However, she told me that I was welcome to e-mail her if I had any more questions.

The SSO website contains a pdf file on Regulations and Information for a solo swim. One must register a swim by June 15 or eight weeks before the crossing, whichever is earlier. I deemed it highly unlikely that I'd be swimming in Lake Ontario before June 1, which would give me no more than two weeks to decide for sure whether I'd be ready for summer 2007, another reason to postpone the swim until summer 2008.

∽

Ever since I moved to Kingston in 1999, I had been a fanatic about long-distance cycling in addition to cross-country skiing and long-distance running, both of which had been a significant part of my life even before I moved to Kingston. I am frequently on the lookout for physical challenges which would push my physical capabilities to the

edge. When I initially decided that I wanted to swim across Lake Ontario, the plan was to do it for my personal satisfaction, for the challenge, and to stay in shape – until people started to tell me that it made more sense to do it for a charity. Asperger's Syndrome was a logical choice since I am personally affected by Asperger's Syndrome. Three benefits would result from this feat:
- it would raise financial support for the Asperger's community; (2)
- it would raise awareness of Asperger's Syndrome
  it would raise awareness of Asperger's Syndrome
- it would demonstrate that people with Asperger's Syndrome are, in fact, capable of unusual feats (i.e. it would help dispel any myths that people with Asperger's Syndrome are handicapped and unable to accomplish what the average person is capable of accomplishing)

When I trained for my first running marathon, I had to make several lifestyle changes to make it happen. Training for a swimming marathon requires a much more substantial lifestyle change than training for a running marathon.

※

I'm sensitive to distractions in any new environment, especially a new job. I had been on contract for over two years and was unsure how long my job would last. There was certainly the possibility that my current job would come to an end before I could bring my dream desire to completion two years later. I hoped that either (a) the job would keep getting renewed for the next two years (which is what happened); or (b) when I find my next job, I would explain to the interviewer what I'm doing and why I'd like to start the job *after* the swim (unless I really like the job or am offered an irresistible salary).

One roadblock was that I would have to find people who would be willing to accompany me in a canoe, kayak or other marine vessel while I trained, since it would be too dangerous to venture too far from shore without a boat.

The main roadblock to accomplishing my dream's desire would be the cost. This would include fuel for the boats, boat rentals (if necessary), hotels and meals for the crew, plus advertising.

Any discouragement resulting from those roadblocks didn't last long. The following incident gave me more than enough motivation to want to overcome the roadblocks. A co-worker had a calendar on his desk with a picture of a six-year-old child with his back turned.

The page was titled, "Priorities" with the following quotation underneath: "A hundred years from now it will not matter what my bank account was, the sort of house I lived in, or the kind of car I drove, but the world may be a different place because I was important in the life of a child." By swimming across Lake Ontario, I would have an impact on the Asperger's community and would hopefully make a difference in the life of at least one child. There were going to be times when I wouldn't want to train but I'd train anyways because I knew that would make things easier in the long run. There would be times when I'd want to quit the goal altogether; the fact that I was doing it for a cause quickly made me dismiss that thought each time.

Prior to setting the goal to swim across Lake Ontario, my swimming had been confined to open-water swimming in the summer for enjoyment and triathlon training. As part of my training to swim across Lake Ontario, I decided that I would:
- do a few open-water training swims that summer (longer than my usual training swims required to train for a 2-kilometre triathlon swim);
- swim in the pool regularly throughout the winter for the next two years;
- continue to spread the word of my dream desire, paying extra attention to peoples' reaction, especially when I first start to tell them. (I would eventually tell everyone but would be selective on whom I told first);
- recruit more people to paddle beside me in a canoe or kayak.

I wouldn't know whether swimming across Lake Ontario was remotely feasible unless I trained. I wouldn't train super-hard unless I really wanted to do it. I wouldn't make up my mind that I really wanted to do it unless I had confidence that I'd succeed.

A by-product of setting this schedule was that I unknowingly made a firm resolution that I would give it everything I had: 100 percent, if necessary.

It is easier to train when you have people to be accountable to. People are more likely to support your efforts towards your goal if they know you're serious but they won't believe you're really serious until after you've trained for a while. Therefore, the most difficult part would be the initial stage when I began to train and had the burden of showing people that I was serious.

On August 26th, 2006, I undertook my very first training swim towards this goal; I swam from HMCS Cataraqui to the ferry dock on

Wolfe Island, a distance of 5.25 kilometres, with John C. accompanying me in his kayak. Before the outdoor swimming season ended, I completed three swims of similar distance.

When I went home to Deep River on Thanksgiving weekend, I had already given up hope of doing any more open water swimming until the following spring. However, after my mother and I hiked up Mount Martin, I swam for 20 minutes and the water was certainly bearable. On Thanksgiving Monday, my mother kayaked beside me while I swam in the Ottawa River for 70 minutes, noticeably shivering for several minutes after I came out.

Chapter 13

Hypothermia?

"If you stop every time a dog barks, your road will never end."
—Arabian Proverb

    Peter Snell often gives me a ride to work. When I told him about my dream desire to swim across Lake Ontario, he commented that being in the lake for several hours could lead to hypothermia. He made it clear that he thought I could do it and didn't want to discourage me but he pointed out that it's easy to overlook something important like hypothermia even when you're being cautious.

    On August 26th, 2006, a week and a half after Peter issued this warning, I swam to Wolfe Island. This was my first major training swim toward the project. When I swam to Wolfe Island, I felt chilled before the two-hour mark so I wondered whether I could swim across Lake Ontario without going into hypothermia. Despite feeling chilled, I had high hopes that I would achieve my dream of swimming across Lake Ontario for the following five reasons:

- My stroke would be more efficient and I would be able to travel further with less energy;
- I would have worked up a tolerance to cold water;
- I would coat my body with Vaseline before the actual crossing;
- I planned to eat Access Bars before and during the swim, which would help me withstand the cold water. Access Bars, manufactured solely by Melaleuca, are designed to help convert fat into energy and swimmers report that they help to keep up their energy so they don't feel as cold;
- Although I was chilled when I swam to Wolfe Island, I was far from hypothermia and I could have continued swimming for some time. I was shivering when I came out of the water, but I was fine as soon as I dried off and put on warm clothes. In fact, I started to overheat while I paddled John's kayak back to the mainland.

    On Thanksgiving weekend, less than two months after I had informed my parents of my dream desire to cross Lake Ontario, my mother and I canoed across the Ottawa River and then hiked up Mount Martin. Meanwhile, my father had stayed at home to clean the sailboat before putting it away for the winter. While my father was in the driveway, Mr. Fulford ran by and chatted with my father who informed Mr. Fulford about my goal.

Mr. Fulford was concerned and asked, "Does Jay know what he's getting himself into?"

My father replied, "I don't think so."

One of Mr. Fulford's friends had swum across Lake Ontario. Although he completed the crossing, he unwittingly went into hypothermia and spent two days in the hospital. I found out later that although he didn't know he was in hypothermia, his Swim Master had known and chose not to abort the swim because the swimmer was so close to finishing. This swimmer was from the Caribbean and, although he had been to Canada before and knew how cold Lake Ontario could be, he probably did most of his open-water training in the Caribbean. He would not have been acclimatized to the cold water. I had been researching hypothermia ever since my brush with it when I had swum across Wolfe Lake the previous May[27]. [*Forgey, 1985*] (See also Appendix L.)

My mother warned me that the swim would cost a lot of money and asked me more than once, "Are you sure you want to do this?" Change is often challenged. There are many examples of people who face disbelief or disapproval when they undertake a goal, but those who doubted become supporters later on. Once my parents knew I was determined to accomplish this goal, they understood that I wouldn't be swayed by anyone's opinion. They knew they either had to stand behind me or stay out of it. My mother and father turned out to be two of my best sources of support for the swim.

A woman I met through a friend had swum across Lake Ontario and when I connected with her, she told me that she had suffered moderate to severe hypothermia at the end of her swim. I know of at least one other person who had encountered the same problems by the end of a long swim. I mentioned my concern about hypothermia to Vicki. As is typical of me, I kept making more and more paraphrases of the same basic concern.

Vicki's reply, August 30, 2007:

From what I have heard from you, it does not appear that hypothermia is going to be a huge issue. You have told me the

---

[27] This close-call experience is described in Chapter 9 – "Pushing my Limits".

temperatures you have dealt with, and you seem to handle them well. This does not mean that you shouldn't remain aware of the issue; just remember, if you feel cool or are shivering, you are still fine. If you listen to your body, you will know what is too cold. If you are miserable, shivering uncontrollably and can't find any resolution you are getting close. Tell your crew that if you stop making sense in conversation, can't answer simple questions, stop being able to perform the stroke at the same level (hips and feet drop well below the surface), these are all signs of hypothermia, and things I would look for if I was concerned about hypothermia in a marathon swimmer.

As a marathon runner, I have always felt fit to the point that if I'm cold, I can generate heat through physical activity. I felt that hypothermia was highly unlikely to become an issue during any of my short training sessions. The body has a remarkable ability to heal itself. Whenever something goes wrong, the body will signal danger, as well as assist itself in remedying the problem: shivering is an automatic response to being cold. When I'm sleep-deprived, my internal "heat-generating mechanisms" don't work as well. I suspected that during the last hours of the swim across Lake Ontario, I would be so focused on finishing the swim that I wouldn't necessarily be doing whatever was necessary to prevent and respond properly to the onset of hypothermia.

Vicki's reply, October 19, 2007:

You have spoken so often about your worry about hypothermia, but with what you tell me, it isn't that big an issue for you. You obviously have the capability of withstanding cold water. You now need to stop focusing on that as a major risk, and just advise your crew of the risks so they know how to handle it in the unlikely event you become hypothermic.

When I was in grade school, my sister and I had front row seats to a Corey Hart concert in Ottawa. About a month before the concert, my cousins came to visit and one of them said, "Corey Hart will *not* sing 'Sunglasses at Night' at his concert. I can promise you that." My mother said, "If Corey Hart does sing that song, Jay's going to say, 'But Rory said he wouldn't sing it.'" That's exactly what happened. I said that largely because my mother said that I would. After what Vicki had said, I wondered if my mother would be thinking, "If Jay does go into hypothermia, he's going to say, 'But Vicki said I wouldn't go into hypothermia.'"

Chapter 14

A Risky Adventure

"He who risks nothing has nothing and is nothing."
—*Leo Buscalia*

On Friday, September 29th, 2006, my friend Jens, who was one of my roommates from university, came to visit me in Kingston from Kitchener. The next day, Jens paddled my kayak beside me while I did a training swim. It was an old white-water kayak that my mother had bought used twenty years earlier and had recently given to me. When Jens and I arrived at the lake with my kayak and the other safety equipment, we noticed that the waves were three feet high because of the strong wind. Jens asked me, "Are you sure you want to do this?"

I told him I wanted to go ahead because I had to be prepared for all kinds of bad weather when I swam across Lake Ontario and I wasn't going to be swayed from trying. I was more concerned for Jens. Several times, I had gone kayaking by myself and I'd had trouble getting the kayak away from shore: the waves would push the kayak back into shore faster than I could get into it and get control, and then it was too shallow for the kayak to float. Each time this had happened, I'd been fine once I got the kayak out far enough from the shore. We didn't have that problem this time because I was there to hold the kayak in place until Jens got into the cockpit and started paddling.

Jens and I proceeded away from shore towards the westernmost tip of Simcoe Island, which is about 6.4 kilometres away from our starting point by Pleasant Point. Because of the rough waves, I frequently swallowed water and started coughing. Then I would say to Jens, "I'm okay; I just swallowed some water," and we would proceed. At least once, I got slapped in the face by a wave. Jens was able to keep up with me but not without paddling hard. He was thinking, "I hope Jay gets tired soon. I'm not sure how much longer I can keep this up." Jens was saddled not only with the responsibility of going as fast as I was, but also with staying near me and keeping the kayak pointed towards our destination.

After swimming for 45 minutes, I decided to turn around and head back; I had never swum that far in high waves before. More urgently, I felt chilled and didn't want to be too far from shore without enough body heat to make it back. We both thought that the return trip would be easier since the waves would be behind us and would help bring us toward shore. Jens had paddled hard on the first half of the trip, but on the return trip, the waves were pushing the kayak towards the shore faster than they were pushing me since a kayak has less resistance to the water than a swimmer does. Jens kept getting ahead of me and could not back-paddle fast enough to stay beside me. About two minutes after the turnaround point, Jens figured that if he turned the kayak around, he could paddle forwards facing me and would be better able to stay beside me. When Jens tried to turn the kayak around, a wave hit the kayak broadside and it capsized. When he got out of the kayak, he immediately handed me the spare lifejacket, knowing that if I subsequently got into trouble, he wouldn't be able to get to me in time with the lifejacket. Then Jens blew his whistle twice.[28]

    I had inserted a beach ball into both the bow and stern of the single-compartment kayak to keep it afloat if it flipped over. Minutes after the upset, the beach ball in the bow floated out of the kayak and blew away. Luckily, the beach ball in the stern fit more snugly and kept the kayak afloat with one end pointing straight up. However, with one end submerged, the kayak was very difficult to move. Jens and I swam for shore, carrying the paddle and the throw rope while pulling the kayak. At least once, Jens suggested that we abandon the kayak but I didn't want to let it sink if we could prevent that. I continued to pull the kayak with one hand and hold the paddle with the other hand, using only my legs to kick. I tried tying the throw rope to the loop at the end of the kayak so I could tow the kayak, but the knot came loose and I didn't notice until the kayak was several metres back. I swam back for the kayak and then continued pulling it for a short while, but realized that I wouldn't catch up to Jens while towing the kayak. I didn't know how well Jens could withstand the cold water and was concerned that he might go into hypothermia. Reluctantly, I abandoned the kayak, knowing that I might never see it again, and caught up to Jens.

    We kept heading for the shoreline, not caring where we ended up. About one hour after the upset, we finally made it to someone's home on the Pleasant Point shoreline. I tried to run up a concrete boat ramp, but slipped and fell, gashing my shin. Jens, who wasn't yet out of the water, crawled up the ramp. When he got out of the water, he felt waterlogged and had to stand still for a few seconds while the excess water dripped from his clothes. We ran barefoot through the yard and

---

[28] One blast of a whistle means, "Where are you?" Two blasts means, "Come to me." Three blasts means, "I need help."

onto the road. On both the swim to shore and the walk that followed, Jens and I were both more concerned for the other person than ourselves. Within minutes, a family drove by in a pickup truck. Shivering, I flagged the driver down, told him what had happened, and he agreed to drive us home. Jens and I hugged onto each other to help us keep warm in the open back of the pickup truck.

Jens and I both took a hot shower and donned warm clothes when we got back to my house. Our next concern was recovering the kayak. We didn't want to waste any time, so we called the Canadian Coast Guards, to see if they would rescue the kayak and what they would charge us to do so. The coast guards rescue people, but don't normally rescue a kayak. They made an exception in this case, concluding that a floating kayak could be a hazard to other boaters. We walked back to the shore and noticed the kayak barely ten metres from the shoreline. I could have easily swum into the lake and pulled the kayak back, but the coast guards had already arrived. The coast guards lifted the kayak out of the water, deposited it on the shore, and then left so quickly that I had barely enough time to thank them. Jens and I carried the kayak, along with the warm clothes I had left at the starting point, back to my house.

The first time John C. saw me after he read my diary entry on the above event, he asked me, "Do you want the lecture?"

I said, "Yes."

John reminded me that I had felt chilled when he accompanied me on my swim to Wolfe Island at the end of August. That had been over a month earlier, so John wanted to know how could I have possibly expected to make it to Simcoe Island that late in the season. John's main comment was that I should stay close to shore when doing training swims.

I asked, "How close?"

John replied, "100 yards."

John's advice might seem like a contradiction. He had paddled beside me all the way to Wolfe Island. How is it that John was telling me to follow rules that he hadn't followed himself? John has lots of experience and clearly knew what he was doing, whereas Jens had very little experience kayaking.[29] It's scary to think what could have

---

[29] If my stroke rate or pace had started slowing down or I had shown any signs of hypothermia, John would have known when to abort the swim and head for the nearest shoreline. John wouldn't have ventured too far from shore without being aware of this possibility. Jens, on the contrary, did whatever I told him to do, and if I were too fatigued to make it back to shore, Jens wouldn't have known until it was too late.

happened if Jens had been unable to stay near me. That would have defeated the purpose of having someone accompany me in a kayak. Experience and advice had proven that it is better to stay close to shore so that if the swimmer and boating companion get separated, they can head to shore more quickly and safely reunite. The benefits of swimming too far from shore seldom outweigh the costs. The rule I adopted at this point was, "Whenever there is any doubt, stay close to shore."

Chapter 15

Embarking on a Training Regime

"By the yard, life is hard. By the inch, it's a cinch."
—American proverb

Even though I had been participating in triathlons for several years, what I couldn't do was swim fast or maintain the front crawl stroke for long periods. It would be more correct to say that I *didn't want to* maintain the front crawl stroke because I wanted to breathe when I wanted, not when the stroke rhythm dictated I should breathe. After the 2-kilometre swim in the Kingston triathlon in August 2006, my record for maintaining the front crawl stroke was two or three minutes. In addition, whenever I did front crawl, I'd breathe only to the right and breathe every second stroke. When I got tired of doing front crawl, I'd switch to another stroke, such as breast stroke, back crawl, or side stroke.

A former coach of the Kingston Masters Aquatic Club (KMAC) had told me years ago to learn to breathe on both sides, reasoning that most triathlons are "out and back"; if there were waves, I'd have to breathe on one side on the way out and the other side on the way back to avoid the waves hitting me in the face. (At that time, the only swimming I did was in triathlons.) I tried breathing on the left several times, but each time, I thought I was going to suffocate so I gave up and went back to breathing only to the right.

One characteristic of Asperger's Syndrome is that I require structure. Before I committed to swimming across Lake Ontario, I didn't have the discipline or the desire to go to the pool regularly throughout the winter. I rarely swam during the winter; I would wait until the lakes were warm enough to begin my training for the swimming part of a triathlon. I could tread water and swim well enough to get from one point to another, so that was good enough for me. This explains why I ranked so poorly in the swimming section of the triathlon in comparison to the cycling and running. As soon as I decided to swim across Lake Ontario, I knew that I'd need to continue my swimming regimen throughout the winter.

On Thanksgiving weekend of 2006, I swam for over an hour in the Ottawa River. After that swim, it didn't take me long to decide that it was my last time in open water for the season and that my training would happen at indoor pools until the spring.

Later that October, I went to the pool at the Kingston Military Community Sports Centre (KMCSC) and swam the front crawl stroke non-stop for 45 minutes. This was by far the longest I had maintained the front crawl stroke.

On October 31st, I paid my first visit of the year to the Kingston Masters Aquatic Club and officially joined the club in November. I had not been to a KMAC practice for over three years.

In November, I tried breathing only to the left. As always, I felt like I was going to suffocate but I forced myself to do it anyway. The only reason I forced myself to adapt to breathing both ways was that the SSO Regulations and Information manual cautioned that swimmers would get a sore neck crossing the lake if they always breathe to the same side. I knew that I'd have to breathe only on the left for a while to get used to it. I wondered what might happen if I abstained too long from breathing on the right; I might get used to breathing only on the left and not want to go back to breathing on the right. Luckily, Trish, a KMAC coach, suggested the solution that most triathletes already know: breathe every three strokes and alternate sides when breathing. This is called bilateral breathing.

The first time I tried breathing every three strokes, I gasped at the end of every length when I brought my head up and it was quite a feat to swim 100 metres breathing every three strokes. I simply wasn't used to receiving that little oxygen. Less than a month later, I was comfortable with bilateral breathing, so comfortable, that I felt I could go on forever. Looking back, learning bilateral breathing was much easier in a pool than in open water.

As I was learning the bilateral breathing, I set a goal to swim for 90 minutes to see if I could maintain the front crawl for that entire time. My next goal was to swim 180 lengths in 90 minutes by March 31, 2007.

On December 20, 2006, I swam front crawl non-stop for eighty-five minutes and then treaded water for two minutes. I was 9.5 minutes shy of my targeted pace. I breathed every three strokes and at the end of every lap I touched the side of the pool as I took a breath. At the time, it felt like it was a huge accomplishment to be able to maintain the front crawl that long, regardless of my speed. I felt like I could have gone another half hour, but I predicted I would get tired (i.e. shoulder fatigue, among other things) shortly after that.

excerpt from e-mail message from Vicki, December 11, 2006:

I think if you are not able to swim 6 hours of front crawl comfortably (and feeling like you could go on forever) by April, you should consider focusing on the summer of 2008.

    I had already told Vicki in my initial letter to her in October 2006 that I was aiming for 2008; I had never intended to undertake the crossing of Lake Ontario in 2007 as Vicki had thought. I had no hard feelings towards Vicki over this. She hadn't known me very long and she was already doing me a favour by taking time out of her busy schedule to offer me advice.

    In early January, I again swam the front crawl uninterrupted for 90 minutes and got a cramp in my foot during the last length. With less than 25 metres to go, I maintained the front crawl despite the pain. The lifeguard suggested that I hadn't been drinking enough water. A few days earlier, I got foot cramps during the KMAC workouts. I decided that the next time I got a foot cramp while swimming the front crawl stroke, I would switch to the breast stroke to see if that eliminated the pain. I found out a few weeks later that swimming the breast stroke for 200 metres would eliminate the pain after which I could resume my front crawl. Artillery Park, the pool where I attended KMAC and the only municipal swimming pool in Kingston, had a two-hour lane swim every weekday morning. I committed to a two-hour "time trial" once every two weeks, usually on a Tuesday or Thursday, after attending the KMAC workout. I tried to swim as many lengths as possible within the two hours. Occasionally, I was lucky and had an empty lane at KMAC so I could swim front crawl uninterrupted for longer than two hours.

    One day, after lane swim, I decided to attend an aqua-fit class to check it out. I met Jane and we got talking after the class. I told her about my goal to swim across Lake Ontario. She was very supportive and offered to paddle beside me during some of my training swims. As an added bonus, Jane has experience with hypothermia and is very knowledgeable about how to recognize the signs of hypothermia.

    Part way through the winter I stopped touching the side of the pool during the time trials, even though I swam faster when I made contact with the sides. I turned in an arc at the end of each length in order to mimic the crossing as much as I could. I stopped touching the sides on my speed workouts for a while but, partly to add variety and partly at the coach's suggestion, I resumed touching the sides for speed trials. On March 31st, I was three minutes shy of my goal to swim 180 lengths in 90 minutes.

The Gatineau Loppet used to consist of classic races and ski-skate races on the same day until recently when the format was altered and all classic races were held on Saturday and all ski-skate races were held on Sunday. Three years earlier, I participated in both the 53-kilometre classic race and the 53-kilometre ski-skate race. I participated in both races again in 2007. This had been my plan, as part of the running sabbatical, even before I decided I wanted to swim across Lake Ontario. I had a minor cold for a few days afterwards, which may have caused chest pain during my swimming practices. I tried every different stroke I knew, but no stroke change would alleviate the pain; I was forced to sit on the deck for a few minutes every so often. What would I do if this happened on the crossing?

There were times when I didn't want to go to swimming practice. Reminding myself, "I am doing this for the children," was usually enough to keep me motivated. Each time I reminded myself of the children and focused on my enjoyment of swimming in general, I felt a renewal of motivation.

In April, I travelled to Calgary for a week to visit my sister Claire. While I was there, I was overjoyed to learn that the swimming pool at the Southern Albert Institute of Technology (SAIT) was open for lane swimming for two and a half hours each day. I swam the front crawl non-stop for the full time, finishing fourteen minutes shy of my usual target pace of three kilometres per hour. I could easily have switched to the breast stroke for five minutes and then swum the front crawl non-stop for another hour.

At the beginning of May, I found out from an acquaintance that Progress Fitness Centre in Kingston has two lanes available for swimming at all times. I would have gone to Progress Fitness Centre sooner if I had known about it; all winter, I'd been hoping to find a pool with a longer lane-swim. The only drawback is that the deepest part of the pool is 1.35 metres and I can barely tread water without touching my feet on the bottom. Despite this drawback, I was very happy to have a place for longer lane swims. I swam for about five hours the first time I went. Later in May, I did one more long swim at Progress Fitness Centre before beginning my training in Lake Ontario. I only did the front crawl, except for about 700 metres of breast stroke, because my shoulders were getting tired. As a marathon runner, I knew that through practice, I could condition my muscles so that my shoulders wouldn't get tired.

During the winter of 2007, I practised my front crawl in various swimming pools using bilateral breathing. I still had no answers to the following questions:
- a. Could I maintain my front crawl for long distances in open water?
- b. Could I breathe bilaterally for long periods of time in open water?
- c. Could I maintain my front crawl in three-foot waves?

I had to proceed with what I knew so far and have confidence that everything would work out.

Chapter 16

How Safe is Safe?

"Why not go out on a limb? Isn't that where the fruit is?"
—*Frank Scully*

In September 1999, two months after I moved to Kingston, I swam to Cedar Island and then toured the island in the hopes of bringing back old memories from when my parents used to take my sister and me in our sailboat to St. Lawrence Islands National Park in the Thousand Islands. There is a lot of boat traffic (motor and sail) around these islands, and a swimmer risks being hit. I regularly swam to Cedar Island and back about twice a year – more for the swim than the tour. This was part of my triathlon training. Each time, I made sure to let someone know where I was going and roughly when I would be back. Then I always let them know when I was back home safely. When I decided whom to tell, I only had a small selection of people to choose from because I didn't want to tell anyone who would possibly criticize me since I don't like being criticized. I had basically divided my friends into two groups: those who would criticize me and those who wouldn't.

Each time I swam to Cedar Island, a red flag went up in my mind. Years ago, my mother had told me not to swim alone and she explained that, "If you get tired and get a cramp, you could sink before we even knew what had happened." My friend's father once told me, caringly but firmly, "If you try to swim without an escort boat beside you, you're a dead duck." He explained that I'd likely be hit by a motorboat since a swimmer without an escort boat is all but invisible to boaters. I knew I was breaking a safety rule by swimming alone, but I made a supreme effort to keep as many other safety rules as possible, such as not to swim at night and to exit the water at the first sign of being chilled.

I have told several people that I don't like being criticized and, when people told me not to swim to Cedar Island unaccompanied, I took that as criticism and stopped talking to those people about my lone swims. The message was quite clear: "You criticize me and I won't talk to you about this anymore." Michelle, my co-worker, used to be a lifeguard. I explained to her that I don't like being criticized and when she told me not to swim to Cedar Island alone, I took it as criticism. She later told me that she didn't intend her words to be critical. She went on to say that if she had told me to go ahead with my swim and something had happened to me, she would feel terrible. However, if she told me not to swim, and I swam anyway and something happened to me, she could honestly say to herself that she had done her part. One of the safety rules she had always taught as a lifeguard was to swim with a buddy.

Nicola, a friend who lives in Calgary, also disagreed with my swimming to Cedar Island alone. When I told her that I interpreted such disagreement as criticism, she apologized. She told me that an acquaintance of hers had been very fit (i.e. he did triathlons and marathons) and was a good swimmer. He swam to a distant island alone and, while swimming laps around the island, had a heart attack and drowned. Nicola told me that she was happy when I called her because it let her know that I was still alive. Nicola suggested that I pray that I'd find more swimming partners.

I found the hassle of finding an accompanying paddler or swimming partner was more trouble than it was worth. It required planning in advance and coordinating our schedules. Asperger's Syndrome makes it more difficult for me to discern the circumstances under which it is appropriate to ask someone to paddle beside me. Haunted by the fear of being rejected or yelled at, a carryover from my younger years, I always try to do as much as possible without being dependent on someone else.

The tables turned in the summer of 2006 when I set my goal to swim across Lake Ontario. I took the initiative to recruit more paddling volunteers, partly because I knew I had been breaking a safety rule by swimming unaccompanied, but perhaps more because I knew I'd be doing longer training swims and needed a boat to carry my food and water.

I mentioned to Nicola my dilemma of not wanting to train without someone paddling beside me but needing to train in open water in order to complete the swim across Lake Ontario. Nicola suggested that I contact Special Olympics and mention my need to them. Since I was going to be doing the swim for Asperger's Syndrome, it would be in the best interests of Special Olympics to help me spread the word for paddling volunteers. I had never heard of Special Olympics before Nicola mentioned them. I wrote a letter to Special Olympics (see Appendix F) and they were very helpful. They let me attend their once-a-month executive meeting and, despite having a long agenda to cover, they let me speak first. We talked for half an hour about my need for volunteer paddlers. Louise, the volunteer swim coach for Special Olympics, sent out a mass email message, advertising my need.

I set my goal to swim across Lake Ontario in the summer of 2006 and started serious training at the end of August with limited paddling volunteers. I spent the entire winter thinking, *I will need to do several open water training sessions next summer and no one person will have time to accompany* me in every session. I hope to find lots of people who are willing so I can rotate through them. I put up posters (Figure 16-1) advertising my need for paddling volunteers. I reasoned that the only way I wouldn't find enough paddling volunteers was if there weren't enough people who were willing. If there were people who were willing, I would find them. I was prepared to commit to making repeated trips to Deep River to get my mother to kayak beside me and also to several trips to Toronto to have Peter Wong paddle beside me. If I couldn't recruit enough paddling volunteers in the greater Kingston area, I would seek paddling volunteers in neighbouring communities, and purchase a car in order to facilitate transportation, if necessary. Nothing was going to stand in the way of my open-water training.

I ended up finding lots of people who were willing to accompany me on my swim trials. People leapt at this opportunity to support my dream and there was no shortage of paddling volunteers. I felt I could never have had too many paddling volunteers in my roster since there was always the chance that people will drop out, move, or be too busy. Also, it never hurts to have backups. I like to be well prepared.

When I first started recruiting paddling volunteers, at least one person seemed hesitant to kayak beside me on my training swims because, if I got into trouble, he wouldn't know how to help me. Except in the unlikely event that I had a heart attack or went into hypothermia quickly, having access to a spare lifejacket was all I needed.[30] The main safety reason for being accompanied by a boat is to make the swimmer more visible to other boats. If I were going into

---

[30] Peter Snell and I had a lengthy discussion when I told him that, if I'm in trouble, my first line of defence will be to have the paddler throw me the spare life jacket. Peter replied that I should have a plan in place detailing the entire process from when I start to be in trouble to when I get the life jacket on. For example, how would I signal to the paddler that I'm in trouble? How would he pass the spare life jacket to me? In rough water, I may not want to get too close to the canoe/kayak and the paddler may not be able to stop paddling long enough to pass me the life jacket with the end of the paddle. If the paddler drops the life jacket in the water, the wind could blow it away. Peter also mentioned a floatation cushion, which would be easier to hug than a life jacket and therefore more suitable if I simply needed to rest for a few minutes before proceeding with my swim.

hypothermia, I'd feel chilled and would have lots of warning so I would be able to swim to shore before I was in danger. Two other reasons for having a boat accompany the swimmer are to carry food and water and to help point the swimmer in the right direction.

I don't think I have ever swum to Cedar Island unaccompanied without wondering at least once while in deep water, "Am I going to make it back to the mainland alive?" When you're wondering whether you're going to make it back alive, that tends to take the fun out of the swims. I told this to Jess, one of my paddling volunteers who had responded to my appeal for volunteer paddlers. Jess said I should let her know the next time I planned to swim to Cedar Island and that she would paddle beside me. If anything happened to me, my other friends who had cautioned me would feel sad, but would eventually get over it and wouldn't feel responsible. They'd think, "I told Jay not to swim to Cedar Island unaccompanied. It was his choice to do it anyway." Jess, however, would probably beat herself up for the rest of her life thinking, "I should have pushed harder with my offer to accompany Jay on his swims."

Sharon lives within walking distance of the entry point near Kingston for my swim to Milton Island. In 2005, I swam to Milton Island and stopped at Sharon's house afterward for a visit and some water. Sharon reprimanded me for swimming alone. In 2007, I told Sharon the good news that there was no shortage of paddling volunteers. She seemed happy for me but commented that, if I did the swim unaccompanied and the unthinkable happened, the motorboat driver would feel guilty for the rest of his life. Deep down inside, I knew that I was breaking a safety rule and could end up dying. I had promised myself that I would stop swimming unaccompanied (and certainly any distance far from shore) if people would either (a) paddle beside me or (b) help me find volunteer paddlers.

It has been pointed out that even with a kayak beside me I am not completely safe. After all, what would I do if I had to be pulled out of the water? Lois seemed concerned and unhappy that I swam to Wolfe Island accompanied by only one kayak. Lois is an educational assistant for children with pervasive developmental disorders including Asperger's Syndrome. Six months after my first swim to Wolfe Island I was a guest-speaker in the class where Lois worked. After the students were dismissed at the end of the day, I told the teacher about my goal to swim across Lake Ontario as a fundraiser for Asperger's Syndrome. He was very interested and asked if there were any way

The Ambition of an Aspie

he could help. I told him he could help by paddling a canoe or kayak beside me on one or more of my training swims. Lois immediately voiced her concern by simply stating that what I was doing was not safe. I felt that Lois had discouraged the teacher from helping me and spent two hours writing a four-page letter to Lois. This letter, which is copied in Appendix G, can be summarized with three points:

1. If I go into hypothermia swimming to Wolfe Island without having sufficient warning to swim to shore and get out of the water, I should not even be thinking about swimming across Lake Ontario.
2. The chances of me going into hypothermia by swimming to Wolfe Island in August, when I'm accompanied by a one-person kayak, are smaller than the chances of me dying riding my bicycle to work in the summer.
3. Most importantly, if you don't retain anything else from this letter, please remember this: I am doing this for the children.

It was later pointed out that this third point was an emotional appeal on my part and that the end doesn't justify the means.

By profession, Lois is striving to help children with Asperger's Syndrome and, totally independently of Lois, I was attempting to swim across Lake Ontario (which is certainly no small feat) in order to raise awareness about Asperger's Syndrome. I had hoped that Lois would not let her concerns interfere with my goal. I questioned Lois several months after the fact.[31] Her reply amounted to: "By all means, keep up the open-water training swims. Just stay close to shore. Both John C. and Vicki Keith have told you to stay close to shore and they're both very knowledgeable about water safety." Lois's argument explains why she was concerned when I swam to Wolfe Island but it doesn't explain why she voiced her concern when I informed her co-workers about my need for paddling volunteers.

---

[31] I was in "panic mode" when I initially informed Lois's co-workers about my need for paddling volunteers. At the time, I still wasn't sure I'd have enough paddling volunteers and was aware of the possibility that I might have to abandon my dream to swim across Lake Ontario if the lack of paddling volunteers made it impossible for me to train. Therefore, I was quite desperate to recruit as many paddling volunteers as I could.

How Safe is Safe?

Figure 16.1

DO YOU ENJOY CANOEING/KAYAKING?

I AM TRAINING TO SWIM ACROSS LAKE ONTARIO AS A FUNDRAISER FOR ASPERGER'S SYNDROME
www.aspergers.ca

I AM LOOKING FOR PEOPLE TO ACCOMPANY ME IN A CANOE OR KAYAK ON MY TRAINING SWIMS

I WILL SUPPLY THE CANOE/KAYAK

IF INTERESTED, CONTACT JAY @ xxx-xxxx
or
xxxxxxxxx@xxxxxx.com

77

Chapter 17

Plunges and Open-Water Swimming 2007

"For many are cold, but few are frozen."
—source unknown

    We had another Navs reunion in Montreal at Gunnar and Chantal's apartment in January, 2007. They had a newborn baby so we went to Montreal rather than Karen's house in Toronto. Karen and I drove back to Kingston on Sunday and after sitting inside a hot car for three hours, I decided to go for a plunge into Lake Ontario. I wanted a swim partly to cool off, but more to acclimatize myself to the cold water. The plan was to immerse myself once every two weeks throughout the winter. Lake Ontario had not frozen the previous year and, with the mild start to the winter in 2006-07, there was no reason to believe it would freeze that year either. As it turned out, Lake Ontario did freeze shortly after my January ducking, so that was my last open water plunge until the spring.

    Throughout the winter I kept an eye on Lake Ontario, anxiously awaiting the day I could jump in, and perhaps swim. On March 27th, I saw an opening in the ice just off the RMC peninsula that was large enough for my whole body. That was the first time I had seen an opening of that size so I planned to take a quick dip the next day. Within two minutes of leaving my house to go to work the following day, I realized that I had forgotten my old running shoes that I wore for winter plunges. I used shoes so that I could run in and out quickly. I had entered the water once before in bare feet and stayed in the lake just long enough to immerse my entire body. However, I had to walk on the rocky shore so slowly, that by the time I came out of the water my feet hurt. I debated going back to get my shoes but decided not to waste time and vowed to bring my old running shoes the next day.

 I took my first plunge of the season on March 29th. Only three days before, the lake had been completely ice covered. On March 29th all the ice had broken and drifted south. I ran in and out of the water as quickly as I could.

    On April 4th I planned to stay in as long as I could and practice my front crawl. Where I entered the water, it was too shallow to do the crawl. After two strokes of breast stroke, it was deep enough to do the front crawl stroke but, by then, I had to get out of the frigid water that was about 39F.

I had two reasons for taking the winter plunges:
1. I wanted to acclimatize my body to the cold water; and
2. I needed to know by testing the water temperature regularly when I could start my training. In other words, I was striving to jump start my open water training swims and also "extend" the open-water swimming season as much as I could.

My goal was to take a plunge once a week, carefully picking sunny days. I went to Calgary for a holiday from April 5th until April 15th. On April 20th, I actually swam. I only stayed in the water for twenty seconds but, after coming out, I warmed up quite quickly and then went back in the water for another twenty seconds.

On the weekend of April 28th-29th, I went home to Deep River. For the entire winter, I had high hopes that Corry Lake or Tee Lake, two smaller lakes in the Deep River area that warm up much sooner than the Ottawa River, would be "warm enough" by late April. I was optimistic about this for three reasons:
a. Nine years before, my mother and I both had a comfortable swim in Corry Lake on May 16th.
b. I was more resistant to cold water because of my winter plunges and other training in recent years.
c. I don't need the water to be as warm when training as I do when swimming for enjoyment.

On April 28th, the water temperature of Corry Lake was between 46° and 50°F. I stayed in for just under three minutes but scraped my chest against a metal stake. Anaesthetized by the cold water, I was unaware of the scrape until my mother saw my chest after I came out of the water. I was shivering and quite chilled but the energy exerted during the canoe ride after the plunge suppressed the shivering. The next day my mother and I went to Tee Lake and I tried again to do some open water training. This time, I could only stay in the water for two minutes, but my mother and I had an enjoyable canoe ride afterwards.

The following weekend was the annual open house for Frontenac Outfitters with free test paddling in Pearkes Lake. Frontenac Outfitters is one of Canada's largest on the water canoe/kayak retail store. My friend and I test paddled some of the canoes and kayaks. After the store closed at 5:00pm, I went back to the lake for a swim. Just as I was about to enter the water, clad only in a speedo, bathing cap and swimming goggles, an older woman who was driving by, pulled over, rolled down her window, and said "Hi, sexy!" She probably thought that I couldn't possibly be intending to swim that early in the season so she figured I must be wearing a bathing suit to show off my body. With the water temperature at 63F, I was actually comfortable. For the first time in my life, I did the front crawl in open water with bilateral breathing and had no difficulties. I stayed in for 20 minutes. The only reason I didn't stay longer was that my friend had to leave.

On Saturday, May 12th, George drove me to his sister's house, picked up his canoe, and then proceeded to Round Lake near Battersea where he paddled the canoe solo to accompany me while I did a 50-minute swim once around the perimeter of the lake. The water temperature was 57F. I wasn't ready to quit and I could have swum longer, but I didn't want to take any big risks because I still didn't know how much my body could handle or how long it would take me to recover.

On the May long weekend, I went to Deep River with a friend. My friend and I paddled across the Ottawa River while my mother paddled her kayak. We tried to climb Mount Martin but didn't get very far on account of too many fallen trees blocking the path. I managed to take a few short swims in the Ottawa River on both the Ontario and Quebec sides. On the Monday, the three of us went to Tee Lake where my mother and my friend canoed beside me while I swam. I am adamant about stretching before my swims, so my mother and my friend paddled the canoe until I finished stretching. When I got in the water, I made the same mistake I had made a year ago at Camp Iawah: I left my towel and warm clothes on the shore with the result that I would not have a towel and warm clothes in the canoe with me if I needed them. As I swam, I stayed close to shore so that, at any time, I could get out of the water and ride back in the canoe, if needed. This time, I was aware of the danger and ended the swim where I had started. I swam for a total of one hour. The water temperature was 55°F but my shivering stopped as soon as I dried off and put on warm clothes.

On May 23rd, George and I returned to Round Lake. This time, I swam around the lake twice, and with minimal chill. On May 24th, with my open water training swims in the smaller lakes well underway, I decided to attempt my first Lake Ontario swim of the season. The water temperature was approximately 53°F where I entered on the west shore of the RMC peninsula but it would have been colder on the south shore. I swam around the peninsula to the east side, then turned around and swam back, carefully staying within ten metres of shore almost all the time, ready to get out if it was unsafe to continue. I had made a rule to exit the water after 75 minutes regardless, judging this to be a small enough increment after my previous trial of swimming for 60 minutes in 55°F water only three days before. After 65 minutes, I saw the ferry go by and lifted my goggles, wondering if I'd be able to see a friend on the ferry. The goggle strap broke and, only intending to swim for another 10 minutes anyways, I came out of the water. It was a sunny day and, with the air temperature at 22°C, I blindly assumed I'd warm up as soon as I came out. How wrong I was. I almost hadn't bothered bringing a towel to the lake. Less than sixty seconds after coming out of the water, I began shivering violently, almost out of control. I dried off, hurried into the building at RMC, got changed and bundled up with pants, long underwear, a T shirt, sweatshirt, and windbreaker. The ventilators in the building weren't working very well so, fortunately for me the building was hot.

Earlier that afternoon, I had informed my co-worker Kim that I might go for a swim. When I got back to work, still shivering, I went to her office to let her know that I had done the swim and was still alive. (I know that Kim cares about me and that's why she coaxed me to wear a wetsuit during the swim across Navy Bay.[32]) Poor Kim was taken aback. She was concerned and brought me to the coffee room to make sure I got a warm drink. En route, with a partly suppressed smile on her face, Kim pointed her finger at me and said, "Don't do this again. That's a rule."

email message from Jay to Kim, sent the next day, May 25, 2007:

I seemed fine (and stopped shivering) after I microwaved some food that I had in the fridge in the coffee room. I left work still wearing my sweatshirt and windbreaker but I took them off as soon as I got outside – and I did sweat while riding my bicycle, which meant that my body was generating heat and releasing heat.

Thank-you for your concern and advice. It will be at least a week before I try swimming in Lake Ontario again. Until then, it's the swimming pool or smaller lakes.

Jay

---

[32] The story about swimming across Navy Bay will be mentioned in Chapter 26.

Kim's reply, May 25, 2007:

I'm glad to hear that you're doing okay.

excerpt from e-mail message from Jay to Vicki, May 30, 2007:

My open water swimming (in the smaller lakes) is well underway. Last Thursday, I swam for an hour and five minutes without a wetsuit along the shoreline of the RMC peninsula. I was shivering violently within minutes after coming out of the water but I warmed up as soon as I ate something hot. If it hadn't been sunny out, I wouldn't have done the swim. Please correct me if I'm wrong: no matter how cold I get or how badly I'm shivering, there will be no long-term damage AS LONG AS I DON'T GO INTO HYPOTHERMIA. (I know that what I do after I get out of the water is perhaps more important than what I do in the water.)

Vicki's reply, May 30, 2007:

Lake Ontario is still quite cool to be swimming in. I usually recommend 60 degrees or warmer. It is not necessary to put yourself through violent shivering. That is the first step to hypothermia and you are probably pushing yourself too much.

Chapter 18
Spring 2007

"A true friend knows your weaknesses but shows you your strengths; feels your fears but fortifies your faith; sees your anxieties but frees your spirit; recognizes your disabilities but emphasizes your possibilities."
—William Arthur Ward

After Louise sent the mass email message regarding my need for paddling volunteers, Richard Cadman, a triathlon coach, replied with the offer to let me come to his home and swim in Dog Lake[33]. A week later, a volunteer from the Special Olympics offered to paddle. Before I knew it, I had more paddlers than I ever imagined.

Knowing that the smaller lakes in the area would warm up before Lake Ontario, I made a list of all the smaller lakes where I could potentially swim. There were ten such lakes. (See Figure 18-1.) I had friends and relatives who lived on some of these smaller lakes. I asked these people if I could visit them and whether they would paddle beside me. Then I rotated among those friends and relatives. That way, I was only imposing on the lake owners once and I'd be sparing the paddlers who had volunteered for my Lake Ontario trial swims. Despite the fact

Table 18-1 – List of Smaller Lakes

Lake	Nearest town
Corry Lake/Tee Lake	Deep River
Wolfe Lake	Westport
Gould Lake	Sydenham
Pearkes Lake	Sydenham
Higley Lake	Outlet
Colonel By Lake	Kingston Mills
Dog Lake	Battersea
Loughborough Lake	Inverary
Chippego Lake	Verona
Round Lake	Battersea

[33] Lower Dog Lake was created in the 1800s when the Rideau Canal system was built. It is approximately 4.5 metres deep at its maximum depth. Due to its shallowness, it is one of the first lakes to warm up in the spring.

that I had many volunteer paddlers, I still assumed a worst-case scenario that resulted in those who had volunteered only being able to accompany me once or twice in training before my final swim across the lake.

On June 2, 2007 I cycled about 35 kilometres to Richard Cadman's home on Dog Lake near Battersea, arriving in time to start swimming at 8:00 a.m. with a group of triathletes who meet weekly. Richard has two floatation markers: one that is 250 metres and the other, 500 metres from the dock. Since no one else was training for anything longer than an ironman swim, they all stopped at about the 4 kilometre mark while I kept swimming back and forth between the dock and the floatation markers, covering 13 kilometres in 5 hours and 41 minutes. There wasn't a cloud in the sky and I didn't feel cold or shiver at all. I had put on sunscreen but my shoulders and upper back were still red.

One kilometre away from home, I stopped at Al's house to borrow his canoe to use for the next day's swim. The canoe did not have a yoke[34] so I tried to carry it by using the central thwart like a yoke and, within 100 metres, I put the canoe down to give my arms a rest. When things don't go according to plan, nine times out of ten I stop and assess the situation and this was no exception. As I was trying to decide how best to proceed, Steve S., who just happened to be visiting Al, happened to come along. He knew exactly what I wanted to do and offered to help me carry the canoe to my house. Steve's wife followed with their car and brought all of my gear, including the lifejackets and paddles so I didn't need to make another trip for them. During the walk, Steve brought up the subject of recruiting paddling volunteers. I told him that I had divided all my potential recruits into four groups, according to their level of enthusiasm for the task:

Group 1: I am excited and I can't wait to paddle beside you. I would be disappointed if you never ask me to paddle beside you.
Group 2: I am willing to paddle beside you but I'm equally willing not to do so. I won't be disappointed if you don't ask me.
Group 3: I could paddle beside you but I'd prefer not to. Ask me only if you're stuck.
Group 4: I absolutely will not paddle beside you.[35]

---

[34] A yoke is a crossbar at the centre of the canoe with a semi-circle cut in the middle. A person will place the canoe with the semi-circle behind his/her neck during a portage so that the entire weight of the canoe is on the person's shoulders. This keeps the person's hands free to assist with balancing the canoe while portaging.

[35] This group may seem like it shouldn't exist since anyone in group 4 wouldn't sign up. However, there is always the possibility that people will change groups and I am a firm believer in considering all possible outcomes, no matter how unlikely they may seem.

Before I'd explained any more, Steve told me that he was in Group 2.

In the worst case scenario I outlined above, possibly no volunteer would paddle beside me more than once or twice during the season and not everyone who had volunteered would be in a position to follow through with his/her commitment, so I'd need to recruit more paddling volunteers than the actual number of training sessions. But what would happen if I got too many volunteers? People might be disappointed if I never asked them to paddle beside me. That is why I created the four groups. If I found a few people in Group 1 plus several people in Group 2, things would work out well, maybe even swimmingly, because no one would be disappointed. As it turned out, the outcome couldn't have been better. A few people in Group 1 were willing to paddle beside me several times, which meant that when we decided who was able to come, I'd simply rotate among those willing paddlers and, occasionally, resort to people in Group 2. Nicola commented that through the process of recruiting and scheduling my paddling volunteers, I was learning people-management skills.

Later, when an organizational committee formed to help coordinate the swim[36], their message was, "Jay, you focus on the swimming and the interviews with the media. Leave everything else to us." It was suggested that I would free up even more energy by having someone else set the schedule of paddlers. Despite my case of Asperger's Syndrome, I can usually discern all of the following information quite quickly:

- how long a person was comfortable paddling in one sitting
- how often s/he was willing to volunteer
- whether s/he would prefer a canoe or kayak
- whether s/he would prefer the bow or the stern
- how much notice s/he would typically need
- how long s/he generally took to respond to email messages

Conveying all of this information to the person doing the scheduling would actually be more work than doing the scheduling myself. Also, when I recruited new people, I would have to communicate with them anyway to let them know what they were required to do and answer any questions. No one knew what I needed better than I did. Besides, what if a paddler cancelled at the last minute? The schedule coordinator would have to alert me in any case,

---

[36] See Chapter 24 for details.

and then try to find a replacement. I wouldn't know whether or not to keep myself psyched up for the training session while these alternate arrangements were being made. For all these reasons, I decided to do the scheduling of paddlers myself.

∽

On June 3rd, I undertook my first real training swim in Lake Ontario. The water was calm and I stayed in the water for one hour and fifty minutes. I was shivering when I finished.

On June 5th, I walked 500 metres to Lake Ontario carrying Al's canoe by one gunnel, walked back home and then brought the lifejackets, paddles, other safety gear and food and drink for the swim. I paddled Al's canoe solo approximately 7 kilometres from my house to the starting point at Murney Tower museum in Kingston. The lake was reasonably calm during my trip, but the wave height increased to two feet just before I arrived. Also, it had begun to rain. I met Jason and Jess at the starting point. They were two volunteer paddlers who had met neither me nor each other. I swam along the shoreline and then across the Cataraqui River and arrived at RMC in fifty minutes. I spent the next hour swimming back and forth along the shoreline of the RMC peninsula. At each point along the way during my training, I learned valuable lessons. After this swim, I decided that the next time I would rather rent a canoe along the shoreline and meet my volunteers there than take the time to carry Al's canoe for 1.5 kilometres and then paddle it solo all the way downtown.

Prior to setting the goal to swim across Lake Ontario, when motorboats created wakes or it was windy and the waves were rough, I would tread water or do head up breast stroke until the waves passed in order to keep an eye on them and also to avoid swimming the front crawl in rough conditions. If I resorted to this technique while crossing Lake Ontario, I knew I would never make any progress unless the lake was completely calm, which is very unlikely for Lake Ontario at any time. If I switched from the front crawl to the breast stroke, I would not only lose speed but I wouldn't generate heat fast enough to combat the coldness of the water. I had spent the entire winter working on my front crawl in a swimming pool not knowing whether I would be able to maintain that stroke in big waves or even whether I'd be able to breathe bilaterally in open water. This was my first time swimming in rough water that season, so I didn't want to let any discomfort prevent me from at least trying the front crawl in rough waves. I quickly came to the conclusion that I would rather do the front crawl than the breast stroke any time there was rough water.

At this point in my training I could breathe comfortably on both sides. I knew that if I breathed on the leeward side, I could avoid the waves hitting me in the face. This was what the Masters coach had tried to tell me six years before. However, always breathing on the leeward side required me to breathe every two or four strokes. Breathing every two strokes seemed too frequent then and I wasn't comfortable breathing every four strokes because I needed to get oxygen more frequently. Breathing every three strokes seemed ideal.

I left the canoe at RMC while I went to work for the rest of the day. On the way home, I decided to brave the task of paddling the canoe solo on the ten kilometre trek from RMC all the way back to Pleasant Point in two-foot waves. Highly inexperienced at solo canoeing, I paddled more than one hundred strokes at a time on the same side and kept the canoe in one direction, but, unfortunately, not the direction I needed to go. Several times, I was closer to Garden Island than the mainland. I had the physical strength required to power the canoe but I didn't have the skill to steer it. More than once, the waves hit me broadside and somehow I managed not to capsize. I was relieved to finally pull the canoe up on the shore. I telephoned a close friend (thank goodness for cellphones) who graciously came with his van to drive me and the canoe back home. Interestingly, when my friend arrived half an hour later, the lake had calmed down. After that frustrating and exhausting experience, I have no desire to paddle a canoe solo in any major lake ever again.

On June 9th, Jens came to visit me. He had told me in advance that he would not paddle beside me if the waves were as rough as the last time he'd gone with me on Lake Ontario and I didn't blame him.[37] Instead, he said he'd be willing to put my kayak on top of his car and drive to one of the smaller lakes. This time, Lake Ontario was reasonably calm so I proceeded with the original plan of swimming in Lake Ontario that day. I swam to Snake Island, an island almost invisible from the shoreline and consisting of rocks and bird droppings. It was risky, not to mention a violation of John C.'s instructions to stay within 100 metres of shore, but I wanted to show Jens that Snake Island

---

[37] See Chapter 14 for Jens's last experience kayaking beside me.

does exist. On the way back to shore, I informed Jens that I was cold and needed to get out of the water as soon as possible. We headed straight for DuPont and I was shivering a lot in the water during that return trip. This had never happened before and part of me wondered if I might have to give up on my dream desire. Once again, I was determined that I would not fail this mission; I reaffirmed my vow to give my training for this crossing nothing less than 100 percent. When we reached the shore, Jens ran back to the starting point along the shoreline while I paddled the kayak. By the time I arrived at the starting point, I had generated enough heat to stop shivering.

The concern of not being able to handle cold water didn't last long; three days later, Jason and Jess paddled beside me again. This time, I swam for three hours and fifteen minutes and didn't feel the slightest chill. The lake was calm and Jason took some pictures. In anticipation of needing to rest my muscles during the crossing, I practiced travel stroke, something I learned in swimming lessons but hadn't done for years. Travel stroke consists of three drown proofs[38] followed by a kick and a pull; the slower the swimmer travels, the better. I didn't want to try this in a pool in case others thought I was drowning.

On June 16th, Rob arrived at my house at 4:00 p.m. to paddle beside me on my longest swim so far in Lake Ontario: I went almost all the way to the Brother Islands that are halfway between Amherst Island and the mainland and then back again. I did not feel chilled. I could have swum longer but it was getting dark.

On June 23rd, I undertook a point-to-point swim starting at Ewen and Sharon's house on Faircrest Blvd (about five kilometres east of RMC) intending to finish at Fairfield Park in Amherstview. I was completely comfortable for a few hours but then felt chilled. The water was 66F, clearly colder than it had been a week ago. Before long, my quadriceps felt tight. I had originally estimated the total swim time to be nine hours but increased that time to eleven hours. I learned from this trial that my time estimates for my open-water swims in colder water was too optimistic.

I was all set to do the swim without an escort boat until a few days before, when Oliver, a volunteer from Special Olympics, and his girlfriend Kelly, agreed to accompany me in their canoe. Before I'd heard from Oliver and Kelly, I traversed the entire route by bicycle in order to pick locations where the spotters could conveniently hand me

---

[38] A drown proof occurs when swimmers relax their body; causing their head to go beneath the surface for two seconds or less, before they bring their head above the surface.

food and water. I created a timeline of approximate arrival times at all of the landmarks where I would stop for refreshment. The reason for picking this route in the first place was a carry over from when I thought I might have a shortage of paddling volunteers. I wanted to give people who are afraid of water a chance to assist with my training so I asked those people bring food to the shore. This way, my supporters could meet along the shoreline with a backpack full of food. As it turned out, these spotters weren't needed since I could receive food from the canoe.

I aborted the swim just past DuPont, after swimming for six and a half hours: my longest swim to that point. Then I rode in the canoe to the foot of Bayridge Drive[39] where my friend Thomas met us to give Oliver a ride back to where he had parked his car on Faircrest Blvd. Oliver and Kelly would have gladly paddled longer if I had asked them.

In order to continue swimming for long periods, I had to eat and it was necessary to tread water while I was eating. Although the tightness in my quadriceps was bearable while doing front crawl, the discomfort was more noticeable while treading water. This made eating and drinking more difficult. I tried switching to back crawl in order to use a different set of muscles but felt dizzy when I resumed front crawl again, so I was hesitant to try back crawl again.

Vicki Keith had given me advice on a number of previous occasions, so I emailed her about this dilemma.

excerpt from email message from Jay to Vicki, June 27, 2007:

I tried giving my shoulders a rest by doing breast stroke but I got super-chilled and had to resume front crawl less than ten seconds later. A few times, I switched to back crawl and, when I resumed front crawl, I felt dizzy. Is this common?

Vicki's reply, June 28, 2007:

When you move from back crawl to front crawl especially in open water, you may feel dizzy for a short while. That is normal.

On July 24th, I swam for three hours. Part of me wanted to quit within the first half hour (for safety, not for comfort) because I was getting chilled and didn't want to strain my body. I got more

---

[39] Bayridge Drive is located at the bay immediately west of Everett Point.

comfortable during the swim. I was shivering within minutes after coming out, but not uncontrollably. The lake seemed to be getting colder. Two weeks earlier, I had swum for 3 hours and 15 minutes with minimal chill, even though I had goosebumps during the swim. I had rented a canoe from Ahoy Rentals so when I returned the canoe I sat inside their shop for several minutes to get warmer. I had to borrow a sweatshirt that I returned the next day. The owners told me that the next time I rented from them I could leave some warm clothes in their building during the swim.

I used to own a car so I know how expensive it can be. Owning a car during the training process would have saved me the cost of renting a canoe. I knew it was cheaper for me to pay to rent a canoe closer to my entry point on the lake rather than own a car. The cost of the canoe rental didn't bother me when I considered the relative expense of owning a car.

I did not swim again until July 1st when I went home to Deep River for the annual Navs summer reunion when I swam across the Ottawa River.[40]

On July 7th, I made another attempt at the point-to-point swim from Faircrest Blvd to Fairfield Park in Amherstview. Two weeks before, it was rather unusual to find two people willing to paddle beside me for the entire stretch. I was prepared all along to recruit several paddlers and have them do shifts. This time, I had difficulty finding enough paddlers, largely because I didn't plan the swim soon enough. My main reason for attempting the point-to-point swim again so soon was to train for the 24-hour marathon swim at Camp Iawah the following weekend.[41]

At my request, Thomas picked me up at 7:15 a.m., drove to Amherstview to borrow Brandon and Cynthia's canoe, put the canoe on the roof of his car and drove the 24 kilometres to the starting location on Faircrest Blvd., picking up the first shift of paddlers along the way. I had given Thomas a detailed list of instructions. He set the entire day aside to shuttle the paddling volunteers back and forth.

I set up a total of four shifts of paddlers. Tim and his girlfriend Tracy paddled the first shift. This shift wasn't too difficult because the water is calmer earlier in the morning and that section of the lake is more sheltered.

It took me exactly two hours to swim to the St. Lawrence Pier at the southeast tip of the RMC peninsula. This was the first transfer

---

[40] See Chapter 20 – Navs reunion '07 for more information about this swim.
[41] The marathon swim at Camp Iawah is described in Chapter 21 – Camp Iawah.

point where Steve S. and Rob took over and they proceeded to the shore by the Kingston Psychiatric Hospital. The water was reasonably calm until the Portsmouth Olympic Harbour, about one hour before the next transfer point. However, it got rougher gradually enough for Steve and Rob to experiment and find techniques that enabled them to maintain control of the canoe.

When the third shift of less-experienced paddlers took over, the waves were over three feet high. The paddlers seemed to have difficulty communicating. Within minutes, and barely 20 metres from the dock, the swim was aborted because the paddlers had so much difficulty controlling the canoe in the high winds.

I telephoned Greg, the paddler for the fourth shift, to say that the swim had been called off and I didn't need him. However, Ashley, his seven-year-old daughter, had been looking forward to the canoe ride and really wanted to paddle. Because they were so keen, I had them meet me at the Kingston Psychiatric Hospital. When Greg and Ashley arrived, I was happy to get back into the water and continued my training swim. By this time the wind had died down and the lake was almost completely calm. I swam for an hour and a half, ending back at the Kingston Psychiatric Hospital. Ashley was the youngest of all my paddling volunteers.

∽

At least three times throughout the summer, I practiced treading water holding a brick to prepare for the feeding times – as recommended in the SSO Regulations and Information manual[42]. Each time, Kristine came down to the water with me and I ate my entire lunch treading water while Kristine handed the food to me from the dock one piece at a time. My swimming snacks consisted of: grilled cheese sandwiches, scones, cookies, yogourt, and bananas. Once, when Kristine noticed that I was struggling eating my yogourt, she suggested that I park the spoon in the yogourt container once in a while to free up one hand for treading water. This worked well and allowed me to rest.

To train for eating in open water, I got two bricks: a 6.5 lb brick and a 13.5 lb brick. Treading water holding the smaller brick for ten minutes was relatively easy. Ninety seconds was the longest I had ever

---

[42] This file may be obtained by going to http://soloswims.com/sso.htm and then clicking "Download - SSORI Registration Forms - 598k PDF" or, as of this writing, going directly to http://soloswims.com/SSORIr06a.pdf

managed with the bigger brick, after which I literally started sinking in which case Kristine immediately took the brick out of my hand. When I finished with the brick, I would often put my feet up, lie on my back and use my hands to scull, mimicking a float but resting my leg muscles.

∽

When I attended a monthly meeting in March 2007 for the Special Olympics, Bill, one of the executive members who works at RMC, mentioned that the RMC sea cadets come to RMC for six weeks every summer and would likely be willing to help me. Bill showed me the HMCS Ontario building where I could talk to the cadets' leaders. I explained to them who I was and my goal to cross Lake Ontario. They set up a schedule from 8:00 a.m. to 2:00 p.m. on July 10th to organize three paddlers to accompany me. The leader was happy to spare three people for the day, especially since canoeing and boating was what they would be doing anyways. The person in the middle didn't paddle but read a book or sometimes slept. The cadets took turns paddling and, while I swam, two of them switched positions in the canoe while the third person continued paddling. It took me exactly two hours to swim from the RMC boathouse to the summer ferry dock on Wolfe Island. Then I proceeded west to the winter ferry dock and then back to the RMC boathouse, for a total swim of six hours.

On August 1st, the RMC sea cadets once again accompanied me in a canoe from the RMC boathouse to the Wolfe Island summer ferry dock, over to the winter ferry dock and then Knapp Point, and back to RMC for a total swim of eight and a half hours. Swimming from the boathouse to the summer ferry dock, a distance of slightly more than five kilometres, once again took me exactly two hours.

On August 5th, I took part in the annual Deep River triathlon, a tradition I had seldom missed since my first year participating in 1990. I completed the one kilometre swim in 17 minutes and 48 seconds, knocking about four minutes off of my usual time. That still wasn't fast enough to catch Mr. Fulford, who bested me by four minutes in the cycling segment. I managed to catch up to him halfway through the running course and finished four minutes ahead of him. This was the first time I had ever crossed the finish line ahead of Mr. Fulford in a triathlon. Mr. Fulford and I had been rivaling each other for years about who could cross the finish line first. This was a real milestone for me! All my swimming training was paying off!

August 8th was the fourth and final time that the RMC sea cadets paddled beside me. As always, the cadets let me pick the route. We followed the same route as the previous week, but in the reverse direction: I swam to Milton Island, across to Knapp Point on Wolfe Island, and then parallel to the Wolfe Island shoreline toward Garden Island. At 2:30 p.m., before reaching Garden Island, I estimated it would take an hour and a half to swim back to the boathouse. I headed back immediately because I'd told the sea cadets we'd be finished by 4:00 p.m. On account of the rough waves, and possibly my fatigue, it took me two and a half hours to swim back to the RMC boathouse. We arrived at 5:00 p.m.

Chapter 19

My First Night Swim

"An expert is a person who has made all the mistakes that can be made in a very narrow field."
—Niels Bohr

    At around 11:00 p.m. on Friday, June 15, 2007, after I'd had a 90-minute nap, John C. picked me up at my house and drove me to HMCS Cataraqui where I started my night swim. Then John drove to the Cataraqui Canoe Club where he stored his sea kayak, launched it there and paddled to HMCS Cataraqui to meet me. The section of the Cataraqui River located at the Cataraqui Canoe Club contains so many weeds that it is unpleasant for swimming, so I entered the water at HMCS Cataraqui at 11:30 p.m., and started swimming.
    The plan was to swim continuously for 24 hours later that summer. What would happen if I started swimming at 9:00 a.m. and felt dizzy at 10:00 p.m.? I wouldn't know whether the dizziness was caused by swimming at night or swimming continuously for 13 hours. Therefore, I planned a few hours of night swimming when I was well-rested, several weeks before the 24-hour attempt. This was one of these shorter night trials.
    Not long before that night in mid-June, I thought I would be hurting for paddling volunteers and would have been happy to have any volunteer who was willing paddle beside me during the day. However, there are few people I would trust to paddle beside me at night and John was one of them. He had plenty of experience kayaking and owned a headlamp and other safety equipment.
    At first, I had trouble seeing John's kayak and I unsuccessfully tried to use the shoreline of the RMC peninsula as my guide. About an hour later, when I was able to orient myself better in the dark to following the kayak, John commented that I was following him much better than at the beginning of the swim when I had kept veering off course while he had been travelling in a straight line.
    We went around the south side of Cedar Island and continued proceeding east towards Milton Island. We arrived back at HMCS Cataraqui at 3:00 a.m. after swimming eight kilometres. Minutes before I came out of the water, a man drove by in a motorboat. John had heard the motor so he knew that the boat was there. Because John

was unaware that the light on the stick at the rear of his kayak had burned out, he assumed that Chris, the driver of the motorboat, had seen him. When John heard the motorboat get within 80 feet, he turned his head towards Chris to see where the boat was, and shone his headlamp directly at Chris. That was when Chris realized our presence and he barely had time to avoid hitting us. Chris drove his motorboat beside us as he yelled to us that he could have split the kayak in two. Chris was undoubtedly shocked, but nonetheless relieved that no collision had occurred. John was also shocked at the near collision, but reasoned that Chris probably thought that no one would be on the river at that time of night and might have been travelling faster than he ordinarily would have been. Neither John nor I have met Chris since this encounter.

John proceeded to paddle his kayak back to the Cataraqui Canoe Club. I was prepared to get out of the water and do the 20-minute walk from HMCS Cataraqui to the Cataraqui Canoe Club where John had parked his car. John was going to drive back and get me, but Chris graciously offered to give me a ride back to the Cataraqui Canoe Club. While I was riding in Chris's motorboat and John was on the shore, Chris yelled at John to turn around. John did, and Chris commented that when John was turned around he was completely invisible since his headlamp was shining in the opposite direction. If John's head had been facing forward in the kayak that had no tail light and Chris had come right behind us in the darkness, he would have smashed right into us with no warning. We all realized that we had narrowly escaped a potentially disastrous collision that night.

After Chris let me off at the dock, John drove me home and we both got some well-deserved rest.

Chapter 20

Navs Reunion 2007

"A good friend can tell you what is the matter with you in a minute. He may not seem such a good friend after telling."
—Arthur Brisbane

The fourth annual Navs reunion took place on the July 1st weekend in 2007. This was the first year that my parents were present for the reunion, not including 2004 when only Karen and I attended. On the Friday evening, Gunnar and Chantal arrived first. About an hour later, Karen and I arrived. John P., who had flown into Ottawa to attend a funeral, arrived by bus on Saturday afternoon. Peter, who had other plans for the weekend, arrived Sunday evening on his motorcycle.

My life revolved around my project to train for my swim across Lake Ontario and almost all of my spare time was spent either training, planning my training, or communicating with my paddling volunteers. I still had to hold down my full-time job. I was happy to meet and socialize with the various volunteers during my training. It was all I could do to spare one weekend away from my training to host this reunion.

Monday was the day we'd set aside to cross the Ottawa River and hike up Mount Martin. Gunnar, Chantal and their nine-month-old son left for Montreal when Karen, John, Peter and I departed for the hike. Peter and I carried my mother's kayak to Pine Point beach where Peter started kayaking and I began swimming across the river. Pine Point beach is the entry to the Ottawa River shoreline that is closest to my parents' house, but it is not the shortest route to Indian Point across the river. I didn't mind the extra distance because I needed all the training I could get. Karen, John and my parents headed to the marina and went across the river on the sailboat. They caught up to us in the sailboat and stayed with Peter and me for the remainder of the crossing. It took me one hour and five minutes to reach Indian Point. According to the boating chart, the distance is three kilometers although I had travelled partially downriver. When we reached Indian Point, Karen joined me in the water and we both swam another twenty minutes to the starting point of the hiking trail. The water temperature was 61°F – too cold for comfort for most casual swimmers. Karen was shivering when she came out, but she warmed up reasonably quickly.

The previous year, July 1st had seemed to be the ideal weekend for our reunion: it was a long weekend and was the perfect time of year for swimming and hiking. May is too early for swimming in the Ottawa River and Karen and Peter have a tradition of doing the Kingston triathlon on the August long weekend, so the holiday weekend in July worked out well. The 2007 reunion timing was the wrong time of year for both: the river was too cold for casual swimming and there were too many mosquitoes on the hiking trail. Because of a storm the autumn before, too many fallen trees blocking the trail made the hike very unpleasant. Also, the water level was so high that John and my mother couldn't walk the usual route along the shoreline to get to the trail but had to make their own trail through the forest. My father waited at the sailboat where it was anchored and did some cleaning.

After we returned to the house, Karen drove John back to Toronto, where he would be staying for a week, and dropped me off in Kingston en route. During the car ride, Karen, John and I talked for practically the entire trip about the logistics of organizing my swim. Ever since I had set the goal to swim Lake Ontario, the entire Navs gang was very supportive of my goal. They were totally confident that I could complete the crossing. They had known me for so many years that they knew I would have the discipline to train for this project. I had already been diligent with my training for one year. Training for the swim was one thing, but getting all the details organized to ensure that my swim would be successful was something else.

Karen and John intended to give me encouraging advice, but it ended up sounding so regimented that I found their advice overwhelming. I listened anyway because it was well-intentioned and I knew in my heart that it was what I needed. Karen and John strongly recommended that I find someone else to organize the swim. This would not only free up more time for me to train but might result in engaging corporate sponsors, marinas that might provide boats, and companies that might make in-kind donations like food or gasoline. These businesses would be much more likely to show interest if they were supporting an organization instead of an individual. I understood and agreed with the point of professionalism and having a larger cause for my swim. A request for goods or financial support from me or one of my friends as an individual would be much weaker and less likely to get support than a request from a representative calling on behalf of a charitable organization like Kerry's Place Autism Services.

When I told my friends that Kerry's Place Autism Services had a summer student working for them, Karen pointed out that KPAS might be more than happy to ask their summer student to help me in organizing my swim and it certainly wouldn't hurt to ask, especially since KPAS was supportive of my goal.

Chapter 21

Camp Iawah

Q. What do you call a goal without a deadline?
A. A wish.
—source unknown

When I first set the goal to swim across Lake Ontario, I thought that the most difficult task would be finding people to paddle beside me on my training swims. I knew that arranging volunteers when I did night-swim training would be particularly challenging. I had learned from the accounts of other distance swimmers that night swimming is the hardest portion of a marathon swim, but I wouldn't know exactly how hard it was without trying an overnight swim. I knew the summer staff and full-time staff who worked at Camp Iawah because of my volunteer work there over the previous two years, and I thought some of the summer staff [43] might be willing to paddle beside me. I was prepared to make trips to Camp Iawah and do some of my swims at Wolfe Lake. I planned to do a 24-hour swim at some point over my summer training in 2007, and I hoped there would be enough people at Camp Iawah to accompany me. I needed the camp staff's consent to provide me with a rotating shift of paddlers for the 24 hours. At first, I was afraid to ask, but I got along well with the staff so I figured the worst they could do was say no.

Emily G. and Emily F., two of the summer staff whom I knew through volunteering, were very supportive of my goal to swim across Lake Ontario, were in favour of the idea of me doing a 24-hour swim at Camp Iawah, and agreed to help me coordinate the swim. Emily G. was in charge of the Camp Iawah boathouse where the canoes, paddles and lifejackets were stored. For safety reasons, at least one paddler should have a headlamp on at all times during the night and Emily G. had her own headlamp.

The Camp Iawah staff discussed the issue. Steve L., the team leader for the team of Directors at Camp Iawah, who made the final decision, agreed to my request and gave me permission to use one or two canoes as well as paddles and lifejackets. Steve made it clear to me that the full-time staff were overworked at that time of year so

---

[43] The summer staff, who are mostly high-school and university students, come to Camp Iawah only for a summer job, in comparison to the full-time staff who work there year-round.

The Ambition of an Aspie

Camp Iawah did not have the resources to supervise my swim or provide paddlers. He imposed the following two rules:
1. if I asked the summer staff, I had to make it clear that the swim was my idea and not Camp Iawah's; and
2. the summer staff could not interfere with their staff duties in order to help me.

When I arrived at the camp on the evening of Thursday, July 12th, I spread the word to the summer staff and posted a sign-up sheet on the bulletin board for people to take the various shifts, which were two hours in length, starting at 10:00 a.m. Friday morning, and have two people in the canoe at all times. This would require 24 paddlers – less, if people were willing to paddle more than one shift. At breakfast time on Friday morning, I made an announcement about the 24-hour swim and asked people to sign up for a paddling shift.

I entered the water at 10:15 a.m. on Friday, when there still were many empty slots on the sign-up sheet. Before long, the sheet was completely full; word got around and the summer staff were more than happy to help me out.

At the beginning of each shift, I introduced myself to the new set of paddlers and then asked them for their names. This made the swim more interesting since I hadn't met many of the people who paddled beside me. On each shift, I followed the shoreline to the north, crossed the lake, followed the opposite shoreline, and then crossed back to arrive at the dock in time for the next shift of paddlers to take over.

At the beginning of the second shift as I waited for the next shift of paddlers, I took a feeding break – I had arranged for the previous shift of paddlers to leave some of my food on the dock for me – and then I kept swimming back and forth a little way along the shoreline, careful not to touch the bottom. Twenty minutes later, two paddlers showed up. My guess is that no one had signed up and the first set of paddlers managed to recruit someone.

It rained heavily at times during the afternoon. We were on the opposite side of the lake and we had to stay close to shore – to the point where I was hitting bottom – so that we could abort the swim immediately if there was thunder and lightning.

Once night fell, I swam back and forth along the shoreline, trying not to drift too far from shore. One of the canoeists carried a walkie-talkie and kept in contact with another staff member on land. At about 9:00 p.m., I asked him to bring a cup of hot chocolate to the dock.

When we arrived at the dock a few minutes later, several summer staff and a few full-time staff had arrived at the dock with flashlights and a mug of hot chocolate, possibly to check that I was still fully conscious and not too fatigued.

After midnight, one of the summer staff who had paddled beside me on the previous shift offered to swim beside me in order to pace me. Without considering the consequences, I agreed to the arrangement. Swimming for 14 hours is a feat in itself and making decisions for other people was too difficult for me at that point; I was so focused on making sure I kept swimming around the dark lake that I didn't think to say no. The other swimmer was better rested and swam noticeably faster than I did, but he graciously kept pace with me.

At 12:30 a.m., Peter V. came down to the dock and announced that Camp Iawah was calling the swim off. One of the paddlers asked, "Why?"

Peter explained that, even though my swim was not a Camp Iawah event, it was happening at Iawah, and there were liability issues: the camp nurse wasn't happy with the idea.

I had been swimming for over 14 hours: from 10:15 a.m. Friday morning to 12:30 a.m. Saturday morning. I didn't feel cold, but I had goose bumps in the water and I shivered slightly after I came out. As Peter was walking with me back to the main building, he encouraged me to take a warm shower. When I arrived at the main building, two summer staff members kept watch on me, told me which dorm they were in, and encouraged me to knock on their door if I needed anything. I found it curious that I shivered more as soon as I stepped out of the shower than I had after getting out of the lake, but I warmed up quickly after getting dried off and putting on warm clothes.

I woke up in time for breakfast the next morning; I didn't sleep from then until I arrived home because everyone wanted to hear my story about the swim – and I was happy to tell it to them. As soon as I entered the dining hall for breakfast, Steve L. said, "Congratulations." He reached out to shake my hand and commented on my spectacular achievement of swimming for fourteen hours.

After breakfast, Steve asked me, "Do you want to hear Camp Iawah's opinion of your swim?"

I replied eagerly, "Oh, please tell me."

Steve encouraged me to continue the training, told me that he had every bit of confidence that I could complete my swim across Lake Ontario, but pointed out that Camp Iawah was not the place to do it.

He told me that when I was doing marathon swim training, I had to make sure I had someone who was qualified in diagnosing hypothermia. Steve pointed out that hypothermia is best diagnosed by someone else because it clouds the brain to the point where the swimmer can't think clearly. He asked me if I had verified that the summer staff were qualified to diagnose hypothermia and also inquired if Camp Iawah had given me a pledge sheet. Several of the summer staff had been under the impression that Camp Iawah had endorsed my swim event, when clearly, it had not. This could have been what caused the summer staff to be so eager to paddle beside me, since they thought that by doing this, they were helping me with my training and also supporting Camp Iawah. I listened intently but made no comment, other than to let him know that I understood his reasoning. Although his viewpoint was valid, in my opinion I had taken no unnecessary risks. It is true that hypothermic victims don't know that they're in hypothermia. However, I believe I know my body well enough to know that, before I become hypothermic, I will go through a "window period" of warning that is sufficiently long to avoid hypothermia, as long as I react accordingly when I receive the danger signals.

Although I was somewhat disappointed at not being allowed to continue my night swim, I was not angry with Camp Iawah for aborting the swim and I probably would have done the exact same thing had I been in its situation. Despite the premature termination of the swim, no one could take away the psychological advantage I'd gained by knowing that I could easily have swum longer. I was happy to have gotten some night-swim training done.

I slept soundly for six hours when I arrived home.

❧

Peter told me the next summer when I was volunteering at Camp Iawah again that what had really concerned the staff during my night swim was that one of their summer staff employees had been in the water with me. This made sense because when Steve and I were emailing each other regarding the logistics, Steve had pointed out that Camp Iawah generally did not allow night swimming. It should have been clear to me that when Steve agreed to my request, he was making an exception for me – not for the summer staff. This is consistent with SSO's rule that no pacers are allowed in the water with a swimmer at night.

I know now that it would have helped immensely if I'd had a trainer to oversee the details of my training. That way, I could have focused on the swimming and left all the other decisions – such as when to allow pacers, clarifying the rules for the summer staff, and deciding when to abort a swim to avoid hypothermia – to the trainer. However, there are very few people who are certified as marathon swimming trainers and it's difficult to find them where and when you need them. I wasn't sure that I was ever going to find a trainer and I refused to put off the swim across Lake Ontario indefinitely just because I didn't have a trainer. Once again, I reaffirmed my commitment to my goal: I would not fail in my mission to swim across Lake Ontario because I was prepared to give it 100 percent of my effort.

Chapter 22

Chippego Lake

"The spirit is willing..."
—*Matthew 26:42*

On May 26, 2007, Heather made a special trip to her in-laws' cottage, located on an island on Chippego Lake, to canoe beside me while I swam. Heather would have canoed solo, but I was able to find someone to paddle with her so she would have some support and company. Heather picked up my friend and me at around 1:30 p.m. and then drove us to the lake, and then brought us to the cottage in a rowboat. I started swimming at 3:00 p.m. I swam the perimeter of the lake which took 2 hours and 50 minutes. Then I swam to a specific point and back, adding on another 20 minutes. I was shivering when I came out of the water but warmed up quickly. The only reason we ended the swim when we did was that Heather had to get back to Kingston for a concert.

I had previously given Heather a copy of my planned training schedule for the summer. After that swim, Heather brought up the subject of my training and suggested that I come to the cottage again for a weekend to do a 24-hour swim. I thought this was a great idea and we discussed how we would arrange a schedule of paddlers and I would tread water during each transition of paddlers. This swim happened on the weekend of July 20-22, 2007.

Two weeks before this marathon swim, Heather, her stepson Nate and I got together for dinner to discuss logistics including the number of people we needed, menus, and the food we'd need to purchase for the crew. Because the cottage is on an island, Heather or her in-laws would have to bring the paddlers from the mainland to the island. Heather preferred people to do a double shift, staying overnight if necessary, which would mean less transportation of paddlers to and from the island. She preferred they stay overnight because she worried that people would get lost driving to or from the cottage area at night. This was difficult to arrange because people have busy schedules and most of them preferred to come, do one shift and leave.

The previous weekend, after the marathon swim at Camp Iawah, Steve L. had strongly recommended that I have someone who was trained in diagnosing hypothermia to accompany me on long training swims. I wasn't sure how to respond to Steve's advice. One extreme would be to ignore it completely. The other extreme would be not to do any training swims – not even two hours along the shoreline in August in broad daylight – without a trained individual with me. I tried to find a few people who might be able to help with this, including John C., who was unable to stay overnight, and Jane, who was not available. I tried to find a balance between these two extremes. I decided to keep swimming until I felt chilled and then make the decision – while I could still think clearly – to come out at a certain time no matter how cold I felt. I hadn't felt the slightest chill swimming at Camp Iawah the previous weekend, even after dark, so I hoped I could complete the 24-hour marathon swim at Heather's cottage without getting seriously chilled.

Table 22-1 list of boats and crew for marathon swim at Chippego Lake

	type of boat used	paddlers/crew
6:00 a.m to 9:00 a.m.	canoe	Colleen K. and Heather
9:00 a.m. to noon	canoe	Sara and Alicia
noon to 3:00 p.m.	canoe	Sara and Alicia
3:00 p.m. to 6:00 p.m.	canoe	Colleen K. and Louise*
6:00 p.m. to 9:00 p.m.	canoe	Lois and John C.**
9:00 p.m. to midnight	pontoon boat	Heather, Chris and Robert
midnight to 3:00 a.m.	pontoon boat	Nate, Craig and Isaac ***
3:00 a.m. to 6:00 a.m.	pontoon boat	Joan, Earl and Matt

*Lois and John C. for the last half hour
**Joan and Heather for the first half hour
***swim aborted at 12:48 a.m.

    Heather, Joan (Heather's mother-in-law), Colleen K. (whom I met at Kingston & Area Christian Singles prior to setting my goal to swim across Lake Ontario) and I arrived at the cottage Friday night and stayed overnight. The next morning, I finished a big breakfast including fruit, hot oatmeal, cold cereal, and oatmeal scones one hour before starting the swim. I began swimming at 6:05 a.m., after stretching and applying sunscreen and Vaseline. Feeling energized from the big breakfast, I didn't need to eat for the first three hours, but had several drinks. Heather and Colleen paddled the canoe beside me around the perimeter of the lake for the first three-hour shift while Joan prepared breakfast for the morning crew, including Sara and Alicia, who arrived in time to eat breakfast before their double shift from 9:00 a.m. until 3:00 p.m.

Just after Sara and Alicia took over paddling, Joan brought me a bowl of hot oatmeal. Treading water, I held the bowl with one hand while eating from a spoon with the other hand. We went around the lake once and arrived back at the cottage at noon. Before going around the lake again, Sara and Alicia took a break for lunch while I treaded water. I took a few short feeding breaks and swam back and forth along the shoreline until Sara and Alicia returned to the island dock. I was unaware that the water at the dock at the mainland was neck deep, so I swam with a plastic dish into deeper water in order to avoid touching bottom. I even ate a hamburger while treading water – a risky move during any prolonged aerobic activity – but I figured I was already pushing it by attempting two 24-hour swims eight days apart, so I'd chance eating the burger. With the big swim one year away, I felt I could afford to take all kinds of risks.

Louise, the volunteer swimming coach for Special Olympics, and Colleen paddled beside me starting at 3:00 p.m. At 4:30 p.m., my wrist started hurting. The pain was certainly bearable, but it was enough to cause concern. I had never had my wrists hurt while swimming; it was almost always my shoulders that got tired first. My wrist continued to hurt for the remainder of the swim.

John C. and Lois arrived at 5:30 p.m. and took over paddling while Louise swam beside me for a while. About half an hour later, Louise and Colleen went home and Heather and Joan temporarily took over paddling while John and Lois ate supper. My body temperature felt fine until 8:00 p.m. when I started feeling chilled. John suggested we move to a sunnier place and this worked until it got dark. Around 9:00 p.m., I reapplied Vaseline to my entire body without getting out of the water. At Camp Iawah, I had not used Vaseline, except under my armpits to prevent chafing.

At 9:00 p.m., Heather, her husband Chris, and Robert took over. With the onset of darkness, a pontoon boat with an electric motor became my escort boat instead of the canoe, and three people were assigned to each shift instead of two. John C. and Lois had other commitments so they headed back to Kingston.

We were miles from a hospital at the island cottage and there were no trained paramedics nearby. Chris's son, Nate, was a lifeguard. He was the only person we had with any certification, so I knew it was imperative to get out of the water well before I felt any signs of hypothermia. Avoiding hypothermia means not only knowing when to get out of the water but also what to do after you've gotten out of the water.

You can reduce the chances of going into hypothermia by swimming faster to generate heat. I claim that two of the reasons I felt chilled were (1) my wrist was hurting and I couldn't do the front crawl as efficiently (2) we kept wasting time trying to agree on which landmark to aim for when I could have been doing front crawl. Also, I may have been taking feeding breaks too frequently. The longer you stop, the more time you have to get cold or stiff. Despite my wrist pain, I actually found it was a relief when I could finish eating and resume my front crawl since that stroke uses the muscles much more efficiently than treading water does.

During the 9:00 p.m. to midnight shift I felt chilled, so I promised myself I would quit at 1:00 a.m. or 2:00 a.m. regardless of how I felt, and get out of the lake. It's never a good idea to keep trying to swim one more hour at a time after you first feel cold. My plan of setting a time limit wasn't foolproof either: I was simply making a conservative estimate of how long I would last in my chilled state, while being ready to get out of the water earlier if I saw fit.

The crew and I had to sort out our confusion from time to time about the next point to head for. I had to stop swimming for about 20 seconds every 5 minutes to reach an agreement about where we were heading. The crew was concerned about getting separated from me. Glow sticks, which are used on almost all crossings of Lake Ontario, certainly would have helped.

The crew had been very encouraging and kept telling me not to quit saying, "You can do it. We have faith in you."

At least three times, I said, "The spirit is willing but the flesh is weak."

Each time, Heather corrected me and said, "The flesh is strong!"

I don't give up very easily and would never end a swim on the spur of the moment, except if I were drowning or in excruciating pain. Whenever I've considered the possibility of quitting, I've contemplated it for a while and then informed my crew how I was feeling. During this swim, Heather and the others kept encouraging me to keep going, expressing their confidence that I could do it. It was on the 9:00 p.m. to midnight shift that I had made a firm decision not to complete the

24-hour swim. Heather, Chris, and Robert knew by then that I don't quit easily. Therefore, there was no point trying to quit on that shift because they knew I had this "weakness" and would dissuade me from quitting. My chances of terminating the swim – and thus fulfill my promise to myself to get out of the water before 2:00 a.m. – were much greater on the next shift. Another reason for not quitting during the 9:00 p.m. to midnight shift or at the transition before the shift change was that introducing myself to each new set of paddlers was one of the most enjoyable parts of the swim. I'd feel badly if some paddlers got psyched up to paddle beside me and then didn't get that chance because I ended up quitting. By continuing part way into the midnight to 3:00 a.m. shift, I would only disappoint one set of paddlers.

After the swim, I explained to a number of people why I had stopped at 1:00 a.m. My mother and Jess asked me what would have happened if – given that I'd decided at 9:00 p.m. to quit at 1:00 a.m. – I'd gone into hypothermia at 11:00 p.m. I replied that I have a rough idea on when I reached the danger point. In addition, the repeated discomfort of the cold water reminds me of the danger; encountering hypothermia before 1:00 a.m. was a chance I was willing to take. Someone else asked me what would have happened if I'd accepted Heather's encouragement to keep going beyond 1:00 a.m. and then had gone into hypothermia at 3:00 a.m. That was certainly a possibility, which is why I rejected Heather's encouragement to continue swimming.

I pointed out that even if I had managed to swim for 24 hours, I would have lost the physical benefit by the following year when I was doing the Lake Ontario crossing. One volunteer pointed out that I'd have the psychological benefit of knowing that I could swim for 24 hours. If I had swum for 24 hours in Chippego Lake and still had energy left, I might have felt the urge to swim for 25 or more hours.

At this point in my training, I was striving for duration, but in crossing Lake Ontario, I would be striving for distance. If I only wanted a long time in a lake, I could just tread water for 24 hours. I had to build up my stamina and speed over time. While crossing Lake Ontario, there would be an incentive to move forward and keep feeding breaks to a minimum: the sooner I completed the crossing, the sooner I could get out of the water, get warm, and get some sleep.

"I didn't want to pull a muscle and drown," I pointed out.

Robert replied, "We'd have pulled you out. That's what we were there for."

In hindsight, I was being overly dramatic. My body would not have sunk, at least not right away. Even though I couldn't breathe in the floating position, it wouldn't take much flotation assistance to keep my head above water. When I asked people if they'd paddle beside me, some replied that they wouldn't know how to help me if I were in trouble. I assured them that all they had to do was throw me a lifejacket when I asked for one. If I were ever in trouble, that would be my first line of defense and I had never yet had to resort to asking for a lifejacket.

At midnight, when Nate, Craig and Isaac took over for Heather, Chris and Robert, Heather said to the new shift of boaters: "Jay wants to quit at 1:00 a.m. Don't tell him when it's 1:00 a.m. Tell him that it's 12:30 a.m., then tell him that it's 12:40 a.m., then tell him that it's 1:15 a.m. Then he'll think that he made it past 1:00 a.m. and he will keep going!

Prior to this swim, I had not informed Heather about my concern of going into hypothermia.[44] Therefore, I cannot conclude in the least that Heather was not concerned for my safety – only that I was more concerned than she was. There was no point trying to discuss this concern while I was treading water because I'd lose even more body heat.

By taking a feeding break at 12:30 a.m. and then swimming back to the cottage, I figured I'd arrive at the cottage at 1:00 a.m. when I planned to quit. After my 12:30 a.m. feeding break, I firmly announced that I was quitting. The crew asked me if I wanted to get in the boat but I told them I'd swim back to the cottage. I figured that I'd arrive back there at quitting time. Given that I was quitting solely to avoid hypothermia, sitting on the boat would make me more cold, I reasoned, so I figured I might as well keep swimming to generate more energy and warmth. The crew radioed Heather to say I was coming back.

Heather replied, "Don't let him come back!"

Immediately, Heather got a hot drink and headed for the rowboat so she could bring me the hot drink before I made it to the dock and then convince me to change my mind. She was just a bit too late: she was getting into the rowboat just as I was getting out of the water.

I had swum back much faster than I swam out. With the "finish line" straight ahead, I was willing to put forth extra energy despite the

---

[44] My case of Asperger's Syndrome often makes it difficult for me to communicate a concern without sounding overly concerned. The reason I did not inform Heather in advance of my concern of going into hypothermia was that I didn't want to risk having her conclude that swimming for 24 hours without a paramedic nearby was too risky and the swim being cancelled.

wrist pain. Heather commented that I was "motoring" on the last stretch. I asked her how she had known this.

She answered, "I was watching you."

Heather's comment gave me confidence that I could summon more energy when I needed to or when I knew the finish line was near. This was important information in my training.

At 12:48 a.m. when I made it to the dock, I stood up in waist deep water. Robert was there and he's a very strong man: without me having to ask, he immediately lifted me onto the dock and helped me walk up the stairs. I was shivering quite noticeably when I came out of the water. When I got inside, Heather and the others wrapped me in blankets and encouraged me to keep moving. I walked around the kitchen table several times and Nate kept walking backwards around the table in order to look at me, talk to me and keep me company. Twenty minutes later, after having a warm meal, the shivering stopped. The crew was marvelous and could not have done anything better.

I concluded that if I was thinking of quitting and needed someone to convince me to change my mind, Heather would be the one. I had confidence in her judgment that it was safe for me to continue. I decided then and there that I wanted Heather on the support boat during my Lake Ontario crossing. The SSO Regulations and Information document says that there comes a time during almost every marathon swim in which the swimmer begs to come out; therefore, it's important to have family and friends who care about the swimmer and want what's best for him and can encourage him to continue swimming.

֍

The next day, I felt much less stiff than after a 42-kilometre running marathon and my wrist felt fine. The crew who had stayed overnight went water-skiing, swam casually, socialized, and told jokes.

On July 25th, I cycled to Frontenac Outfitters to test paddle the 17-foot sea kayak that I would later buy. Every fall, Frontenac Outfitters sells their entire rental fleet at a discount price. While at Frontenac Outfitters, I went for a dip at Pearkes Lake and after swimming for five minutes, I could feel the tightness in my shoulders.

On July 26th, the RMC sea cadets had agreed to paddle beside me for eight hours. I was fine doing front crawl but, during the feeding times when I had to tread water, the inside of my right ankle hurt. I quit the training swim after two hours. Just before I quit, my ankle started to hurt while doing the front crawl.

On July 28th, one week after the swim at Chippego Lake, I participated in the 13-kilometre Swim for the Cure in the Severn River and showed no side effects from the swim a week earlier.

Part of me regretted having quit the 24-hour Chippego Lake swim prematurely. Lake Ontario would be colder and rougher so I was worried that if I couldn't handle 24 hours in Chippego Lake, I would have trouble handling 30 or 36 hours in Lake Ontario. I was certainly willing to keep training to achieve my dream goal despite my misgivings. I was also conscious of having to pace my training. I didn't want to wear myself out to the point where I'd hinder further training for too long. I knew I wouldn't care how tired I felt when I finished or how many days it took me to recover after I swam across Lake Ontario, but I had to be careful at this stage of my training. Swimming for 19 hours was a noticeable jump from my previous longest swim of 14 hours, so I was quite pleased with my progress. Barely two months before when I had first found out about Progress Fitness Centre's openly available lane swimming, my longest swim had been three hours. Despite several setbacks and disappointments, I felt I would have been ready to attempt my crossing of Lake Ontario in 2007. However, I had already decided to wait until 2008.

Chapter 23

Swim for the Cure

"Small opportunities are often the beginning of great enterprises."
—Demosthenes

The Swim for the Cure was held on July 28, 2007, in the Severn River. I found out about the Swim for the Cure because a similar event had once been held in Deep River and I came across an article I'd kept about the swim. My mother had participated in that event. Whenever I try to clean my room, I make sure I don't throw away anything without knowing what it is I'm discarding. I tend to reread newspaper articles I've kept, before throwing them away. Several months before the 2006 Swim for the Cure, I was cleaning my room and came across an article from the Deep River newspaper on the Swim for the Cure, I noticed the website address[45]. I checked the website and found out that the swim was held annually in Severn River at the end of July. The website said nothing about another Swim for the Cure in Deep River and I didn't have a clue where Severn River was located. I didn't want to travel to Severn River and I didn't really want to swim 13 kilometres.

When I set my goal to swim across Lake Ontario, I remembered the Swim for the Cure. It was held on July 29, 2006 – only ten days away – and I had seriously considered doing it that year. Several questions entered my mind:
- Where is the Severn River?
- What is the nearest big town?
- Was there anyone I knew in the area with whom I could stay?
- Who could paddle beside me?
- Is it feasible to find a willing paddler this quickly?
- Could I handle a 13-kilometre swim on such short notice – given that my longest swim to date was less than three kilometres?

I decided against doing the Swim for the Cure in 2006 but quickly promised myself that I would do it in 2007. Over the next twelve months, I spent hour after hour reading the website to find out more about the swim, studying maps to find out how to get there, and communicating with Debbie, the organizer.

---

[45] www.swimforthecure.ca

Peter Wong had agreed to be my volunteer paddler about a year before the swim. Karen also likes open-water swimming so I told her about the Swim for the Cure. She decided she would participate a few weeks before the swim. Karen and I agreed that she could use Peter to accompany her as long as I could find another paddler. My next choice for a paddling companion was Jens. He had a family reunion but was willing to take time away from it to paddle beside me. Jens's brother Luke was also quite enthusiastic about helping. I borrowed Debbie's canoe and her friend, Jo Ann, offered to paddle in the canoe with Luke, in which case Jens wasn't needed.

The night before the event, I drove to Karen's house in Toronto and Karen made a pasta supper for Luke, Peter, and me. The four of us spent the night with our friend, Cheryl, and her husband, Andrew who live on the outskirts of Port Carling.

We got up the next morning at 6:00 a.m., ate breakfast and then left the house at 6:30 a.m. Luke and I arrived at Severn Falls just before 7:30 a.m. Karen and Peter, who unfortunately got lost en route, arrived an hour later. I had thought they were following Luke and me but they had fallen behind. Steve, Debbie's husband, took Luke and me upriver in a motorboat to the start at Swift Rapids where I registered. Steve returned to Severn Falls to transport Karen and Peter to the starting point after their late arrival. The registration process was quite simple; with a small number of participants, the organizers were able to give more attention per participant than in a big event. Neither Luke nor Jo Ann was comfortable in the stern, but they worked it out and were able to keep the canoe near me.

I started swimming at 8:00 a.m. It took me 20 minutes to get to the 1-kilometre marker and I reached the 3-kilometre marker at 1 hour and 3 minutes when I took my first feeding break. After that, I generally refueled every 40 minutes. I slowed down over time, which is typical of me. It only took me 15 minutes to get from the 10-kilometre marker to the 11-kilometre marker. Either the current had really helped me, or the markers weren't positioned properly. I finished with a time of 5 hours and 53 minutes and felt completely relaxed. This was slower than my time of 5 hours and 41 minutes when I had swum the 13 kilometres in Dog Lake in June, but the Severn River is rougher despite having a helpful current. The fact that my body was still tired after the 19-hour swim in Chippego Lake on July 21st-22nd was another possible contributing factor to the slower time. My initial reason for participating in the Swim for the

Cure was to train for my swim across Lake Ontario, so I wasn't too worried about the time.

Marilyn and Colleen, two registered Swim Masters of Solo Swims of Ontario, Inc., also participated in the Swim for the Cure. I had hoped to meet them and get some advice regarding my upcoming swim across Lake Ontario, but, unfortunately, they had started their swim before I arrived and left before I finished because their paddlers had to leave.

After I had some refreshments, I rode with Steve in his motorboat to check on Karen. I swam out to meet her and then finished the last 200 metres beside her. After she finished her swim, Karen, Peter, Luke and I stayed around to chat and have a snack. Then Luke drove to his girlfriend's cottage while I rode back to Toronto with Karen and Peter.

Overall, I really enjoyed the Swim for the Cure. Part of me wishes I had participated in 2006, despite having only ten days notice. In hindsight, I probably made the right decision not to participate that year, especially since I had never maintained the front crawl stroke for more than two minutes, could only breathe to the right, wasn't sure that I could complete 13 kilometres and didn't want to impose on someone to paddle beside me on such short notice. Besides, I hadn't yet felt ready to tell people of my ambition to swim across Lake Ontario except for trusted friends like Karen and Peter whom I knew would be supportive. If I'd been asked what had motivated me to participate in the gruelling 13 kilometre swim in 2007, I would have replied, "Jenna Lambert swam across Lake Ontario. This is the least I could do."

I resolved to participate in the Swim for the Cure again, regardless of whether it is held in Deep River or the Severn River.

Chapter 24

Starting an Organizational Committee

"Obstacles are those frightful things we see when we take our eyes off the goal."
—Henry Ford

I had to pass through Toronto on my way home from the Swim for the Cure, so I spent two days in Toronto to visit a few organizations that might be able to provide boats or assist with the other organizational details for the swim. During this time, I also made a trip to Niagara-on-the-Lake to watch another candidate, Samantha Whiteside, start her Lake Ontario crossing. I wanted to offer my support to Samantha and get a glimpse of the starting location for my swim. I also hoped to get some idea of what was involved in organizing and training for a marathon swim.

Before the crossing started, I was able to talk to Samantha's Swim Master, Colleen Shields. Colleen pointed out that the swim coordinator did not need to have experience; the main requirement was that this person needed the interpersonal skills required to associate with boat owners, sponsors, and the other people involved with the organization.

Colleen also commented that I should focus on core strength. The only things that came to mind were weight lifting, sit-ups, and stability ball exercises. With my case of Asperger's Syndrome, I can do well at something once a well-defined regime has been set, but in the absence of such a regime, things are likely to fall apart. I had no idea how often I should lift weights or how long each session should be. Unless I really knew what I was doing, lifting weights could do more harm than good. My triceps and upper-chest muscles were often sore for a few days after bench-pressing, especially if I hadn't done that for a while. I didn't want to risk throwing my swimming training out of whack. My high school cross-country ski coach had told me that most weightlifting is done anaerobically – implying that it is not as beneficial as cardiovascular exercises such as running and skiing. Without a trainer, I concluded that I'd be better off to forget weightlifting and core exercises altogether and spend as much time as I could afford swimming or just relaxing. Meanwhile, I would continue to look for a trainer and occasionally lift weights as I saw fit.

Throughout high school, I lifted weights almost every day. Every year, during the first week of school when I resumed my usual routine, my upper-chest muscles would be sore for a few days.[46] During high school, as I got heavily involved with the cross-country running and cross-country skiing teams, my interest gradually shifted from weightlifting to cardiovascular activities: cross-country running and cross-country skiing.

In August 2007, Colleen K. told me that during my 19-hour swim at Chippego Lake, she had been talking with Heather and Louise, two of the other paddlers, about how they could pool their resources to help me organize my swim across Lake Ontario. Colleen works for Ongwanada, Heather works for Extend-a-Family, and Louise works for Community Living, three community-support organizations. This gave me the idea of forming an organizational committee instead of having one key organizational person. A few other people immediately came to mind and they were quite happy to join the committee. I had been following my swimming pool regime all winter not knowing how I was going to organize my Lake Ontario crossing; I kept training on faith that things would fall into place as time progressed. Striking the committee was the answer to this vital part of the planning for my crossing.

The committee agreed to meet once a month. It took a while before everyone got to know each other, but things went much more smoothly once the committee had been established. It was too difficult for ten people to get their schedules to jive and to coordinate all the various aspects of the planning so a new approach was taken. A master steering committee was established with several subcommittees under it. There were subcommittees for the following tasks: media and promotions; fundraising; recruiting volunteers; organizing the details of the actual swim; and hospitality that covered organizing the fun day at Marilyn Bell Park the day of my crossing. The steering committee consisted of the leaders of each of the subcommittees. That way, the steering committee would know what was going on overall, and each subcommittee could focus its efforts on one particular aspect of the organizing for my Lake Ontario crossing.

---

[46] As was mentioned in the Introduction on page xxv the reason I lifted weights so diligently was to help me defend myself physically; being different, I was the target for teasing and bullying.

Chapter 25
Fall 2007

"Many people are like ten speed bicycles. They have a lot of gears which they never use.

—*Charles Schultz*

On the Labour Day weekend, 2007, Karen, Peter and I went to Ottawa to compete in the annual Canadian Iron 226 (ironman distance)[47] triathlon as a team: Karen cycled; Peter ran and I swam. I completed the 3.8 kilometre swim in 1 hour and 19 minutes.

After the race in Ottawa on Saturday, I went to Deep River. On Sunday, I swam in the Ottawa River for four hours with my parents accompanying me in their 23-foot sailboat. For a while, they powered the boat with the sail, having only a small percentage of the sail exposed in order to maintain the desired speed. This motivated me to maintain a constant speed; otherwise, I'd "lose" the boat. When I ate, I fell behind, but when I was finished eating, I had both hands free and they'd steer the boat so that I could catch up. When I wanted a drink, I knew I wouldn't have both hands free when I finished drinking because I had to hold onto the drink bottle until I could pass it to someone. My father told me to hang on to the ladder.

Being a play-by-the-rules person, I told him that holding on to anything would be considered cheating because I knew I would be disqualified if I did that on the actual crossing. Eventually, my father started the motor.

excerpt from email message from Jay to Marilyn, May 7, 2008:

On the actual crossing, is it permissible for the sailboat to use the sail for power and the swimmer to swim beside the sailboat? This will motivate the swimmer to maintain a constant speed. Has this been done? I know it won't happen for any extended period of time. (This is assuming the wind pushes the sailboat in the desired direction.) During the training session I didn't care where we went because I just wanted the time/distance.

---

[47] Although the race is the same distance as an ironman, it cannot be called an ironman because it is not sanctioned by the World Triathlon Corporation, a private company in the United States which "owns" the term "ironman".

Marilyn's reply, May 21, 2008:

We do not allow sailing during the big swim. You do not want to swim one more meter than you have to.

The next day, my parents brought the canoe to Tee Lake and paddled beside me while I swam for two hours.

In mid-September, I purchased a 17-foot sea kayak from Frontenac Outfitters so my paddling volunteers in Kingston would have something to paddle beside me that was more comfortable than the whitewater kayak that my mother had given me in the summer of 2006. I went out in that kayak every weekend that I stayed in Kingston. (She bought a sea kayak when she decided to stop whitewater kayaking.) Generally, I am frugal with my money, but I don't mind spending money on something useful. I had lived in Kingston for seven years by 2006 and had never been on the water except to train for triathlon swims and several times in boats with the RMC sailing club. Someone told me that living in Kingston and not sailing – or kayaking, in my case – is like living in the Rocky Mountains and not downhill skiing.

On September 22nd, I made a third attempt to swim from Faircrest Boulevard to Fairfield Park in Amherstview along the shore of Lake Ontario. I set up three shifts of paddlers. Once again, Thomas set the entire day aside to shuttle the paddling volunteers back and forth. In anticipation of being in the water for 11 hours, I coated my entire body with Vaseline.

The swim started at 7:15 a.m. despite waves that were often higher than one metre. We couldn't predict how big the waves would get further along the swim where the lake is wider or later in the day when it often gets windier. After an hour, Brandon and Sara who were both uncomfortable in the stern at the best of times, headed for shore. They were unable to keep the canoe near me so that defeated the purpose of having a canoe there at all. Submerged from the neck down, I was unable to see how much water was in the canoe. As soon as we arrived at the shoreline, I saw the amount of water that was there and was surprised that Brandon and Sara hadn't called a halt to the swim sooner. The three of us carried the canoe through someone's yard until we reached a municipal road. I called Thomas from my cell phone to tell him where we were and what had happened. Thomas drove the three of us and the canoe to the transfer point to meet the second shift of paddlers. While Sara, Brandon and I were waiting at the transfer point for Mike and Alex, Sara told me that was only her second time in a canoe; the first time was during my 19-hour swim at Chippego Lake. What adventurous spirit! I didn't want to say no to any willing volunteers but I also didn't want to put any of my paddling volunteers in discomfort or danger. I didn't want to risk Sara's safety so I didn't ask her to paddle beside me again in Lake Ontario. I did, however, ask her to paddle beside me in some of the smaller lakes to give her some more canoeing experience.

I had originally added "No experience necessary", thinking that I didn't want people to decide not to help just because they weren't experienced paddlers. It was pointed out that advertising that could actually discourage people from volunteering because people who might be interested might wonder about my safety standards if I'd let just anybody paddle beside me. I decided to leave "No experience necessary" off the poster at that point to see how many volunteers I got.

Mike and Alex, the second shift of paddlers, managed to control the canoe and keep it near me for three hours despite the four-foot waves before aborting the swim at DuPont. I was hesitant to ask for food or water because I didn't want to risk Mike and Alex losing control of the canoe; I waited until Alex offered, which she did at strategic places such as near a dock where the waves were calmer. I didn't feel any chill during the swim. I called the bow paddler who had agreed to paddle with Mike for the third shift, to tell him it was too windy to continue the swim so he didn't need to come. I was disappointed being shut down on my third attempt to complete the point-to-point swim. In fact, perhaps swimming for three hours continuously in four-foot waves was more beneficial to my training than swimming for eleven hours in flat calm water. In addition, I had the psychological advantage of knowing that I could have swum longer in the rough waves.

I went home to Deep River the weekend after Thanksgiving. (My mother had been in Calgary visiting my sister over the Thanksgiving weekend.) On Sunday afternoon, with my mother paddling beside me in her kayak, I went for a swim in the Ottawa River even though I'd come down with a cold the day before. I lasted just over half an hour. Two days later, back in Kingston, Jason and one of his classmates paddled beside me in a canoe. I was still feeling sick and thought about cancelling. Even after Jason and his friend showed up, I debated telling them that I had changed my mind and decided not to swim. Swimming in cold water when I wasn't feeling well was definitely risky, but I knew that if I played it safe and didn't do any open-water swims until I recovered from the cold, I'd lose the acclimatization I'd built up and would have to quit open-water swims altogether until the spring. I was quite sure when I got into the lake that this would be my last open-water training swim of the season. I swam for 1 hour and 20 minutes. On October 21st, which was a sunny day, I swam for 25 minutes in 61F water without shivering. The only reason we stopped the swim was because of the three- to four-metre waves and Jane, who was paddling beside me in my new 17-foot kayak, was often unable to reach the water with the paddle. We were in the bay between Everett Point and Pleasant Point and the waves would even be rougher in the open and Jane was getting cold, so we quit.

    Later that week, Jason canoed beside me with a different classmate. When I came out of the water, my shivering was very noticeable. One of my coworkers was very concerned when she saw me back in the building all bundled up and shivering. She understood why when I explained to her that I had been swimming twice a week and, since Lake Ontario would cool down gradually, I would go through a danger period before I underwent any harm. I explained to her that it was highly unlikely that I would feel fine after swimming for one hour one day and then encounter hypothermia after swimming for an hour three days later. If I swam in Lake Ontario for one hour on September 15th, went to the Caribbean for one month and then swam in Lake Ontario for one hour on October 15th, then my coworker would have had reason to be alarmed.

Chapter 26

Navy Bay Swim 2007

"Many of life's failures are people who did not realize how close they were to success when they gave up."
—Thomas A. Edison

I swam the 250 metres across Navy Bay for the United Way on November 2nd. I did the swim to support the United Way, but also to test my body and learn how much cold I could handle and what hypothermia symptoms I should watch for. Swim Master Vicki Keith had informed me that the body can increase its tolerance to cold water through practice so I wanted to test my capacity to handle cold water.

I was very disappointed that I hadn't swum across Navy Bay in 2006. That year, another coworker, James, swam across Navy Bay – which he had promised to do if a certain amount of money[48] was raised. James had invited others to join him swimming. I had leapt at the opportunity to join him and was all set to go until two hours before the swim: Rej, the United Way representative for my department, talked me out of doing it because proper safety measures were not in place. Earlier that week, Kim had spent time playfully trying to persuade me to wear a wetsuit, claiming it was too dangerous to do the swim without one. Michelle and Kristine had also expressed their concern. Several days later, another coworker, Phil, told me he had informed Rej that I shouldn't swim without a wetsuit. Rej took full responsibility for not allowing me to do the swim and didn't even mention Phil.

I was determined that I wouldn't be talked out of it again in 2007 and I devised a plan. I would continue my open-water swims as late into the fall as I could – which I probably would have done even if the Navy Bay swim had never come into play – and then I'd swim across Navy Bay and back twice a week until at least one of the following occurred:
- It was November 30th.
- Navy Bay froze over – which was unlikely before November 30th.

---
[48] Members of the department had made pledges and donations to the United Way. James promised to swim across Navy Bay only if the pledges and donations totalled a certain amount by a given date.

- I participated in an organized swim across Navy Bay, or a similar swim.
- I was shivering uncontrollably.

I was determined to continue doing short open-water swims until I hit a danger point. I needed solid criteria as to what would classify as a danger point. That way, if the water got too cold to handle, I would have experience with symptoms of hypothermia and would no longer swim for longer distances in Lake Ontario. I also wanted to prove to myself that I could handle the swim across Navy Bay since I'd been discouraged from doing it the previous year.[49]

We had an unusually mild autumn in 2007, so I continued my open-water swims longer than I would have imagined. I swam for 65 minutes in 54F water on October 29th, four days before the swim across Navy Bay. This reassured me that I would have no problem handling the five-minute swim across Navy Bay.

I had originally planned to keep the swimming event within the department, but when I mentioned it to Dave D., the United Way representative for all of RMC, he was more than supportive of the idea. A few other people wanted to swim with me and one of Dave's colleagues promised to provide a powerboat. With the military supporting the swim, they had access to all kinds of resources. It was commented that the swim might even become an annual event.

Near the beginning of the United Way campaign, I had braced myself for Kim's negative reaction to my idea to swim again this year, and gathered the courage to tell her my plans to do so. At lunch time, I told Jennifer within Kim's earshot. Kim asked me if I was going to wear a wetsuit. My face turned red in embarrassment. I replied that I had been afraid she would ask that question. I resisted answering the question and told her that I had swum for three hours on the weekend without a chill. Kim jokingly replied, "You're not answering my question."

Jennifer interjected, "She wants you to say, 'Yes, Kim, I will wear a wetsuit.'"

Kim still remembered the incident from May 24, 2007[50] when I had been swimming in Lake Ontario and showed up at her office shivering violently.

---

[49] This was not a foolproof plan since the water temperature has been known to fluctuate by several degrees from one year to the next.
[50] The 'May 24' story was mentioned in Chapter 17.

On some of my cold-water swims, it hurt too much to put my face in the water. I couldn't comfortably do the front crawl without putting my face in the water, so I'd resort to head-up breast stroke. Your body is at a more vertical angle when doing the breast stroke and a wetsuit provides so much floatation to the legs that it is difficult to maintain such an angle. I've heard it said that it's difficult for first-time wetsuit users to do breast stroke. It could have been more difficult to swim with a wetsuit than without one.

The morning of the swim, I paddled my kayak to work. I did this because I wanted to have my own personal escort boat beside me at all times, not only for safety but also to point me in a straight line; and I didn't want to be told that we didn't have enough support boats. Over a month prior to the swim, I told Jane, one of my paddling volunteers who is very knowledgeable about hypothermia, about my idea to swim across Navy Bay. I asked her if she'd paddle my kayak during the swim and she agreed to do so. I had asked Dave D. beforehand if a powerboat and a kayak were sufficient for seven swimmers and he thought they were enough. I wanted to make sure I was allowed to swim that year so I'd brought up the idea early and provided the kayak and paddler.

I never talked about the swim when Phil was around. One hour before I was to do the swim, I walked into the coffee room and Phil brought up the subject and said he was concerned. Just before the event, I walked by my supervisor, Brent, and Phil in the hallway as I was carrying my kayak paddle, two lifejackets and all the other safety equipment, and Brent said, "Please be careful."

Prior to the swim, I ran around the bay to the starting point while everyone else rode in the powerboat – except for two participants who swam both ways. I wanted to be independent; all I needed was one person to paddle my kayak beside me. Running around the bay also generated heat and made my body more resistant to the cold water.

There was a crowd of about one hundred RMC employees plus about ten of my paddling volunteers. My mother drove to Kingston specifically to watch the swim. I enjoyed the swim and was excited to share the good news with Vicki Keith.

email message from Jay to Vicki, November 2, 2007
subject: Swim Went Well

Vicki:

The swim went well. The conditions couldn't have been better. The bay was flat calm and it was sunny with little wind. I measured the water temperature at 54.9F. I could discern with my sense of touch that the water was cold but it didn't make my body feel cold (probably because I had been psyched up for several weeks). I wasn't even shivering when I came out and I didn't bother showering; I simply put on some clothes and drank hot chocolate.

There were seven swimmers and only one of them wore a wetsuit.

Regards,

Jay

Vicki's reply, November 2, 2007:

Congratulations Jay!!!

I don't think you have to worry about hypothermia. If you can handle that, you should be fine in Lake Ontario.

Have an amazing day!!

Vicki

  I approached Phil a few days after the swim and told him that I was scared of him. I mentioned that I appreciated his concern and the fact that he cared about me but went on to explain, being as friendly as I could, that by interfering with my plan to swim across Navy the year before, he had made it more difficult for me to proceed with my swim across Lake Ontario. I made it clear that I had refrained from talking about this year's swim across Navy Bay when he was around because I was afraid he'd try to talk me out of it again.
  "I'm the bad guy," Phil replied, to summarize our discussion.

          ◈

  On November 5th, three days after swimming across Navy Bay for the United Way, I undertook my final open-water training swim of the season. I stayed inside Navy Bay, but the bay was so rough that, within 20 minutes, my two canoeists called it quits and brought the canoe out of the water, while I continued swimming back and forth along the dock. One of the paddlers tied a throw rope to the floatation cushion just in case he had to pull me to the dock. The water temperature was 12°C(54°F), it was late in the afternoon, and it was cloudy. It had been about three weeks since I'd first thought that each open-water swim would be my last. My plan had been to continue the one-hour swims for as many weeks as I could safely endure the colder water temperatures that fall. After 53 minutes in the water, the discomfort was too great to stay in any longer. This was my last open-water training swim of the season.

Chapter 27

Heartbreaking News

"The soul would have no rainbow had the eyes no tears."
—John Vance Cheney

Aside from needing close to one week to get back to my normal training regime, I felt fine after the swim at Chippego Lake in July 2007. Roughly one week later, I made the following points for myself to summarize the Chippego Lake swim and to describe my training status to that point:

- I had swum for nineteen hours.
- Heather told me after the swim that I was swimming at a brisk pace on the final twenty minute stretch back to the cottage; therefore I still had lots of energy at the end of the swim.
- I could have swum longer and still been reasonably comfortable.
- I know I could have gone further even if I had reached a greater level of discomfort.
- After dark, not only did I have to repeatedly stop to negotiate with the crew on the target point but I lost energy wondering whether I might hit hypothermia. On the Lake Ontario crossing, I would leave this worry to the Swim Master and the paramedics.
- One week prior to the swim at Chippego Lake, I swam at Camp Iawah for fourteen hours without the slightest chill and clearly could have swum longer.
- I probably would have been fresher if I hadn't done the marathon swims at Camp Iawah and Chippego Lake too close together.
- At the beginning of May 2007, barely two months before the swim at Chippego Lake, my longest continuous swim had only been three hours.

After doing this analysis, I concluded that I would have been ready to undertake the crossing in 2007 if I had planned for it.

I knew I would certainly be ready by the summer of 2008 if I kept up the same level of training. I did not regret my decision to make this a two-year project instead of a one-year project. If I had planned to swim Lake Ontario in 2007, I would have had to decide that months earlier.

Months earlier, I couldn't have known whether or not I'd be ready and I would have been tempted to push myself beyond my comfort level.

excerpt from email message from Jay to Vicki, August 27, 2007:

I feel confident that I'm ready to swim across Lake Ontario now. (I know that, if I was going to do the swim this year, I would have had to decide that months ago and, months ago, I didn't know whether I'd be ready.)

Vicki's reply, August 30, 2007:

How far can you swim in one hour? As you prepare to complete the Lake Ontario crossing, you need to be able to average about 2 miles (3 kilometres) per hour. This will set you up for a successful swim in approximately 24 hours. I would recommend that you not attempt a crossing until you are able to hold this pace for at least 12 hours.

I strongly believe that anyone who wants to make a lake crossing has the capability, and I feel strongly that you are capable of this task...Solo Swims of Ontario requires that you complete a 16-kilometre trial swim before you attempt a crossing, and you should be able to complete this in under 6 hours without showing any signs of tiring.

Up until then, I had assumed that Solo Swims of Ontario didn't want to sanction just anyone without insisting on safety standards and a reasonable potential for success in a lake crossing. I reasoned that the purpose of holding trial swims was for the Swim Master to assess how well candidates handle swimming distances in open water. I felt that was fair enough. I had no idea that there was a time limit until Vicki told me. Thank-you, Vicki.

Vicki probably refrained from mentioning this guideline too soon lest it discourage me from my goal. This was a completely appropriate time to mention it since Vicki knew that I still had an entire year to work on my speed.

The next chance I got, I returned to Dog Lake for another 13 kilometre swim. This took me 5 hours and 41 minutes, not a minute faster than the last time I had done it on June 2nd. After all the training I had done, I should have been faster, so I was disappointed in the speed of this swim.

Throughout the winter of 2007-08, I planned to do a timed 16-kilometre swim at Progress Fitness Centre, keeping feeding breaks to a minimum, as many times as I feasibly could without tiring myself out i.e. once every six weeks. Then I planned to do a timed 16-kilometre swim in Dog Lake as soon as the water had warmed up enough for me to handle it. Meanwhile, Progress Fitness Centre had agreed to give me complimentary usage of their facilities in exchange for being named as a sponsor for my Lake Ontario crossing.

On December 15, 2007, I made my first attempt to swim 16-kilometres in a swimming pool. My triceps felt tight as soon as I started swimming, possibly because I had been curling at the department Christmas party the day before. Never before had my triceps been tight at the beginning of a training swim. At the nine-kilometre mark, my triceps became unbearably painful and, 100 metres later, I quit. Normally, I wouldn't quit so easily but would have switched to a different stroke. I wanted to mimic the trial swim as much as I could. On the trial swim, I wouldn't dare switch to another stroke because I wanted to be able to show my Swim Master that I could maintain front crawl for a reasonable length of time without getting tired. If I switched from front crawl to breast stroke, my Swim Master might question me and I'd have to say, "My shoulders were getting tired." Given that my shoulders had gotten tired within the first 16 kilometres in a pool, what would happen during the Lake Ontario crossing in open water? Would I even be able to complete the crossing?

Once again, I resolved that I would not fail in my mission to swim across Lake Ontario because I would give it 100 percent of my commitment and effort. On January 5, 2008, I returned to Progress Fitness Centre for another attempt to swim 16 kilometres. This time, I was successful! It took me three hours and one minute to swim the first eight kilometers and 6 hours and 31 minutes to swim the 16 kilometres.

I had visited my parents over the Christmas holidays and swam twice for one hour since the local swimming pool was only open for one-hour lane swims. I didn't want to increase my swim time to six hours too quickly so, on January 3, 2008 (the day after I returned to Kingston), I swam for two hours at noon and then went straight into work. I hadn't brought enough food with me so, by the end of the work day, I ran out of energy and felt sick. Without first going home for supper, I took the bus to knitting class that evening, planning to walk home afterwards. Not only did I have a headache but I was so tired that I just wanted to sleep. Concerned for my health, the knitting teacher offered to give me cab fare to get home. Luckily, someone who forgot to bring her knitting supplies had to leave and gave me a ride home. Training for my goal was taking its toll on me as well as inconveniencing other people. Fortunately, I was able to get some sleep that night and my energy was restored in time for the 16-kilometre swim two days later.

On February 24th, one week after completing two 53- kilometre ski races which were part of the Gatineau Loppet[51], I made my second successful 16-kilometre swim at Progress. This time, it took me 6 hours and 51 minutes to complete 16 kilometres. I wasn't too worried about the time, partly because I knew my body was calling for rest after the Gatineau Loppet and also because my main motivation for repeatedly swimming 16 kilometres throughout the winter was to be confident that I could show my Swim Master that I could swim 16 kilometres without fatigue. I was hoping I could reduce my time, but my years of experience running marathons had taught me that I could definitely improve my stamina through practice.

April 20th was such a gorgeous day that I would rather have been outside kayaking or cycling than indoors at a swimming pool all day. Nonetheless, I completed my third and final 16 kilometre swim at Progress Fitness Centre. This time, it took me 6 hours and 19 minutes, my fastest 16 kilometre so far. I incorporated the body rotation technique which Catriona[52] had shown me as part of the Total Immersion program. This didn't help me go faster but helped me go the same speed with less energy. Near the end of the swim, I sprinted 500m in 11:03. On the actual crossing, using less energy would certainly help but would it help on the trial swim?

In addition to the three 16-kilometre swims, I attempted three four-hour swims (on January 30, 2008; March 2, 2008; and April 27, 2008) with only one feeding break plus one five-hour swim (on April 6, 2008) with two feeding breaks. My reason for doing so was to learn whether my body could handle swimming distances with limited feeding breaks, and thus determine whether I could reduce my time on the trial swim. I did not complete the five-hour swim or one of the four-hour swims because of calf muscle spasms that came on suddenly and were very painful. Progress Fitness Centre does not have a deep end; otherwise, I would have made my way to the deep end despite the pain

---

[51] See Chapter 29 – Return to the Gatineau.
[52] Catriona accompanied me on many of my speed interval sets. The circumstances which led to Catriona teaching me the body rotation technique is explained in the next chapter (Speed Intervals).

of the spasms. I would have spent a few minutes either doing travel stroke (three drown proofs followed by a kick and a pull) or treading water using both arms plus my good leg. Even at the deepest point of 1.35 metres at this pool, if I relaxed my leg that was in spasm, that leg would hit the bottom of the pool. Instead, I sat on the deck for ten minutes and then swam for another half hour before quitting. I suspect it was a lack of nourishment that caused the muscle spasms. After that, I was afraid to reduce the number of feeding times.

The rest of my plan was to find out who my Swim Master would be and strike up a relationship with her like I did with Vicki Keith. Sometimes it takes people a while to get to know me. With my case of Asperger's Syndrome, it is not uncommon for people to mistreat me or get frustrated with me, but then to become very patient with me once they get to know me. For example, one of my former housemates, Ben, wronged me three separate times and is now one of my most valuable sources of advice. (See Appendix H for details.) I've learned that if I can make it through the initial problems that may come up when I'm first getting to know someone, things get easier as we go along. I quickly learn who I can work with and who is unable to work with me because of my Asperger's. It is possible to communicate smoothly and effectively with Aspies by making small but significant changes. The key is to know which small changes are significant.[53]

I knew that it was ultra-important to mention the nineteen-hour swim to my Swim Master well in advance of the trial swim. Otherwise, my Swim Master might say to me after the trial swim, "I'm impressed that you can swim this far and not look tired, but I'm going to have to fail you because you're just not fast enough. You're probably going to get tired and quit half way through the crossing."

If I replied, "But I swam for nineteen hours last summer," that would likely not convince the Swim Master to change her decision.

I thought, "If I can only make it past the initial hurdles with my Swim Master like I did with Ben, it will be clear sailing."

---

[53] Here is an example of a small, significant change. Sometimes I don't want to talk and want to be left alone. At the Ottawa '97 Navs summer program, I sprained my ankle the morning of a job interview. I arrived back at the program headquarters within a few minutes before supper time. Normally, I would have made a special trip back home to change out of my dress clothes to reduce the chances of being asked about the interview because I seldom like to talk about work or the job search after hours. Because of my sprained ankle, I deemed it easier to undergo the questioning. Surprisingly, no one asked about my interview or even commented on my attire. The other Navs participants probably realized by now that I don't like to talk about work or the job search after hours and left the onus on me to talk about it if I so chose.

Chapter 28
Speed Intervals

There is a story about four people named Everybody, Somebody, Anybody, and Nobody. There was an important job to be done and Everybody was asked to do it. Anybody could have done it, but Nobody did it. Somebody got angry about that, because it was Everybody's job. Everybody thought Anybody could do it but Nobody realized that Somebody should do it. It ended up that Everybody blamed Somebody when really Nobody accused Anybody!
    —http://www.netfunny.com/rhf/jokes/88q4/8772.9.html

    Shortly after Vicki broke the news to me about the unwritten time limit of six hours for the 16-kilometre trial swim, I told Vicki that I didn't think I could meet the time limit and asked, "What can I do?"

Vicki's reply, September 26, 2007:

I am glad that you are completing some long distance swims, but you also need to work on speed and speed endurance to get your times to improve.

  8 X 400m strong on 8 minutes
  16 X 200m on 4 minutes
  32 X 100m on 2 minutes

And 25's and 50's on short rest periods are all great to increase your stroke rate and power.

Again, thank-you Vicki. This was priceless advice.
    As a runner, I had done speed work when training for a 10-kilometre race but never when training for a marathon; I'd simply increase my stamina by gradually bringing up my distance to my peak training run of 30 kilometres. Similarly, I blindly assumed that speed work wasn't necessary when training for a Lake Ontario crossing; I resolved to focus mainly on endurance. The fact that I have stamina is partially an illusion; my determination and perseverance are what helps me build my stamina. Unfortunately, determination and perseverance

don't help improve one's speed as easily as they help increase one's stamina.

On November 26, 2007, I swam front crawl at Progress Fitness Centre for three hours non-stop without touching the sides of the pool and covered 8.375 kilometres. I was all but ready to collapse when I finished, in contrast to my two and a half hour swim at the SAIT pool[54] in April, 2007 when I felt I could have easily switched to breast stroke for five minutes and then swum another hour of front crawl. Needless to say, I slowed down over the course of the swim and would have slowed down more if I had continued. In an open-water, six-hour swim, I would need to eat and drink and that would increase my time to do the swim.

Unfortunately, I did not attempt these speed workouts until December 6, 2007, over two months after Vicki made the suggestion. Before this date, I had been doing speed training at the prescribed workouts with KMAC but far fewer sets than Vicki suggested. I joined KMAC to maintain my swimming fitness during the winter. Even after I started following Vicki's suggested workouts, I rotated among the three workouts and did a speed workout once every two or three weeks. At the end of February, 2008, I started doing Vicki's suggested workouts once a week.

During one speed workout at the KMCSC pool on February 27, 2008, Catriona, my co-worker, was also in the pool. She is noticeably faster than me and her presence motivated me to go faster. A few days later, I asked Catriona if she'd swim with me. During my speed workout on March 12th, after I had completed half of the intervals, Catriona swam behind me for the remainder of my intervals, in order to motivate me to go faster.

From this date until June 11th, one week before my qualifying trial swim, I went to the KMCSC pool for ninety minutes at lunch time every Wednesday to do Vicki's suggested workouts (see Appendix O for the results) – in addition to the practices with KMAC. Catriona almost always accompanied me on my speed workouts.

excerpt from an e-mail message from Vicki, March 31, 2008:

I am glad that the speed workouts are helping. I encourage you to continue to work out with Catriona, and to also push yourself when she is not there to make the pace. It will make a difference.

---

[54] The SAIT pool is partially salt water and thus provides more buoyancy to the swimmer.

Catriona carefully explained the Total Immersion technique and took me through a series of Total Immersion drills three separate times. The Total Immersion technique is based on increasing your stroke length by performing the front crawl on your side instead of on your front and by rotating your body from side to side with each stroke. [*Laughlin, 1996*]

At first, I did each interval as fast as I could. That was not a bad idea on my first attempt at interval training because it got me focused on increasing my pace. The purpose of speed intervals is not only to improve your speed but to find the speed that you can maintain over long distances. Catriona encouraged me to go slower on the first interval and focus on my form. My times were slowing down over the course of the workout. It was hard work: I had to increase my stamina and speed while improving my front crawl technique. I needed all the encouragement I could get!

excerpt from e-mail correspondence from Catriona, March 27, 2008:

I have reviewed your interval times posted on your website. The main goal with intervals is to make the last one in the set as fast as the first one. From what I've seen, you are going out way too hard on the first interval. Try to start your workouts relaxed and build up to higher efforts for the last three intervals. Those are the really important ones. Try to swim each 200 on 3:50, so you get 10 seconds rest. If that's not enough rest, maybe you should do them all on 4:05. If you can, try looking at the clock on every lap to make sure you are staying on the desired pace.

excerpt from e-mail correspondence from Catriona, April 1, 2008:

For all interval workouts, it is important not to set out too hard. If the first intervals feel too easy, try to glide more and focus on making your stroke feel smooth and effortless. Don't get too excited at the start because it's the end of the workout that really matters.

Catriona was most supportive of my goal to cross Lake Ontario. I'm glad I approached her at the pool and asked her to help me swim at a faster pace during my interval training. I learned a number of lessons from this experience of asking for help. I found out that it takes time to get the support you need. As I organized my training schedule, I was sometimes reluctant to ask people to help me. I felt that they had to believe in my dream and get to know me well enough to see that I was fully committed to my goal to swim across Lake Ontario. I was afraid that people would not commit to me if they thought I might quit my training and fail to realize my dream. People don't want to intrude or presume they can help, but when asked, they are more than happy to share their expertise or lend a hand. I was very grateful to Catriona for her help and support. She furthered my training and her guidance inspired me to adopt the total immersion technique that increased my pace sustainably for long distances.

When I initially started Vicki Keith's workouts, I had to take more rest between sets than what Vicki perscribed. In early March, I completed two speed workouts without any additional rest. After that, my speed intervals slowed down and I had to go back to taking additional rest. I had hit my peak and then had trouble keeping myself psyched up.

In April, 2008 I found out that Marilyn Korzekwa, M.D., the secretary of Solo Swims of Ontario, would be my Swim Master. After some thought, I informed Marilyn about my concern of failing the trial swim and what I had been doing to improve my time. It was at this point that Marilyn suggested I do one and a half times the number of intervals prescribed by Vicki Keith and do the workouts twice a week. The KMCSC pool was open for 90 minutes at lunch time, barely long enough to complete Vicki's prescribed workouts. I had attempted a speed workout at Artillery Park only once because it was just too crowded for speed intervals. I figured that I'd go to Progress Fitness Centre every Monday and Thursday evening to do the extended speed workouts prescribed by Marilyn. Unfortunately, this meant saying goodbye to my workouts with Catriona.

On April 28th, I went to Progress Fitness Centre for my first attempt to swim twelve sets of 400 metres. My first set took me 8 minutes and 12 seconds. On the second set, I tried to go faster and was clocked in at 7 minutes and 57 seconds so I gave up on the workout. I stayed at the pool and swam front crawl for another hour for exercise. I had never been slower than 60 seconds per 50 metres on my first interval even if I was trying to go slowly. My speed intervals seemed to be faster at the KMCSC pool than at Progress Fitness Centre. I suspected that it wasn't the pool itself that made me go faster, but the motivation

I got from other swimmers in the pool. Also, my swims at the KMCSC were at a better time of day for me. No matter what the other factors were, if the reason for the first slow interval was anything other than my body recovering from the four-hour swim the day before, I was in trouble. I decided I'd be better off going back to Vicki's prescribed workouts once a week.

Two days later, I returned to the noon swim at the KMCSC and did 90 minutes of uninterrupted front crawl, sprinting 400 metres near the end in exactly eight minutes, still following my usual routine of not touching the sides on a long swim. Clearly, my previous workout two days before had been unusual since I had started from rest, tried to go fast *and* touched the sides, and it took me 7 minutes and 57 seconds to swim 400 metres.

The next week, I was noticeably slower after the seventh set so I quit. Marilyn was disappointed when I told her this and recommended that I complete the workout anyway but take more rest. That's exactly what I did. After all, I was pleading with Marilyn not to fail me on the trial swim; therefore, I felt obligated to do whatever Marilyn told me to do. However, if the speed intervals became too slow, continuing the workout wouldn't be much different than doing the remainder of the intervals without any rest and turning the speed workout into a long, slow swim.

I am deeply indebted to Vicki Keith for suggesting the speed interval workouts and for making me aware of the time limit for the trial swim. I shudder to think about what might have happened if Vicki hadn't told me about the six-hour guideline: I probably would have continued to focus on my endurance and wouldn't have done any timed 16-kilometre swims until the spring; I would have felt more confident and wouldn't have felt the need to strike up a relationship with my Swim Master so I wouldn't have found out who my Swim Master was and possibly wouldn't have realized that there was a six-hour time limit until closer to the trial swim date. My Swim Master would likely have told me about the six-hour guideline, but by then it may have been too late to improve my speed.

∽

At a meeting with the organizational committee on February 26th, I got some disappointing news. The detailed planning and administrative set-up for my Lake Ontario crossing was progressing much more slowly than they'd hoped. They asked me if I was willing to put off the swim until the summer of 2009! I have a tendency to interpret questions such as these as statements or demands. Immediately, I said no.

I quickly concluded that the *only* solution was to summon more energy, get more help, scale down the gimmicks of the event and make sure my swim across Lake Ontario happened in 2008. I had been fine with my decision to delay my swim until 2008. My main reason for not doing the swim in 2007 was because I didn't think I'd be ready. My summer training swims would not have been enjoyable if I had been constantly wondering whether or not I'd be ready by August. Also, I would have been tempted to push myself beyond my comfort zone. In the spring of 2008, I couldn't face another delay in reaching my goal.

On February 27th, I woke up at 5:00 a.m. and couldn't get back to sleep. This was later than the time my alarm went off on the days I attended the early morning practices at KMAC and much earlier than I got up any other day. I could not stop thinking about the situation. I wrote an email message, which is given in Appendix I.

Kerry's Place Autism Services eventually hired a part-time employee, Andra, specifically to assist with the project of making my swim happen. I quickly realized I could either continue to get stressed about the lack of administrative organization or focus on something else related to the swim. I chose the latter and went to the pool that day to do another set of speed intervals. Swimming accomplished two things:

1. It eased my mind from the stress of thinking about the organizational problems and allowed me to focus on the physical aspect of making the swim happen. I was the only person who could insure that this part of the preparation would get done.
2. I had to do my part to make sure my trial swim got approved before I would feel right about putting pressure on the organizational committee to make the swim happen this year.[55]

I was pumped after making these decisions and finished my speed intervals faster than I ever had.

I was very excited when I returned to work and went to see my friend Kim. Kim is my co-worker who kept coaxing me to wear a

---

[55] Sadly, the disappointing news about the slow progress of the detailed planning and administrative set-up for my Lake Ontario crossing was what was required to make me increase the frequency of doing Vicki's prescribed speed workouts from once every two or three weeks to every week.

wetsuit for the swim across Navy Bay. She used to tease me about this, but I knew she was seriously concerned for my safety. I knew that Kim would be excited to hear that I had broken my time records in training that day. I burst into Kim's office and said, "Kim! Guess what? I did 32 sets of 100 metres and kept them all under two minutes." Then I went on to say, "I am concluding that you will be delighted when I complete my swim across Lake Ontario. You know that I have to train. You will not show any disapproval of me doing as much swimming as I want in Lake Ontario without a wetsuit between June 15th and September 15th and you will not show any disapproval of me doing as much swimming as I want in the pool at any time of the year."

Pleased with my performance, Kim replied, "I won't show disapproval of you swimming in the lake even outside those times – just concern."

When I had emailed Vicki the next day I informed her that: "I went to the pool yesterday and did 32 sets of 100 metres and kept them all under two minutes."

excerpt from Vicki's reply, February 28, 2008:

Keep working on the training, the one thing I have learned about you through our communications, is that you are determined to accomplish this. There is no doubt in my mind that you will be successful.

It was wonderful to have Vicki's confidence in me and her ongoing support.

I kept thinking about my relationship with Marilyn, my Swim Master. I came to the following conclusion: If I could only get my Swim Master to share Vicki's confidence in my swimming ability, I would be home free.

Chapter 29

Return to the Gatineau

"Before you criticize someone, walk a mile in his shoes. That way, if he gets mad he'll be a mile away – and barefoot."
—Sarah Jackson

    Cross-country skiing has, by far, been my favourite winter sport for many years. During the winters of 2007 and 2008, I was torn between swimming in the pool and cross-country skiing. Because I don't have a car, part of me hoped that it wouldn't get too cold and that the roads would be clear enough for me to ride my bicycle to the swimming practices. The other part of me hoped it would get cold enough for the lake to freeze so that I could ski. The ski trails in Kingston are difficult to get to without a car, so the most convenient place to cross-country ski is on Lake Ontario. Therefore, regardless of whether it turned out to be a cold winter or a warm winter, I was happy.

    Ever since my first time racing in the Gatineau Loppet in 1994, the trails in Gatineau Park have always seemed like skiers' heaven to me. I had never lived in Ottawa during the winter except for my first co-op work term, when I hadn't yet participated in the Gatineau Loppet and therefore didn't deem it as skiers' heaven yet. The net result is that I seldom ski in the Gatineau except to participate in the Gatineau Loppet.

    Each time I participate in the Gatineau Loppet, I am reminded about how much I love to ski on these trails. I don't always take the initiative to make sure I register for the race, train sufficiently for it or plan my schedule so that I can participate so it has not yet become an annual event.

    I participated in both the classical race on Saturday and the skating race on Sunday in 2004. Both days, the options are 10 km, 29 km and 53 km. I participated in both 53 km races. Sunday's race was shortened to 42 km because of the cold. I was disappointed that it took me longer to ski 42 km than it does to complete a 42 km running marathon. I told this to one of my friends in Ottawa who has skied in the Gatineau many times. He replied that the Gatineau course is hillier than any marathon and if running marathons were held on that particular course, people would have heart attacks.

In 2008, after participating in both 53-kilometre ski races once again, the only parts of my body that hurt were the blisters on the backs of both heels. They developed and broke while I was skiing. When I run a 42-kilometre marathon, my quadriceps are so stiff that I have to go down the stairs facing backwards for the next three days because it's too painful to descend stairs facing forwards. With running, your legs absorb the weight of your body with every step. With skiing, your body never leaves the ground and you're working your arms as well.

When I showered after the first race, I yelled in pain when the water touched the broken blisters. For a few days afterwards, even wearing shoes was painful. At work, I walked along the hallways wearing only socks. Only a few people commented. Each day, as soon as I came home, I took my shoes and socks off. Then I removed the Band-aids, put Polysporin on the wounds and walked around the house barefoot for the rest of the day. When I slept, I kept my feet outside the blankets to heal better. In the morning after showering, I would apply Polysporin and then put on new Band-aids.

I suspected that the broken blisters could make swimming difficult but I was willing to try swimming nonetheless. I planned to go to KMAC practice on Tuesday morning and stay for the full two-hour lane swim in preparation for my second 16 kilometre swim at Progress Fitness Centre the following Sunday. I sat on the deck and then slowly and carefully put my feet in the water, expecting pain. I was fine for a little while but, after a number of lengths swimming the front crawl, the blisters became very painful so I switched to breast stroke hoping to alleviate the pain. The blisters from skiing posed a dilemma for me: I couldn't do front crawl or run because of the blisters and couldn't cycle with snow on the roads. What could I do for exercise? Trish suggested I use a pull buoy and swim using only my arms. I took Trish's suggestion and used the pull buoy for the remainder of the KMAC practice but did not stay for the lane swim. Trish asked me if I cross-country ski because I like cross-country skiing or if I do it for cross training. I told her it was because I like cross-country skiing. She sounded like she would have been concerned if I was doing it for cross training.

Thursday was the day I had agreed to return to Lois's school to give my speech to another year of students. I chose not to go to swimming practice that morning because I didn't want to risk being tired for my speech. I had to attempt the 16 kilometre swim without the usual two-hour preparation. As Lois was driving me home from the speech, I told her that I'd almost asked her if I could give my speech without wearing shoes.

Lois replied, "Of course you could have."

Chapter 30
Spring 2008

"Our passions are the winds that propel our vessel. Our reason is the pilot that steers her. Without winds the vessel would not move and without a pilot she would be lost."
—Traditional proverb

I was waiting for the day when I could again take my polar plunges in Lake Ontario. On April 14, 2008, two weeks after the ice broke up, I took a plunge in 41°F water off the PUC (Public Utilities Commission) dock just east of Portsmouth Olympic Harbour. I stayed in for just under 60 seconds. Just before I got out, I had my spotter throw me a lifejacket which I practiced putting on in deep water, in anticipation of getting in trouble when I was far from shore. I did up one of three buckles but didn't bother doing up the other two because it was too much effort and I could float on my back. I made quite an interesting sight swimming to the ladder doing the breast stroke with the lifejacket bobbing over my head.

As I was drying myself, Mr. Michael Lea, a photographer for the Kingston Whig-Standard, just happened to be passing by. I re-entered the water so he could photograph me for the newspaper, but he warned me not to go in again just on his account. I had done enough dips and knew my body well enough to know that on a sunny day, I could swim for a fraction of a minute, come out of the water and then swim for another fraction of a minute. I knew I could probably keep this up several times but I couldn't stay in for very long at one time.

∽

Another 250-metre swim across Navy Bay had been scheduled for April 18, 2008. The absurd idea of the swim was sparked during a conversation I had with a coworker about my upcoming swim across Lake Ontario while in the locker room after a speed workout at the KMCSC pool in January. One of the military members who had helped organize the Navy Bay swim in November 2007[56] overheard the conversation and asked me, partially joking, whether I would do a swim across Navy Bay for United Way in the winter of 2008. The bay

---

[56] The swim across Navy Bay was described in Chapter 26.

was frozen solid and I didn't think anyone wanted me to do the polar bear swim badly enough to break a 250-metre path through the ice, but I became excited about the prospect of doing the swim. I waited a week to let the organizer know that I had taken time to think about it and then approached him to let him know I was interested. He agreed to help organize the swim and to provide the boat.

HMCS Cataraqui, who agreed to supply the boat, was adamant about not putting a boat in the water when there was any chance of scraping the boat against an ice block and I don't blame them.

Once again, I sought the opinion of Joe, a former professor. Unlike a polar plunge in which the water temperature is close to freezing, Joe didn't think the current situation was life-threatening. He did, however, offer the following advice: that I tell the boat crew before the swim, "If I say, 'Pull me out', you should listen to me but, if you think I should be pulled out and I say, 'I'm fine, don't pull me out' you shouldn't pay any attention to me and should go ahead and pull me out." Joe also told me to tell the boat crew that if I stop stroking for five to ten seconds, then they should pull me out.

As always, I asked Vicki Keith for input. Vicki didn't reply until three days before the swim when she asked me about the water temperature. It was 44F (in comparison to 55F when I had swum across Navy Bay the previous November).

email message from Vicki, April 16, 2008:

Wow!

That's pretty cold. I think your main concern will be when you get out that you have a warm place to go immediately when you finish – a car with the heat full on or something like that. Also, if your support staff keep your towels heated, and then have them ready to throw over your shoulders and wrap around you when you are done that would be smart.

I have to say, this is quite a risk. I wish you the best of luck, but I usually discourage cold swims like this because the risk is so high.

Take care of yourself!!

Vicki

It was crystal clear to me that if Vicki had to make the decision, she would say, "Don't do it!" For obvious reasons, Vicki wouldn't make the decision for me. Both my sister and John P. said, "If Vicki doesn't think it's a good idea, I don't think you should do it."

One of the officer cadets who accompanied me on the Navy Bay swim in November wanted to swim with me. However, as a cadet, he required approval from his squadron commander. The issue reached the director of cadets who called the whole thing off for safety reasons.

email message from Jay to Vicki, April 17, 2008:
subject: Polar Bear Swim Cancelled

Tomorrow's polar bear swim has been cancelled. The director of cadets has called it off for safety reasons. It may get rescheduled for a later date but I will let the organizers make the next move. I forwarded your last two email messages to the organizer (I hope you don't mind) who forwarded them to the director of cadets. Thank you for your concern and advice.

Please rest assured that I am NOT disappointed. There is a part of me that says to play it safe, forget the polar bear dips altogether and not even stick my toe in Lake Ontario until the water temperature reaches 55°F (60°F is safer) – and keep swimming in the pool until then. That's what the pool is for. Taking this safety precaution will, I estimate, decrease my chances of successfully swimming across Lake Ontario by less than one percent. (And it could increase my chances.)

On another note, it is comforting to know that I have people around me (such as yourself) who care about me and are not afraid to voice their opinion. I rest assured that no one in my department would have thought of me as a coward if I had backed out at the last minute.

Vicki's reply, April 17, 2008:

Thanks Jay, I am relieved.

I am glad that you will not be in the lake tomorrow. I agree with 55°F and prefer 60°F.

Thanks for the update.

Have an amazing day!!

Vicki

Experience has shown 55°F to be a safe cutoff for me since I have swum in 55°F water for one hour and, although shivering, my body bounced back to a normal temperature quite quickly; I knew that it was sensible to be cautious. It is always necessary to be cautious while swimming, but the level of caution has to be increased with colder water; it is vital to know when to get out of the water. If it was a sunny day with little wind and I was "pumped" for a swim, I would have been willing to go in at as low a temperature as 53°F, but I would have taken extra precautions if I had done a swim at that temperature.

It had been sunny and calm for several days so on April 18th, the scheduled day of the swim, the water temperature was 46°F.

෴

On May 4th, the final day of the annual Open House at Frontenac Outfitters, I did my first open-water training swim of the season but I felt I should get the owner's permission first since Frontenac Outfitters was providing the kayaks to accompany me, and also for liability reasons. Pearkes Lake is about 21 metres deep at its maximum depth and is therefore one of the first lakes in the area to warm up, if not the first. Frontenac Outfitters is one of Canada's largest on-water canoe and kayak store. Two of my paddling volunteers each paddled a kayak beside me. With the abundance of canoes and kayaks, this is the one training swim where there is no limit to the number of people who can paddle beside me. All I ask is that no one hit me over the head with a paddle! John C. couldn't paddle beside me because he had agreed to help the owner organize the open house. Just as I was leaving the store to go to the lake, which is barely 200 metres from the store, John C. said, in his usual half-joking but half-serious way, "Stay close to shore, Jay." Pearkes Lake is not very wide so it is impossible to venture too far from shore.

The water had been 63°F on the same weekend in 2007. Pearkes Lake was 57°F when I entered it on May 4, 2008, and I swam for one hour. I felt chilled at first but, as usual, I got used to it. I would have liked to swim longer and the only reason I got out was that the person who drove me there had to get back to Kingston. I was shivering quite noticeably when I came out.

Two days later, on May 6th, I took another plunge in Lake Ontario. By this time, the water temperature had reached 52°F. I was prepared to get out after five minutes and told my spotters that I would stay in the water for a maximum of ten minutes. After ten minutes, I concluded that I was ready to commence training in Lake Ontario. It seemed to me that five minutes was the magic time period: either I was in so much pain that I would want out within five minutes or my heat-generating mechanisms would kick in and I would be able to withstand that water temperature for some time. I informed one of my paddlers that day that I was ready to start swimming in Lake Ontario, although I waited for another week.

On May 14th, I started my Lake Ontario training. I swam along the shoreline of the RMC peninsula for one hour and twenty-one minutes, starting and ending at the boathouse. I was surprisingly comfortable some of the time but quite chilled the rest of the time. The water temperature was 58°F at the boathouse but probably varied by a few degrees over the course of the swim.

On May 17th, I undertook my second training swim in Lake Ontario. I swam for one hour and fifteen minutes and would have preferred to continue swimming for as long as two hours but my kayaker wanted to stop. The water temperature was 56°F (13°C).

On May 19th, I returned to Richard Cadman's home to undertake a 16-kilometre trial swim in Dog Lake, which I had planned to do ever since Vicki Keith had informed me about the six hour time limit my qualifying swim. Jane and Shannon paddled Richard's canoe beside me for the first seven kilometres and then Mike and Shannon paddled the last nine kilometres. I took only five feeding breaks, the second and fifth of which were liquid only. It rained during part of this time.

Less than an hour after entering the water, I could not keep my fingers together. The first kilometre took me 21 minutes. I had slowed down to 28 or 29 minutes per kilometre near the end. I sprinted the last kilometre in 23 minutes and had enough energy so that I could have kept swimming longer. I did the front crawl for the entire 16 kilometres and it took me 6 hours and 51 minutes. (See Table 30-1 for my interval times at each kilometre.) The water temperature was 59°F. I was comfortable for some of the swim but not all of it. As with many of my open-water swims, my tolerance to cold water and my determination to finish were more than enough to override any discomfort. Although I felt only mildly chilled while in the water, I was shivering quite noticeably within minutes after I came out; I immediately headed for a warm shower. After I had showered and changed, Richard and his wife treated us all to some barbecued hamburgers

Table 30-1 Lap times for 16-kilometre time trial in Dog Lake

distance	time	distance	time
0.5km	0:10	8.5km	
1.0km	0:21	9.0km	3:37*
1.5km	0:32	9.5km	
2.0km	0:43	10.0km	4:05
2.5km	0:55	10.5km	
3.0km	1:06	11.0km	4:44
3.5km	1:18*	11.5km	
4.0km	1:32	12.0km	4:57*
4.5km		12.5km	5:14
5.0km	1:55	13.0km	5:28
5.5km		13.5km	5:42
6.0km	2:23*	14.0km	5:57*
6.5km		14.5km	6:14
7.0km	2:47	15.0km	6:28
7.5km		15.5km	6:39
8.0km	3:11	16.0km	6:51

* feeding break

On May 23rd, despite being sick with a cold, I had Kristine come down to the water with me. I ate part of my lunch and held a brick while treading water. I stayed in the water for 13 minutes. I was noticeably shivering when I came out, even after getting bundled up. So, at Kristine's suggestion, I ran around the soccer field a few times. That suppressed the shivering.

A few hours later, I did another training swim, following the same route I had followed nine days earlier. So far, it had not rained the day of or the day before any of my Lake Ontario swims. This time, the rainfall the day before was the main reason for the water temperature dropping to 50°F. After 30 minutes, I turned around. After 40 minutes,

I firmly announced to my paddler that I was getting out of the water and would run back to the boathouse to warm up. I was confident that I could have swum for another five minutes or so, but I had stayed within metres of the shoreline because I didn't want to push myself and take unnecessary risks. One year before, I would have wanted to get out of the water quickly at 50°F; 54°F had seemed to be the magic temperature at which I could withstand the discomfort but during this swim I realized that I had built up a tolerance to colder water.

On May 25th, I was still feeling a little bit under the weather and thought of cancelling the swim, but went ahead with it. This was my fourth training swim in Lake Ontario for the season. I swam for one hour, starting and ending at the water purification plant, with Dave K., whom I had never met before, paddling my kayak beside me. The water temperature was estimated to be 52°F. I wasn't shivering when I finished the swim, but started shivering noticeably within a matter of minutes. I instinctively wanted to make two statements without realizing at first that they contradicted each other:
1. I'd know when I needed to get out of the water; and
2. I didn't know I'd be shivering that violently; otherwise I wouldn't have stayed in the water that long.

Luckily, Rob and two of his friends just happened to be nearby playing catch. Rob had paddled beside me on a few of my training swims the year before. If Rob and his friends hadn't been there, I probably would have kept running after the swim in order to generate body heat. One of Rob's friends, Chris, offered to bring the car near me but I ran with him to his car to keep myself warm. Chris turned the heater on full blast and commented within a short time that the car felt like a sauna. Chris offered me three more layers that I put over my torso. Rob had to get out of the car because he was getting too hot and I was still shivering. I stayed in the car for 15 minutes until I felt warm. Chris and Rob strongly recommended that I bring gloves and a hat the next time. I had paddled my kayak the five kilometres from my house to the water purification plant. I was more than willing to paddle the kayak back home, reasoning that paddling would help generate heat, but Rob and the others insisted that I leave the kayak at Dave K.'s parents' house and they gave me a ride home.

On May 30th, I picked up my kayak from Dave K.'s parents house, where I'd stored it since the weekend, and I paddled it to work. At lunch time, Catriona paddled my kayak beside me while I swam. We crossed Navy Bay and followed the Fort Henry shoreline for a while.

Then we crossed over to Cedar Island where the channel was much narrower. I swam to the westernmost tip of Cedar Island and then the last kilometer back to RMC. At this point, I wasn't too worried about being too far from shore. Although I was quite chilled, I had been handling the cold water well in my training to this point; I was confident that I wouldn't become too numb or go into hypothermia without any warning. I definitely went out of my comfort zone but I thought it was necessary to do this in training in order to reduce the chances of encountering hypothermia on my crossing. I had left the keys to my office in a locker and did not have enough dexterity in my hands to open the combination lock, so Catriona had to open it for me.

On June 4th, I swam for 1 hour and 50 minutes. The water temperature was about 58°F. My paddler and I ventured west along the shoreline from my house, cutting across a few bays. On the way back, I was concerned that I wouldn't be able to swim all the way so I retrieved my towel and warm clothes from the kayak and ran back to the starting point. I was no longer shivering when I met my paddler back at the starting point, having generated enough heat from the run.

On June 7th, Jens came to Kingston to visit me for the weekend. Partly for a change in swim locations and partly because Jens enjoys ferry rides, I suggested that I paddle my kayak to Amherst Island, while Jens drove his car to the island. Once on the island, Jens paddled beside me while I swam along the southern shoreline of the island. We stayed so close to shore that the waves were breaking and pushing me on shore. At least twice, I brushed against the bottom of the lake and asked Jens to move further from the shoreline. I swam west, against the current, for two hours and ten minutes until the turnaround point and then swam back to the starting point in an hour and a half. That was my longest swim in Lake Ontario for the 2008 season to that point. The water temperature was 58°F most of the time, but 54°F in a few places. While I paddled the kayak back to the shoreline, Jens measured the road distance of the swimming route to be 3.4 kilometres one way, although the actual curving shoreline may have been a slightly longer distance. In a pool, it typically took me 1 hour and 10 minutes to swim 3.5 kilometres; I had a current helping me and it took me 1 hour and 30 minutes. That was potentially bad news. I tried to console myself with the fact that there possibly could have been a side-current as well. These small set-backs are part of the roller-coaster ride of training results. Once back on the mainland, Jens and I had supper at an all-you-can-eat place with two of my other volunteer paddlers.

On June 8th, Jens drove me to HMCS Cataraqui where I met Alicia who paddled her kayak beside me while I swam around the point of Cedar Island. I swam for two and a half hours, my first time in Lake Ontario that season without feeling chilled.

On June 10th, I tried out something that I'd been thinking about for some time: swimming home from work. I paddled my kayak to work that morning and Shannon, who also works at RMC, graciously agreed to paddle beside me on the way home. It was almost 5:00 p.m. when we started. Things went more or less smoothly until the shoreline by the Kingston Psychiatric Hospital where the waves got much rougher and Shannon considered stopping the trial. As we passed Lake Ontario Park, I informed Shannon that it was time to make a decision. If we kept going, we would have to keep going for a while before the next convenient place to set foot on land. We decided to proceed.

At 9:00 p.m., when we reached Carruthers Point, Shannon and I made the mutual decision to abort the swim. We had two more kilometres to cover and one more bay to cross before our destination just past Pleasant Point. Nightfall was only a few minutes away; Shannon wasn't comfortable being on the water at night, let alone spotting a swimmer; and I wasn't crazy about taking any unnecessary risks. We put my kayak on the cart that I kept in its stern and we towed my kayak through DuPont's private property. This area was totally unfamiliar to Shannon, but I was familiar enough with the surroundings to get us back to civilization, even in the dark. If anyone had confronted us, I was prepared to explain how we had gotten there and the purpose of my training. I was confident that the owners wouldn't ask us to go back into the water and exit their property the way we had entered. Shannon and I took turns towing the kayak. It took us at least ten minutes to get to back to a nearby residential area and then another twenty minutes to walk back to my house along a busy Kingston street. Although it wasn't pleasant at the time, looking back, it was quite the adventure.

On June 15th, one week before my trial swim across Lake Ontario, I swam from HMCS Cataraqui to the Wolfe Island ferry dock and back. I did the front crawl the entire time and it took me 2 hours and 27 minutes one way. In comparison, the one-way trip on my very first long training swim had taken me 2 hours and 34 minutes. Not only was the previous trial twice as far as my previous longest swim, but I had also taken two feeding breaks, doing the front crawl only a fraction of the time and never for more than nine minutes at a time and breathing only on my right every second stroke. On the previous trial, the water had been fairly calm up to Garden Island, but after that it had gotten more choppy. This time, the lake was rough. I was concerned. Given that I had reduced my front crawl time by 10 percent within one month after joining the Masters swimming club (a fraction of this gain was obtained from learning to breathe bilaterally), I had high hopes I'd make it in two hours. If the reason for my slowness was anything other than the rough water, I was in trouble. The previous summer, it had taken me exactly two hours to swim from the RMC Boathouse near the mouth of Navy Bay to the summer ferry dock. I hoped I wasn't getting any slower. I could contemplate the reasons all I wanted, but the time had come to start tapering for the trial swim.

I had thought about doing another 24-hour swim that summer. The logistics of picking a time and place were more complicated than I had thought, especially with the restriction that I not do it too soon before the trial swim or the crossing. I asked for Vicki Keith's input.

Vicki's reply, May 27, 2008:

I do not think a 24-hour training swim is necessary. There is no doubt in my mind that you are mentally prepared for the challenges that a marathon swim will produce.

Chapter 31

Meeting Pam

"We are not so much concerned if you are slow as when you come to a halt."

—*Chinese proverb*

Kerry's Place Autism Services was very impressed with my speech the first time I spoke to them in June 2007. They offered to submit a proposal to fund a coach to work with me for one day after I found out how much that would cost. All I had to do was find a swimming coach who was willing to take the time to coach me.

I asked Vicki Keith if she knew of anyone who might be able to provide coaching services. Vicki told me to ask Solo Swims of Ontario. I did so, but they were unable to provide any names. SSO is volunteer-driven and wasn't in a position to undertake another task, even something as simple as finding someone who had the time to coach me. SSO asked me what sort of coaching I was looking for. I didn't know how to answer that question because I had never undertaken a project of this sort before and didn't know what specific type of coaching would be useful. I couldn't give an answer that was much more detailed than, "I want to swim across Lake Ontario." Eventually, I had all but given up trying to find a coach.

I had never met Vicki in person but she had always answered my questions by email. Trish and Andrew, the coaches of the Kingston Masters Aquatic Club, had been observing my swimming for some time, and had given me one-on-one advice. Unfortunately, they had no experience regarding what was required for marathon swimming training. I was probably the only member of KMAC who was training for anything longer than an ironman swim. I decided to combine the email advice from Vicki with the one-on-one advice from Trish and Andrew, and hope that this would be sufficient. Once a candidate registers his swim, SSO provides a Swim Master. I had also resolved to make myself accountable to my Swim Master, after I found out who that would be.

For several months, I had been confident that I had the endurance but needed to work on my speed; my biggest concern was failing the trial swim because of the unwritten time limit of six hours. KMAC, which focus on speed intervals and drills, is largely intended to assist members with speed and technique and that was exactly what I needed.

In February 2008, when I started filling out the application for SSO, it asked for the name of a coach. I asked SSO whose name I should use and they told me to put down the name of the coach who would accompany me during my swim across Lake Ontario. I wondered if SSO had another regulation that prohibited a swimmer from doing a lake crossing without a coach. Once again, I thought my heart was going to break. I told Vicki that I knew she had already told me that she wouldn't have time to coach me, but I asked her if she knew anyone who might. I made it clear that I only wanted to avoid the off-chance scenario in which I ended up not swimming across Lake Ontario because I didn't have a coach. I told Vicki that I hoped she would know someone who would be willing to act as my coach and if she would she please let me know if she did. I didn't feel it would hurt to ask her for a reference.

Once again, I forged ahead. I refused to give up on my dream desire before I had given 100 percent of my efforts to do everything in my power to accomplish this goal. If having a coach was mandatory, I would resort to every trick I knew, including advertising my need in the Kingston and Toronto newspapers. If a coach was not mandatory, I concluded that finding a coach could be more hassle than it was worth, but I had to try. People such as Vicki, who had the expertise to act as my coach, were few and far between and were in such high demand that they'd probably refuse my request regardless of how much money I was willing to pay. Even if I did find someone nice enough to spend thirty hours on the boat and act as my coach, no one other than Trish or Andrew would have sufficient knowledge of my swimming abilities to know how to help me. Both Trish and Andrew were willing to help in whatever ways they could, but, unfortunately, Andrew was going away for the summer and Trish was unable to get time off work.

Vicki's advice regarding having a coach, March 31, 2008:

I don't know anyone who could act as coach, but having said that, if Trish or Andrew is available, it would be good for them to be there. If neither is available, choose someone who is available, who knows you very well, and whom you trust. They can then act as your coach, passing information to you, and helping you make necessary decisions. Your selected coach should be the only person who is allowed to give you distance feedback etc. This stops inexperienced crew passing you misinformation that can be frustrating (I have been told inaccurate distances during the swim and it is very distracting). The important traits in a coach are that they are logical, cool headed and you trust them to make decisions for you if you are unable, or with you if you are able.

I concluded from Vicki's reply that it is not mandatory that a swimmer have a coach, but it is in the swimmer's best interests to have one.

Solo Swims of Ontario suggested that I get a non-swimming friend or relative to act as my coach and have Trish or Andrew bring that person up to date on my swimming background. SSO indicated that it would be helpful if the coach had a swimming background, but it was not essential.

∽

I had never heard the term "Total Immersion Technique" until Catriona had told me about it. Interestingly, Marilyn, my Swim Master, who had been a registered Swim Master with Solo Swims of Ontario for some time, hadn't heard of Total Immersion either. In the process of doing speed intervals with Catriona, she gradually informed me more and more about what Total Immersion was about. Three separate times, Catriona walked me through some Total Immersion drills. One day, I went to the Total Immersion website and noticed a link to "Find a Coach". In mid-May, I emailed a coach named Pam who was suggested on the website, told her I would be swimming across Lake Ontario at the end of July, gave her my website address and asked her if she'd walk me through the introduction workshop to Total Immersion swimming.

Pam replied very quickly to say that she'd be happy to do that, asked me if there were any other ways she could help and said she was at my service.

I replied, "Yes, you can accompany me on the boat for the trial swim and act as my coach for the big swim."

On June 1st, Pam made a special trip to Kingston to give me a day of coaching. Originally, the plan had been for me to go to Hamilton, but no pool in Hamilton would guarantee us our own lane for the entire day. Kingston's Progress Fitness Centre probably wouldn't have made that guarantee either, but I had been there enough times to be confident that, even if there was no empty lane, we'd simply do land drills until one of the lanes was vacated. (Pam had mentioned that we'd do some land drills as well as in-the-pool drills when I'd spoken to her.)

Pam and I met at Progress Fitness Centre when the pool opened for the day. Pam brought her stuffed dolphin and told me that it was to remind me that the swimming drills should be fun. I informed Pam that, in the past, what had often stressed me out more than anything else was that people asked me to explain something when I preferred not to discuss the subject at that particular time. Pam replied that no explanation was needed if I didn't want to do something and that she would not pressure me to explain anything.[57] Pam also made it clear that I was welcome to take a break any time I liked. This would give me an opportunity to eat and let what Pam had taught me sink in or we could use the time to just talk casually.

The very first thing Pam had me do was swim 100 metres my own way. She videotaped me and as she was showing me the video, she informed me about a few ways that I could improve. One of her first points was that I shouldn't reach as far forward before my hand entered the water; my hand should have been underwater already when I reached forward, Pam said. I had recently learned, with Catriona's help, to rotate my body when doing the front crawl. Pam said I was rotating my body too much.

At the beginning of the day, it would take me about 30 strokes (sometimes 32) to swim 25 metres. Pam explained to me that the fewer strokes I did, the better. With full confidence, Pam told me that, by the end of the day, I would have the stroke count down to twenty. Pam repeatedly asked me to swim 25 metres and aim for "this many strokes", cutting my stroke count down a few strokes at a time. Pam graciously shook my hand when I met the interim goal. She was as good as her word; I was able to swim 25 metres using only 18 strokes before the end of the day! Lake Ontario, roughly 50 kilometres wide, would equal 2,000 lengths of the pool. A reduction of ten strokes per length would save me twenty thousand strokes. I was worried that, over the course of the crossing, I would eventually get tired and have trouble focusing on the advice that Pam had taught me.

Pam taught me seven focus points, which are listed in Figure 31-1. She had me concentrate on one focus point at a time. That way, I wouldn't have to worry about too much at once and I could add to what I'd already learned. Often, Pam had me swim more than one length of

---

[57] See Explanations Require Energy in Chapter 1.

Figure 31-1

excerpt from email message from Pam sent June 6, 2008

Here is a recap of the stroke philosophies we want to instill for your trial and Lake swim:

1. On your recovery arm, lead with a high elbow (to at least your goggle line).
2. Your lead arm should be patient (i.e. it doesn't move until your hip initiates the switch which co-incidentally is generally the same time the recovery arm reaches the goggle line).
3. Stay long and tall: reach, reach, reach (especially when you take a breath).
4. Anchor:
   a. elbow up/fingertips down/no break at wrist;
   b. press your weight on your anchor;
   d. keep your anchor to the outside of your body (i.e. you should rotate around your anchor)
5. "Go for the wall" on every stroke!! Squeeze as much out of it as you can.
6. Don't forget to "keep your batteries charged" on the recovery arm (i.e. it isn't allowed to pause even though you are being patient with the lead arm).
7. Spear the targets at 11 o'clock and 1 o'clock and don't forget that the targets are one foot below the water.

Start out each swim session dedicating a length to each of the focus points. Devote ONE focus point per length.

For the remainder of the practice session, rotate through the focus points as you like (i.e. 100m thinking about a high elbow on the recovery; then 100m thinking about a patient front arm; etc. Or you may be more comfortable doing 400m per focus point. This is up to you to decide. The idea is that you should always have a focus point in mind when you are swimming.

Pam's advice over the telephone on June 11, 2008:

Do this on dry land the day before seeing me as a prelude to the day of coaching:

Dry land training

Skate position
Lie on side
Lower arm forward, stretch out

Figure 31-1 continued

Eyes and nose looking down
Other hand on inner thigh

From skate, stroke the dolphin's back
Lead with high elbow until at least goggle line
Dolphin is 8 inches from body

Dolphin switch
Lead with high elbow, switch to skate position on the other side
Think about:
    (a) initiate with hip (this will get core engaged)
    (b) when I initiate switch, lead arm is at 11:00 or 1:00 (i.e. not pointing out)

the pool with the same focus point so that I got comfortable with it. She would inform me as to the point during the 25 metres that I had lost my focus or where I had shown improvement.

While Pam was coaching me, another friend whom I had previously met at Progress Fitness Centre, introduced me to Jean. Jean's philosophy went hand-in-hand with Pam's philosophy; Jean was also happy to spend time with me. After that point, Jean accompanied me on a number of my sets of speed intervals.

On June 13th, I went to Hamilton to a facility called Premier Fitness Centre where Pam spent another day coaching me. During the day, Marilyn, who by coincidence also lived in the greater Hamilton area, stopped by for a visit. This was the first time Pam or I had met Marilyn. While Marilyn was present, I swam 100 metres my usual way, then 100 metres incorporating the techniques that Pam had taught me, then another 100 metres as fast as I could. Marilyn invited me to come to her house later that evening when we could discuss the logistics of the trial swim. After Pam left, I swam 1.05 kilometres in 20 minutes and 18 seconds (42 seconds faster than my target pace of three kilometres per hour), gaining approximately two seconds per 50 metres. I'm not usually that fast, which meant that Pam's coaching was helping me improve my speed. The question was: Would I be able to maintain that technique a few days later?

On July 1st, Pam returned to Kingston for another coaching session. Several times, while Pam was coaching me to concentrate on one particular focus point, she had me swim 100 metres breathing every three strokes and then swim 100m breathing every two strokes, switching sides at the end of every length so that I was always facing her. More often than not, I was faster breathing every two strokes. Ever since I had learned how to breathe bilaterally shortly after I had joined KMAC almost two years before, I had preferred to breathe every three strokes and never wanted to go back to breathing every two strokes until I realized my time was faster with the two-stroke breathing. Pam suggested that I consider breathing every two strokes when swimming across Lake Ontario. I knew I needed a regime. Breathing every two strokes might have worked in a pool when I knew that the end of each length was the time to switch breathing sides, but when I was swimming in open water, I would not have any physical indicator of when to switch sides. I also had to consider that when I was swimming long distances, breathing every three strokes would involve fewer neck twists that would be less tiring; also, I wouldn't have to think about when to switch sides if I breathed every third stroke. July 1st was the last time I saw Pam before the morning of the crossing.

It would have been very helpful if Pam could have observed me swimming in open water other than on the trial swim. On the trial swim, because of the time limit, Pam and I knew that it would have been unwise for her to ask me to stop swimming while she coached me. On any other training swim, Pam would have been totally free to stop me as often as she saw fit and for as long as she wanted in order to counsel me on how to improve my stroke. Pam's coaching during my pool swimming certainly helped but I needed her advice more during my open water swims.

In total, Pam spent four entire days with me, one of which was for the trial swim. Pam drove to Kingston for three of these four days and would have spent two more days with me, but that did not work out. I will always be extremely grateful to Pam for all her expertise and insightful points. Her help in June and July, when my training was in its final stages, was crucial to the success of my Lake Ontario crossing. Without her help, my raising of funds and awareness for Asperger's Syndrome would not have been as substantial. Pam deserves my thanks as well as the sincere appreciation of the young people who will benefit from the funds my swim raised.

Chapter 32

The Trial Swim

"The probability that we may fail in the struggle ought not to deter us from the support of a cause we believe to be just."
—Abraham Lincoln

email message from Jay to Marilyn, April 22, 2008
Subject: concerned about "failing" the trial swim

Marilyn:

Swim Master Vicki Keith informed me last fall that most Swim Masters will expect me to complete the 16-kilometre trial swim in six hours. At first, I thought my heart was going to break. When the dust settled, I would have quit my dream desire of swimming across Lake Ontario right away (and would have informed my organizational committee since they'd be wasting their time) if it weren't for two things: (1) the six hour time limit is only a guideline and is NOT written in stone; and (2) the goal is within reach. My guess is that the purpose of the trial swim is so that the Swim Master can assess (by observing how well the candidate handles swimming distances) whether the candidate is likely to succeed in his/her crossing of Lake Ontario. I also guess that SSO would like to sanction everyone who applies but doesn't want to develop a reputation for sanctioning attempts by people who clearly aren't ready and will end up quitting during the crossing. Very few people apply for a swim across a great lake; it's not like applying for a driver's license or writing an exam in which the number of people that attempt is so great that the examination committee must set certain standards below which they must fail the candidate.

Vicki told me that I need to work on my speed and suggested the following workouts:
  8 x 400 on 8 minutes
  16 x 200 on 4 minutes
  32 x 100 on 2 minutes

The Trial Swim

Lately, I have been going to the pool every Wednesday and alternating between 400s one week, 200s the next week, and 100s the week after. I plan to continue doing so at least until the end of May. One of my co workers, Catriona, is noticeably faster than me and usually accompanies me on my speed workouts. The results of these speed workouts, which are also on my website, are given below. (See Appendix O for the speed interval times.) At first, I focused on completing the workout and my interval times slowed down noticeably throughout the workout. Catriona strongly encouraged me to go slow on the first interval, keep a constant pace throughout the workout (taking extra rest time if necessary) and sprint the last 400, the last two 200s and the last three 100s.

I swam 16 kilometres three separate times over the course of the winter (there is a pool in Kingston with lane swimming all the time). On Sunday, my time was 6:19 and I only took four short feeding breaks. (I'm going to be slower in open water.) At the end, I managed to sprint 500m in 11:03 (without touching the sides) followed by the last 150m easy in 3:52. (I started out at ~63 seconds per 50m. For the longest time during the latter half, I was 75 seconds per 50m but I didn't get any slower than that.)

I slow down over time and my speed on the last half seems to be independent of my speed on the first half (unless I'm obviously trying to sprint on the first half in which case I will wear myself out). Please don't get me wrong; I know that SSO has reasons for having the trial swim and for setting these guidelines.

In December, I swam front crawl nonstop for three hours and covered 8.375 kilometres. For your information, I like to make my distance swims in the pool mimic the crossing as much as I can so I don't touch the sides when I turn. I can't (won't) do the upsidedown flip turns; I turn in an arc at the end of each lap. I do, however, touch the sides when I do speed work.

If I can't meet the six hour guideline, perhaps my next best chance of passing the trial swim is to maintain front crawl for the entire 16 kilometres (minus feeding breaks) and appear completely unfatigued on completion (sprinting the last 500 metres or 750 metres if necessary) and thus demonstrate that I could swim further.

I plan to swim 16 kilometres in Dog Lake in mid- to late May, then do one timed and measured swim in Lake Ontario on June 14 or 15. (One of my recruits lives on Dog Lake and has a floatation marker 500m from his dock and said I could swim in his lake whenever I like.)

I know better than to ask, "Will you sanction me as long as I complete the 16 km without floatational assistance regardless of the time taken?" because that may be interpreted as a request for a license to take as long as I like. In grade twelve English class, the day before the final exam, I asked the teacher, "Am I in any danger of failing this class?" and he replied, "Are you planning to flunk the exam or just stay home?"

For now, please rest assured that I am aware of the six hour guideline and I have been trying to get my time down.

Any comments or question?

Regards,

Jay

Marilyn's reply, April 23, 2008:

Dear Jay,
This is why we have been encouraging you to work on your "core" strength and swimming speed. The more all around core strength you have, the more the joints involved are stabilized and thus strengthened. Swimming involves the whole spine and abdominals and if you can strengthen them through cross training, the better. Speed training is also vital. Interval training is the best way to develop speed.
Yes, I am aiming for the 6 hours. I'm also interested in seeing the time for the first mile be close to the time for the 10th mile.
Why don't you work harder and try 24 x 200 on 4:15 and 12 x 400 on 8:30?
Also, I think you should be doing the interval work twice a week for the next 6 weeks. It's too bad you weren't doing it 2 or 3 times a week all winter.

On an encouraging note, I was able to rearrange my summer so that I am free from relatives the last week of July. (I still have to work as much as possible that week.) An incentive to pass your trial swim.
Have a great day,
Marilyn

In early May, I had a dream that my swim across Lake Ontario was actually happening. (See Appendix J.) It was broad daylight, I could see the CN tower and other lakeshore Toronto buildings, and I was comfortable doing my swimming strokes. I interpreted this dream to mean that my swim across Lake Ontario would be sanctioned and that it would happen. Nevertheless, the dream did not decrease my anxiety that I might fail the criteria to be allowed to do the crossing.

The trial swim date was set for Sunday, June 22nd. In order to be well rested for the trial swim, I decided to taper down my training by swimming for four hours on Tuesday, three hours on Wednesday and resting Thursday, Friday and Saturday. On Tuesday, June 17th, Jacquie, my volunteer paddler, forgot to bring the spray skirt for her kayak. Lake Ontario was quite rough that day so Jacquie was forced to stay inside Navy Bay. Several times, we travelled back and forth between St. Lawrence Pier at the mouth of the bay where the waves became rougher, and the tip of the bay. After two hours, Jacquie's hands were cold and she was forced to abort. But she put my food, water and other belongings on the dock while I continued swimming for another hour, carefully staying within a pole's length of the shoreline.

As I was swimming, I could feel my body running out of fuel. During the swim, I decided that I would go to East Side Marios for the all-you-can-eat pasta special that evening. By the time I got there, my body was over depleted to the point where my digestive system wasn't working very well. While I was eating my fourth plate of pasta, I felt full and probably shouldn't have tried to finish that plate. (I had eaten six plates on a previous visit.) As soon as I finished eating, I went to the restroom and got sick to my stomach. Then I cycled home. The next day, I still felt under the weather but I was able to go to work and then swim for two hours in Lake Ontario after work. I was confident that resting from swimming three days would help me to sufficiently recover from my illness.

On Saturday, June 21st, in order to "fuel up" for the trial swim the next day, I went to the all-you-can-eat breakfast buffet at the Golden Griddle. Later that day, I telephoned Marilyn to tell her that I wasn't feeling well but my preference was to proceed with the trial swim anyway. I felt hopeful that I would be better by Sunday. Even if I wasn't, I knew I could likely complete the trial swim as I had done other training swims while I was sick. A candidate who fails a trial swim is allowed to apply for another trial swim; therefore, I didn't really have anything to lose by attempting the trial swim despite being sick. My concern was that it would be wasting Marilyn's time if I was unable to complete it.

※

Margot, the executive director for Aspergers Society of Ontario, had a surplus of T-shirts with ASO's name and logo and gave me as many as I had asked for. I gave them out to the organizational committee and my paddling volunteers who helped me regularly, as a way of saying thank you for their help. I not only invited them all to watch the trial swim, but encouraged them to come in order to show their support. I asked them all to wear their Aspergers T-shirts. My hope was partly to surprise Marilyn but also to let her know how many supporters I had. I also invited other long-time friends whom I knew were supportive of my swim. I felt that this would convince Marilyn that I was not only building an effective support crew but that, during the actual crossing, I would be less likely to quit because I would feel accountable to all my supporters even if they weren't part of the support crew. I judged that having a large crowd to show their support from the shore would be a very positive sign of my commitment to the swim. About fifteen people in addition to the actual support crew for the trial swim showed up on the shoreline: a few people at the beginning and the rest near the end of my swim .

I had four plans of action for passing the trial swim:
1. hope against hope that I can complete 16 km in six hours
2. maintain front crawl for the entire 16 km (minus feeding breaks) and appear completely unfatigued on completion thus demonstrating that I could swim further
3. hope that I pass
4. plead

The failed attempt to swim for four hours on January 30, 2008 and the failed attempt to swim for five hours on April 6, 2008, both with limited feeding breaks, made me afraid to reduce the number of feeding breaks because I knew that, if I had a muscle seizure on the trial swim, it would be "game over" for plan of action #2. It wouldn't be a problem keeping my body afloat for a few minutes but that would lose time and, unless I could magically regain those lost minutes and get within the six hour point, it would be all I could do to finish the 16 km, hope for a pass, and then plead.

My heart would have broken if I hadn't passed the trial swim to qualify me to cross Lake Ontario, but there were already five benefits to my months of training:

Although it is true that my heart would break if I didn't get to swim across Lake Ontario, there had already been not less than five benefits thus far:

1. My swimming speed and technique had improved significantly.
2. I had made friends with a number of people who helped me during my training and organizing.
3. I had learned more about myself and Asperger's Syndrome in general. During this preparation period, I developed different strategies for interacting with many people and tried a variety of ways to handle my training for this major feat while living with Asperger's Syndrome.
4. I had associated with more people living with Asperger's Syndrome and other "labels": I don't like to refer to Asperger's Syndrome as a disability or handicap so as I met people who deal with a variety of challenges, I became more knowledgeable about the diverse types of people in this world. It is not right to "look down" on people for being different. I've learned that people who do distance themselves from others who are different end up limiting their own growth, experiences and potential friendships.
5. My talks to different individuals and groups about Asperger's Syndrome had already made a positive impact on a number of people.

I was preparing myself for what I would do if failed to qualify in the trial swim. I would thank my committee for all their help and tell them that I would no longer need their help. I could honestly say that I had done my best. I would tell them that I knew that my speed wouldn't improve substantially in the few weeks I had left before the crossing. I'd inform them that the training was taking its toll on me and I could not continue training like this for another year. I knew that

The Ambition of an Aspie

if I could not do my swim in the summer of 2008, I would have to give up on my dream ambition.

Marilyn had asked me to provide a twenty foot powerboat plus another unsinkable boat for the trial swim. My co-worker, Kristine, and her husband, Collin, graciously agreed to provide the use of their powerboat. Marilyn told me that my kayak would suffice as another unsinkable boat. I explained to Marilyn, that because of my abundance of volunteer paddlers, it wouldn't be a problem to recruit someone to paddle my kayak for me. My parents were coming to Kingston to watch the trial swim and my mother had offered to bring her kayak. Shannon agreed to paddle my kayak for part of the trial swim and both John C. and Alicia said they would provide their kayaks. Marilyn told me that two kayaks would be better since that would give her an opportunity to paddle beside me for part of the time and observe my swimming more closely, but we did not need three kayaks so I decided not to bring my kayak. I was relieved because I was still feeling the effects of being sick after Tuesday's swim. I was grateful I didn't have to paddle my kayak all the way to the village of Bath, the location of the trial swim, two days before the trial. My mother still planned to bring her kayak. She would watch me from shore at the start and finish of the trial swim but paddle her kayak a sufficient distance from me and the other kayaks during my trial swim, in order not to interfere with the official support group. I was glad to have her in the water near me for moral support.

As planned, Marilyn, Pam, and the rest of the support crew arrived at Loyalist Cove Marina in Bath, ready for a 10:00 a.m. start. I performed my usual routine of stretching plus coating my body with Vaseline. It was 10:10am when I entered the water, proceeding with the plan to swim west for 8 km to stay clear of the path of the Amherst Island ferry and then swim back to Bath again. Collin, Kristine, Marilyn, Pam and Shannon went in the powerboat while John, Alicia, and my mother paddled their kayaks. The waves were one to two feet high throughout the trial swim. I had actually hoped the lake would be rough during the trial swim for two reasons: it would give me an excuse to take longer than six hours and it would show that I could handle rough waves. John, Marilyn, and Shannon took turns paddling John's kayak while my mother and Alicia stayed in their kayaks for the entire duration of the trial swim. Everyone clapped when I reached the turnaround point at three hours and fifteen minutes. I was instructed to turn around and swim back to the marina.

The return trip was easier since I had the eastward-flowing current pushing me. I was so focused on maintaining the front crawl stroke (and only the front crawl stroke) that I only occasionally wondered why I couldn't see the powerboat during the last few kilometres of the swim. I found out minutes after completing the swim that the powerboat had broken down and had to be towed.

All along, the powerboat had been zigzagging, which interfered with the accuracy of GPS readings. With three kayaks accompanying me, I was able to complete the trial swim despite the powerboat's breakdown. Marilyn paddled John's kayak while my father drove Kristine, Collin, Pam and John back to the marina. Shannon rode back to the marina in the marina owner's powerboat.

In order to demonstrate how much energy I still had, I tried to sprint the last 500m but couldn't; I was able to make progress in high waves but wasn't able to sprint. I arrived back at the marina after five hours and forty-one minutes of swimming. Marilyn instructed me to get out of the water quickly since the clock was still ticking. To make sure I heard correctly, I said to Marilyn, "I'm not getting out until you give me the OK to get out." My reasoning was to demonstrate that I could have swum longer (as opposed to hanging onto a boat as soon as I completed the trial swim). John, who was standing on the wall of rocks, helped me out of the water. My support team congratulated me.

No sooner was I out of the water than Marilyn said with a neutral intonation, "You were under six hours. I guess you pass!"

The water was uniformly 62°F throughout the trial swim; I shivered only slightly and only after I had been out of the water for several minutes.

Marilyn, Pam, and John C. sat down at a picnic table after my successful trial swim to discuss the logistics of the actual crossing, including the equipment and the amount of food that would be required. Meanwhile, I was taking a warm shower and putting on warm clothes before joining the discussion. Marilyn nominated John C. as my swim coordinator. I gave Marilyn an Aspergers Society of Ontario T-shirt to thank her for her contribution, as I did with the other supporters. I had waited until after I had passed the trial swim to give her the T-shirt so nobody would think I was "bribing" her into passing me.

I said, "It's a good thing we stayed close to shore because a kayak wouldn't have been able to pull me out of the water."

John replied, "That's why I've been telling you to stay close to shore."

It makes sense that there had to be a time limit (a soft time limit, in this case); otherwise, the candidate could swim at his/her leisure without any incentive to go fast (or to do his/her best). What probably matters more than the time is whether the candidate can convince the Swim Master that s/he is likely to complete the crossing.

Trial swim report to SSO, written by Marilyn, July 2, 2008

Dear Board,

Jay completed his 12 km trial swim in Lake Ontario near Bath, Ontario on June 22, 2008. The powerboat broke down and had to be towed. Fortunately Jay had 3 kayaks surrounding him and I paddled in one of them after the powerboat was towed away. Needless to say, the GPS readings got all screwed up because of this and he ended up swimming only 12 km. His time was 5 hours 41 minutes. He kept a steady pace, but averaged 2.1 km per hour, which makes it a borderline trial swim. The water, however, was 62 degrees F for most of the swim, the air was 70 deg. And the wind whipped up 1 2 foot waves in his face for the whole outgoing trip and died down and shifted to his flank for the return trip. I figure he would have taken just over 7 hours for the 16 km. He was not at all hypothermic and handled the waves without flinching. Because of his steadiness and great performance in rough conditions, I decided to pass him on the trial swim.

I would like to warn the swimmer's team, however, that if he gets significant waves coming at him on the big swim, because of his slow speed, his rate of forward progress may grind to a halt and we will have to pull him out.

The content of Marilyn's message did not concern me in the least. Encountering big waves was something I had anticipated all along – and had prepared for by undertaking training swims even when Lake Ontario was rough. Nothing could be done to prevent big waves – except pick a calmer day – and that would not be possible the days of my crossing. Ever since my 19-hour swim at Chippego Lake (see Chapter 22), I had felt fully confident that I was ready to undertake the crossing. For several months, my biggest worry was failing the trial swim. Now that I had that worry behind me, I felt much more relaxed.

Chapter 33

Tapering My Training

"Inexperienced athletes are nervous; they focus on results. Experienced athletes focus on preparation."
—Source unknown

On July 5, 2008, I went to the weekend breakfast buffet at Golden Griddle and ate two platefuls of fruit, waited at least five minutes and then ate three pancakes and ten pieces of French toast plus some bacon, sausages, home fries and scrambled eggs - all within one hour. I was eating a lot because I was reaching peak training, after which I would taper down my training. One hour and forty minutes after I finished eating, I entered the St. Lawrence River at Deadman's Bay and swam to Milton Island and back, totalling nearly five hours, with John C. accompanying me in his kayak.

The next day, I undertook my peak training-swim of the season, entering the water at Faircrest Blvd at 8:15am and hoping to swim all the way to Amherstview. I tried not to dwell on my three failed attempts at doing this in 2007. Organizing paddlers can get very complicated. July 6th was one of those days! The original plan was for Alicia to paddle for the first half and Jane to take over at the Kingston Psychiatric Hospital, the closest place to the midway point where the paddlers can conveniently switch. Unfortunately, Jane was sick and cancelled the day before and I had to find a replacement quickly. At my request, Alicia gladly agreed to paddle as far as the water treatment plant on Pleasant Point. The only reason Alicia didn't paddle longer is that she had a soccer game that evening that she needed to get ready for. I made several telephone calls, instructing people to call my cell phone should they not receive the message until the day of the swim. Unfortunately, the person who'd agreed to replace Jane wasn't at home when a volunteer went to pick him up. I was about to call the second person who had offered to take Jane's place but I didn't need to because Thomas graciously paddled the kayak instead.

In 2007, when I was recruiting paddling volunteers, Thomas wanted to help but he wasn't comfortable paddling a canoe or a kayak beside me. He was very helpful, however, by staying on land and driving the paddlers to and from their homes and the lake. He set the entire day aside to help shuttle paddlers, and became the designated taxi driver during each point-to-point swim. On July 6th, when Jane's replacement paddler was not at home and because the lake was flat calm, Thomas didn't mind kayaking. Thomas had some paddling experience but only a limited amount. We proceeded all the way to Bayridge Drive and then turned around to finish at the foot of Lakeview Ave at 6:15 p.m., getting further than I had in 2007, but not as far as my destination of Amherstview. I was in the water for ten hours and covered roughly 20 kilometres. My back was noticeably sunburned and it was painful to use a towel to dry it.

What I ate during 10-hour swim:

> one bottle of Xilarate (600mL)
> 1 bottle of Ensure (250mL)
> 1 bottle of Boost (250mL)
> 1 PowerBar Gel
> 1 maple sugar candy
> 1 banana
> 2 brownies
> 1 oatmeal scone
> 2 oatmeal raisin cookies
> 1 rolled oat shortbread cookie

Now, it was time to taper off the training, with the big swim only three weeks away. I would do one six-hour swim on the next two weekends. I would gradually shorten the mid-week swims ending with a four-hour swim on July 22nd (six days before the crossing) and a three-hour swim on July 24th. I would begin a regime of swimming for six hours once a week, with one or two four-hour swims throughout the week, tapering down to two hours during the last week.

Saturday, July 12th was my rest day from swimming, because I had run 12 kilometres from one end of Kingston to the other with Jonathan Howard who was passing through Kingston during his run across Canada for autism[58].

Once again, I had solicited help from the RMC sea cadets who arrive each year at the beginning of July. Somehow, I didn't connect with the same group of people as I had worked with in 2007. This year, the organizer supplied an inflatable powerboat with two upper year navy officers trained as lifeguards as drivers. They provided a thermal

---

[58] For more information, go to www.runthedream.ca

blanket in the boat in case I needed it. On July 13th, I swam east for an hour and a half and then turned around and came back to RMC in time for the boaters' lunch. While the boaters were having lunch, I treaded water and took a feeding break, but swam back and forth between two docks as much as I could, in order to comply with the SSO's rules that I not use any flotation device over the course of the swim. After the boaters returned, I proceeded with my swim, again swimming east until the turnaround point. I swam for a total of seven hours and fifteen.

On July 20th, two different upper year navy officers from the same group as last week accompanied me. I swam for a total of six hours and twenty minutes.

On Tuesday, July 22nd, Guy and two other sea cadets paddled beside me in a canoe for four hours, following the same format as in 2007, with three people in the canoe. While I had been cycling to work along the RMC campus earlier in July, Guy recognized me and spoke to me, but I didn't recognize him. He told me that he'd paddled with me last summer and immediately offered to paddle beside me again this year. I was very glad to have him help out again.

On Thursday, July 24th, I swam for two hours starting at RMC, and going towards Milton Island and back with Jane paddling my sea kayak beside me. With thunder expected, we carefully stayed within 100 metres of shore, going around the shoreline of every bay when we would have otherwise cut across the bay. We encountered the odd rain shower. A few times, Jane did see lightning towards Wolfe Island, but it was far enough away that she would have had ample time to bring the kayak to shore should the lightning get closer. With the two years of training now completed, there was nothing left to do except undertake the crossing.

Chapter 34

Renting the Boats

"The obsession with tomorrow forfeits today; the focus on today reassures tomorrow."

—source unknown

When I first decided that I wanted to swim across Lake Ontario, I thought the most difficult part of the process would be finding people to paddle a canoe or kayak beside me on my training swims. I spread the word of my need. Several people responded to my request but I had no idea how serious these people were. Less than a month after my first training swim in Lake Ontario in 2007, I knew I had more than enough paddling volunteers to make it through the season.

I went back to the people I had asked to help me recruit paddling volunteers and said, "I don't want to say no to anyone. If someone volunteers to paddle beside me, give that person my contact information but don't go out of your way to recruit any more paddling volunteers."

I thought my second most challenging quest would be finding boats for the actual crossing.

excerpt from an email message from Vicki Keith, August 30, 2007:

Boats are always a challenge. All you can do is e-mail and phone yacht clubs and marinas and ask for their assistance. Also, Organization for Autism and Aspergers may have boat owners who could be interested. That might be the best way to go as you are giving many of these families hope, so they may want to give back to you and your swim.

A lot of candidate swimmers "pound pavement"; that is, they go to marinas in person, find people with boats, and ask the owners if they would be willing to provide the use of their boats.

In October 2007, Kerry's Place Autism Services (KPAS) hosted a conference on autism at St. Lawrence College and brought me in as a guest speaker. Chris, from the Aurora branch of KPAS, was impressed with my speech. She told me it was the best speech she had ever heard and she had been with KPAS for a long time. After meeting me, Chris immediately volunteered to help me with my swim. When she found out I needed boats for my crossing, she told me she would handle that detail; she had connections and would make sure that the boat requirements for my swim were met.

When Chris told me she'd contact boaters, I was unsure about the best way to handle organizing those details. I was torn between the following choices:
   a. I could settle on a date for the swim and then try to find boat owners. I was worried that if I did this, I would run the risk of boat owners not even contacting me because they wouldn't be available on that particular day, even though they really wanted to help.
   b. I could contact boat owners and find out when they would be available, but they might not be able to commit to me until they knew the actual date of the swim.

Because Chris appeared to know several boat owners, I decided to go with option (a) and set the date first. If all the boat owners ended up being unavailable, I would have been more than willing to change the date.

I spread the word that I preferred August 11-14, 2008 for the crossing. It is preferable to reserve four consecutive days in case the swim has to be delayed because of bad weather. With four days to choose from, there was a better chance of getting good enough weather to complete the swim. My initial reason for picking these dates was that I really wanted Karen on the support boat. Karen is a school teacher who often teaches summer school during the month of July.

Mere days before I was about to mail in my registration to SSO, Trish, one of the two KMAC coaches, pointed out that my preferred dates were during the 2008 Olympics in Bejing. That meant that I would be competing with the Olympics for media coverage. Not only would my swim be less likely to appear on the front page of the newspaper, but some of the journalists and media crews would be dispatched overseas during that time.

I didn't want to waste too much time, so I checked with Vicki, SSO, my parents, my sister, Karen, Jens, the organizational committee, and a few others to verify that they were all agreeable to changing the date to July 28th-31st. A few days later, I mailed in my registration. Less than one month later, Chris told me that enough boats were organized for the new date.

After I changed the date for the swim, it turned out that the boat owners who had agreed to the August dates were not available at the end of July. Many of the other potentials declined when they realized that a four-day commitment was required. SSO had purchased two Zodiacs several years before and Chris learned that these could be rented by swimmers for a nominal cost. However, Zodiacs are not very durable, and unbeknownst to Chris, SSO had sold their boats the previous year and weren't in a financial position to buy more. Chris was worried about these new complications, but she didn't want to tell me about them because she didn't want to burden me with worry.

Because of the scramble to find boats, KPAS finally decided to rent them. They were quite glad that they'd shielded me from all the stress of the boat arrangements falling through and being so tough to organize. KPAS signed a binding rental contract for the boats so they were counting on me to complete the swim as much as I was depending on them to finalize all the arrangements. Not only was the contract finalized, but so was the route, so I was very happy that all those details were worked out.

Kerry's Place Autism Services rented a 33-foot Formula One cigar-boat and a 68-foot boat named Precious Lady. Only one crane was big enough to lift Precious Lady out of the water, so she stayed in the harbour in Hamilton all winter. She has 20,000 square feet of living space, four bedrooms in addition to four couches and captains quarters. Bay Port Yachting Club sold two inflatable Zodiacs to KPAS at a discount. After the swim, KPAS sold the Zodiacs and applied the proceeds to the swim. Chris had been prepared all along to rent boats for my swim across Lake Ontario. I was very grateful for her help and for all the organizing that KPAS did to ensure that we had all the necessary support equipment for my swim. I'm also very glad that they spared me the worry as plans to procure boats got more problematic. Everything worked out in the end and I appreciate all that they did to make this happen.

Chapter 35

John C.'s "Discouraging" Opinion

"I show you doubt, to prove that faith exists."
—Robert Browning

John C. was one of the leaders of the Kingston & Area Christian Singles group when I joined it in 2003. I got to know him during the three years prior to 2006 when I set my goal to swim across Lake Ontario. He was one of the first people I contacted for help and his support included paddling beside me on my first long open-water training swim. John C. was one of my most valuable resources and a key player in helping me achieve my dream desire.

◈

John drove me home at 3:30 a.m. on June 16, 2007, after he'd kayaked beside me on my very first night swim. As we chatted, he recommended that I consider changing the route for my Lake Ontario Crossing: instead of swimming the 52-kilometre route from Niagara-on-the-Lake to Marilyn Bell Park in Toronto, he asked me to consider swimming the 34-kilometre route that Jenna Lambert swam from Baird Point, New York to Kingston. John's reasoning was that over 90 percent of the spectators wouldn't know or wouldn't care what the distance was and that a 34 kilometre swim would generate just as much publicity as a 52-kilometre swim. The 34-kilometre swim isn't really "across"; it goes from the east shore of Lake Ontario to the north shore (instead of from the south shore to the north shore) and barely crosses the St. Lawrence River. (This comment is in no way meant to detract from the outstanding accomplishment of Jenna Lambert's swim.)

When John made this comment, I'm not sure whether he was aware that I first decided to swim across Lake Ontario *and then* decided to do it as a fundraiser for Asperger's Syndrome. This meant that I had set a goal of swimming across Lake Ontario and as a secondary benefit, wanted my swim to help to raise awareness about Asperger's Syndrome. I had been committed to the physical feat of the 52-kilometre swim for some time and doing a lesser version of the crossing to help the Asperger's community was not an option I wanted to consider.

◈

With the steering committee's tasks – such as advertising, fundraising, and recruiting volunteers – well underway, I thought it was time I start to seek help for the swim itself. I telephoned John in March, 2008 and we talked for a long time about the logistics, the equipment required, who to pick for crew members, the meal plan for the crew, and what could be done in advance to facilitate the meal preparation. Instead of assuming the load of relaying to the steering committee what John told me, I invited John to come to one of the steering committee meetings so that he could tell the committee what he told me.

John attended the very next steering committee meeting. When it came John's turn to speak, he opened by saying that I wasn't going to like to hear this. John asked Jess, the head for the media and promotions subcommittee, if she had ever stayed awake for 24 hours. John mentioned that, after 30 hours, everything would start to fall apart: drowsiness would set in and cold would set in to the point where hypothermia would become an issue. Apparently, 30 hours was the magic number. I wanted John to tell me what was so magical about the number 30. He did go on to clarify this and said that it was ultra-important that I complete the swim within 30 hours. He went on to urge me to train for a minimum of 15-20 hours per week and I would likely see a resulting increase in my speed. He gave me a set of paddles, worn on the hands, and told me that I wasn't allowed to use them for the crossing; they were reserved for my training swims.

All this time, John was more than fulfilling his duties as swim coordinator by making sure that all the required safety equipment, including boats, was in place. He had been in touch with Chris who had volunteered to find the boats we needed for the swim. Chris kept telling John that we would have boats but didn't specify the exact types of boats that she had been able to secure. The Toronto Port Authority required a form indicating all the registration numbers and specific information about each boat that would be entering the port by Friday, July 11th – two weeks before the swim. Marilyn had warned John that unless a meeting with the boat operators was held by the following Tuesday, the swim would be cancelled. We didn't even have boats, so how could we possibly have had boat operators? Since the trial swim on June 22nd, John told Marilyn that if the swim were rerouted to Kingston, we had enough contacts to find boats within a matter of days; Marilyn had been okay with re-routing the swim to Kingston.

On Wednesday evening, July 9th, two days before the deadline for Toronto Port Authority, John called to inform me about the boat situation.

John C's "Discouraging" Opinion

He said that Kerry's Place Autism Services had rented a 33-foot cigar boat. In the event of an evacuation, no boat could get me to shore faster than a cigar boat; therefore, it certainly met the requirement of reaching a speed of 15 knots, John said. However, no one would be able to sleep on the boat and people would need to sleep during a 30 hour swim.

John asked me how I felt about changing the route. I initially replied that I really wanted to swim from Niagara-on-the-Lake to Toronto. John claimed that the swim might have to be cancelled unless I consent to rerouting the swim to Kingston, whether we liked it or not. He went on to say that SSO would pull me out of the water after 36 hours. The route from Baird Point to Kingston was 34 kilometres, so I would only need to maintain an average speed of slightly under 1 kilometre per hour to get the swim done in 36 hours. John felt confident that I could swim the first 18 kilometres in 9 hours and then slow down to 1 kilometer per hour. This speed would get me across the lake in 27 hours, giving me lots of leeway to cross within the 36-hour limit. John was committed to ensuring the success of my swim: he wanted me to consider switching routes to significantly increase my chances of completing the crossing.

I told my parents about John's recommendation and asked for their input. My father recalled Marilyn asking John to make specific preparations for the crossing after I had finished the trial swim. She told him to make sure there was enough food on the boat for the crew members for 36 hours.

John had asked, "What if he doesn't finish in 36 hours?"

Marilyn replied, "We'll pull him out if he's not close to shore." Marilyn had calculated that, with a start time of 10 a.m., the second night would fall within 36 hours. My parents and I concluded from this discussion between Marilyn and John that she was also concerned about the 36-hour limit.

Vicki had been an invaluable source of advice and I continued to email her from time to time. Because she was one step removed, I knew that she would have a valuable perspective, so I sent her the message below:

excerpt from e-mail message from Jay to Vicki, July 14, 2008:

Someone on my committee seemed to tell me that I will be pulled out of the water if I don't finish within 36 hours. Do you think this is correct? He seemed to say it was because they'll have enough food for the crew only to last 36 hours, although I'm probably missing something. I'm under the impression that, as long as the crew isn't tired and that the swimmer is not hypothermic and is still making forward progress (and there are no other dangers which require that the swim be aborted), the swimmer is allowed to continue (even if s/he is fatigued and/or slowing down). In other words, there is no "time limit"? I have to be careful how I word this because it sounds like I'm asking for a license to take as long as I like. Unlike in the trial swim, it is in my best interests to finish the crossing as soon as possible since, even if I'm not chilled, I will be fatigued.

Vicki's reply, July 14, 2008:

You should not be pulled out due to length of time as long as you are making progress. My last swim (80k butterfly) took 63 hours and 40 minutes. At 36 hours if you are not done, you should be close. Worst case scenario, they can ask a boat to come out and meet the flotilla with supplies.

As always, I found Vicki's advice very reassuring. Here is how I viewed the situation: John wanted me to complete the swim just as badly as I wanted to complete it. He was also supportive of me raising awareness for Asperger's Syndrome. John was most concerned that I might not finish the swim and pointed out the advantages of doing a shorter crossing. Although John worried that I might not complete the route from Niagara-on-the-Lake to Toronto, he didn't want to discourage me by saying so. I think he made one last strong plea in the hopes that I would change my route. I reasoned that the only thing left for me to do was take the longer route and make sure I finished it to prove to John that I could do it. I was determined to use John's attitude to motivate myself to try harder and propel me to success. I sent the following email message to Pam and several others:

John has been urging me to shorten my route from the planned 52-kilometre route from Niagara-on-the-Lake to Toronto to the 34-kilometre route from Baird Point to Kingston.

I read in the SSO Regulations and Information manual that there comes a time during almost every marathon swim in which the swimmer begs to come out. It's easy to say beforehand, "I will finish it regardless of how much pain I'm in or how difficult it *gets." It's easy to say after the fact, "I shouldn't have quit." If you find out during the swim that I am even thinking of quitting, PLEASE DO *NOT* be afraid to tell me, "John will say, 'I told you so.'"*

Part Four
Crossing Lake Ontario

Chapter 36

Crossing Lake Ontario – The First Day

"Pain is temporary. It may last a minute, or an hour, or a day, or a year, but eventually it will subside and something else will take its place. If I quit, however, it lasts forever."
—Lance Armstrong

On Saturday, July 26th, I went to Golden Griddle for the all-you-can-eat breakfast buffet. My appetite was enormous because of all the calories I burned in my training so I had been scouting the all-you-can-eat restaurants in town; Golden Griddle was one of my favourites. I ate my fill but I went easy on the bacon and sausages. I had forty-eight hours to digest the big breakfast before my swim.

On Sunday, July 27th, I called Pam in the morning and we talked for over half an hour, partly about the logistics of the swim but also to carry on a friendly conversation. Talking to Pam certainly helped me stay relaxed. Pam and I had gotten along very well ever since the day we'd first met and I was glad to have her as a coach and friend.

Shortly after lunch, my mother and father arrived to drive me to my cousin Susan's house in Toronto where we met my sister Claire, one of her friends and several of my aunts, uncles and cousins for a spaghetti supper and a family reunion. After the reunion, my mother, father and I drove to Karen's house to pick up Karen and John P. and then proceeded to St. Catharine's where we spent the night. Rob had already arrived in St. Catharine's when we got there; Peter arrived later with his kayak. John had obtained his Zodiac-boat driver's licence that day so that he could be part of the support crew. There had been a thunderstorm the day before and, during the car ride to St. Catharine's, we encountered another thunderstorm. Karen commented, "It can thunder all it wants tonight." Better to get the thunder over with, Karen thought. When we arrived in St. Catharine's, Karen and John, who hadn't yet eaten supper, proceeded to a restaurant with some of the other crew members while I stayed at the hotel to relax. It took me several hours to fall asleep because I was so excited that the day I had long awaited had finally arrived.

◦§

On Monday, July 28th, the first day of the Lake Ontario crossing, some relatives and friends, including Jens, came to Queens Royal Park

Crossing Lake Ontario - The First Day

in Niagara-on-the-Lake to cheer me on. I had originally wanted to start the swim at 8:00 a.m., confident that that would give me enough time to finish the swim before the second night. Marilyn told me that the earliest that I could start the swim was 10:00 a.m.; an 8:00 a.m. start would require the crew to start getting ready at 5:00 a.m.

My mother and father went to the Niagara-on-the-Lake Sailing Club to see the crew off before returning to the beach to see me off. While at the sailing club, my mother pointed at Gord, the Zodiac driver, and said, "Now you bring my boy back."

Meanwhile, I did my usual routine of applying sunscreen and then doing ten minutes of stretching to give my skin time to absorb the

Table 36-1 crew members

Jay	swimmer
Marilyn	Swim Master
Pam	swim coach
John Cr.	large boat operator
Joe	large boat operator
Dave	large boat operator
Stephen	large boat operator
Eden	pacer, lifeguard
Karen	pacer
Peter	kayaker
Rob	kayaker
Andra	Assistant Swim Master, Zodiac driver
Gord	Zodiac driver
John P.	Zodiac driver
Dan	Zodiac driver
Gavin	Zodiac driver
Charlene	nurse

sunscreen before applying the Vaseline. I generally don't get cold swimming in July and August so I'd stopped applying Vaseline to my whole body in my training swims. I still spread it on my armpits and the parts of my face and shoulders which rub while doing the front crawl. Experience has shown that I get rashes within two hours but Vaseline makes *all* the difference. Because I wanted to take every precaution against hypothermia for the arduous Lake Ontario crossing,

I applied Vaseline to my entire body to be on the safe side: hoping for the best but preparing for the worst.

My first thought at the edge of the lake was, "My dream desire after two years of training is actually happening! This is it!" When I entered the water at 10:10 a.m. and started swimming, it seemed like any other long training swim. I knew from the level of excitement I felt, however, that my training was over. This was my swim of a lifetime. I was pumped with a lot more adrenaline than any of my training swim starts because I had the support of a wonderful crew and a crowd of well-wishers. After the first couple of hours, I felt like I was off to a good start. Thanks to the current from the Niagara River, I averaged more than 3 km/h for two hours and that was faster than I had been able to swim in a pool!

At the one-hour mark, I felt fine but the crew encouraged me to have an energy drink. SSO required that one Zodiac travel beside the swimmer at all times. It was necessary to have two Zodiacs. The second one is often used to transport people back and forth between the boats. During dangerous periods such as fog, high winds, dark or if the swimmer gets into trouble, it would be necessary to have the second Zodiac beside the swimmer. SSO suggests that a kayak also accompany the swimmer, but this is not mandatory. Needless to say, it is much simpler to receive food/drink from a kayak instead of from a zodiac. I had one kayak beside me throughout the swim. The food and drink was passed to me from the kayak since that is much simpler than receiving the food and drink from a Zodiac.

Chris had been in touch with a nutritionist so we could plan the food I would need for the swim. Shortly before the crossing, I emailed Marilyn a list of the foods I planned to eat during the crossing. The following was the list of foods and liquids I emailed to Marilyn.

water
Gatorade
Xilarate (an energy drink)
hot apple cider (I will supply the powder)
Boost (an energy drink)
Ensure (an energy drink)

PowerBar Gel
maple sugar candies (I will supply)
dextrosol (i.e. sugar tablets) (recommended by Vicki, I plan not to

eat them except if there are problems with my normal eating routine)
bananas (it takes me ~3 minutes to eat a banana and I know they're not recommended for this reason)
watermelon
Delmonte (or Dole) fruit cups (recommended by Vicki, spoon required)
nutri-grain bars
access bars (a type of chocolate bar ~40g), probably won't use until nighttime (or second day if cold) (I will supply)
instant oatmeal (only if cold or extremely low on energy, spoon required)
hot oatmeal (optional)
yogourt (optional)
chocolate bars (optional) (I will supply)

homebaked goods (I will supply)
rolled oat shortbread (very crunchy, semi-quick to eat)
oatmeal scones
oatmeal and raisin cookies
brownies

Marilyn's reply, July 18, 2008:

Dear Jay,
I am concerned that if you eat too many solids you will become nauseated. Once that starts, it is very hard to get rid of and can lead to vomiting. If we can't stop that, the swim will be over.
Stopping for any reason for over 2 minutes will:
1. make you cold
2. make you stiff
3. make it harder to go on again.
It would be preferable if most of your diet were liquid.
The spoon has to go. The amount of energy required to keep both hands and your head that high out of the water simultaneously is not worth it. If you are cold you will not be able to coordinate holding a spoon. Find another get warm alternative.

    These precautions didn't apply on the training swims because, if I got too cold or stiffened up, I had the option of aborting the swim. My

The Ambition of an Aspie

swims in the spring and fall were largely to test the cold water; these swims were often so cold and short enough that I didn't need solid food. In the summer, I seldom got cold; therefore, taking longer feeding breaks was not a problem. I had wanted the training swims to mimic the crossing as much as possible, but I figured that I could eat whatever I wanted to, within reason. I knew that Marilyn had good reasons for her suggestions, so I followed her advice.

Throughout the swim, most of my food/drink consisted of Boost, Ensure, and power gels and, occasionally, Gatorade, Xilarate, or scones. I didn't eat any bananas which had been a staple of my trial swims. It was a tough choice to drop the bananas because they are a good source of potassium and I was used to eating them while swimming. Again, I went with Marilyn's advice on this because it took me three minutes to eat a banana and that was too long for a feeding break.

Other than my long-time friends Karen, Peter, John and Rob, I had not previously met any of the crew members except for Marilyn, Pam and Andra. Andra had been hired by Kerry's Place Autism Services specifically to assist with this swimming project. Being accompanied by different people added another dimension to the final swim, but I had no time to focus on the people. During my marathon swim at Camp Iawah, I introduced myself to the new shift of paddlers every two hours and then asked them their names. I enjoyed having time to get to know them, but there was no time for any socializing on the crossing. I did not keep track of any change in the Zodiac occupants; I'd notice when my friends were on the boat but, unlike the training sessions, I had no time to talk to the crew. I had to conserve time and my energy resources.

Six hours into the swim, I said to Pam, "I still have every intention of finishing, my heart will break if I don't finish, but I'm starting to have doubts that I'll be able to finish." I had just eaten an oatmeal raisin cookie which I baked myself and felt slightly nauseous. I resisted the urge to vomit and then easily re-grouped and resumed my commitment to accomplish the crossing. However, I was concerned about what might happen later in the swim when my digestive system might not be functioning as well.

Pacers, who take turns swimming beside the swimmer, are not allowed until the fifth hour of the swim. However, the crew delayed putting any pacers in the water with me because I was doing very well. At 5:30p.m., after I had been swimming seven and a half hours, Eden entered the water with me. I had not met Eden nor communicated with her before that point. Chris had introduced me to her. Shortly after Chris learned of my ambition, Chris thought that Eden, a Program Supervisor for the Ministry of Children and Youth Services, and a former employee of Kerry's Place Autism Services, would like to assist with my swim by being a pacer. Eden was keen to do this and re-certified as a lifeguard to qualify to help me even before I was officially sanctioned by SSO to undertake the crossing. Minutes after Eden entered the water, I told Eden a joke.

Q. What do you call a cat that fell into a jug of lemonade?
A. A sourpuss.

I told Eden that there were plenty more jokes where that came from and then I told her to remind me to tell her more jokes after the swim.

Forty-five minutes later, Karen took over for Eden as a pacer. With the eventual onset of darkness, I was handed one glowstick to put behind the strap of my swim goggles. Karen applied another glowstick to the back of my bathing suit using a safety pin. I had been unsure how to attach a glow-stick to my bathing suit since it was difficult to do that by myself, but Pam confirmed that Karen was allowed to pin the glow-stick to my bathing suit.

While Karen was pacing me, I could see the CN Tower and other buildings along the Toronto skyline. While interpreting my dream of early May, which is mentioned in Appendix J, I thought I wouldn't be able to see such a sight until Tuesday. I said to Karen, "Do you see what I see?"

At nine and a half hours into my swim, my hamstring felt tight during a feeding break. I thought I'd be fine as soon as I resumed the front crawl. As soon as I continued with front crawl, both quadriceps suddenly seized up. I wondered if that might be the end of my dream swim. Karen offered to massage my quadriceps when I quickly screamed, "Don't touch me!" I would have been immediately disqualified if another person had touched me in any way that could be considered assistance to keep me afloat. Accidental brushing was OK. I do not give up easily, so I rolled onto my back and sculled with both hands for about a minute. Then someone made a suggestion that I massage my quadriceps. Fortunately, the cramps went away after I massaged my quads.

For two hours before sundown, Marilyn had taken over paddling Peter's kayak. When darkness came, Peter took over the kayak and continued paddling until dawn.

The lake had been very calm until the evening and then the waves increased to 2 feet. Usually it's calmer during the evening and windy during the day. I had been informed after the trial swim that the lead boat would set the course on my actual crossing and stay approximately one mile ahead of me. The nights of my actual crossing were much easier than the three night swims I'd done in 2007 because I only had to focus on making forward progress with a well-lit boat ahead of me as my guide. Nothing unexpected happened during the first night and I still felt completely comfortable except for a minimal chill. Nonetheless, my pace, which had averaged 2 km/h since leaving the Niagara River, had slowed to roughly 1 km/h after the pacers retired for the night. I was not aware of this. Throughout the night, I proceeded with my goal of reaching the other side while thinking, just as I thought after my dream in May (see Appendix J), "If I can just keep swimming until dawn, I've got it made."

Chapter 37

Crossing Lake Ontario – The Second Day

"When you're at your worst, that's the worst time to make a big decision"
　　　　　　　　　　　　　　　　　　　　—*a running club member*

At 6:30 a.m. on July 29th, just after the sun came up, Rob took over Peter's duty as kayaker and Karen re-entered the water. Once again, Karen and Eden took turns keeping me company as pacers, alternating roughly every hour. Rob and Andra also took a turn pacing me even though they weren't listed as pacers. I had started out yesterday wearing tinted goggles which were more suitable in bright sunlight but switched to clear goggles at night. In the morning, Pam offered me the tinted goggles but I declined. I didn't want to waste time and I thought I was close to finishing. At one point, Pam made a comment about my stroke technique and I replied, "At this stage in the game, I don't care." I did not want to invest the mental energy to focus on how to effectively alter my stroke. Pam, knowing that explanations often stress me out, was completely agreeable.[59]

The Toronto shoreline had been visible for some time, so I still thought I could finish before 8 p.m. and possibly even attend part of the fun day which Kerry's Place Autism Services hosted at Marilyn Bell Park from 2 p.m. to 8 p.m. on Tuesday, July 29[th.] That way, the crowd could cheer me on from land and congratulate me upon my arrival. This time had been scheduled with the assumption that I would finish my swim in 30 to 36 hours after my planned start at 8:00 a.m. If bad weather forced the swim to be delayed one day, the fun day would still be held on July 29th to raise awareness for Asperger's Syndrome. Marilyn Bell Park had to be booked in well in advance and it was very expensive so my organizational committee had made the decision to hold the fun day regardless of whether my swim was delayed or not.

excerpt from e-mail message from Jay to Vicki, July 14, 2008:

Kerry's Place Autism Services will be hosting a "fun day" (i.e. put up booths and sell hamburgers) at Marilyn Bell Park from 2pm-

---

[59] I had discussed this with Pam the first day we met (see Chapter 31 – Meeting Pam) after which she quickly made it clear that if I didn't want to explain why I was doing something in a particular way, she was totally okay with that. See also Explanations Require Energy in Chapter 1.

8pm on Tuesday, July 29 (the estimated finishing time of my swim). It has been made clear to me not to feel any pressure to finish during this time. If the swim is delayed, the fun day will still be held for the sake of raising awareness of Asperger's Syndrome.

Vicki's reply, July 14, 2008:

We have done the same thing – It always works out. The weather is the most important aspect of your swim.

∽

  A few times when I was swimming on that Tuesday, I said to the Zodiac driver, "I'm inhaling fumes." Each time, the driver would adjust the Zodiac's position. One time, I could clearly smell the fumes so I simply did head-up breast stroke until my position was clear of the fumes.

excerpt from e-mail message from Jay to Vicki, December 14, 2007:

For the longest time, I did several training swims and was never accompanied by a boat with a gas motor (always either a canoe or kayak or, on one occasion, a boat with an electric motor.) My parents own a 23-foot sailboat. I went home on Labour Day weekend and swam in the Ottawa River. My parents accompanied me with their sailboat and, for a while, they powered the boat with the sail but, eventually, they started the motor. I concluded that I don't like putting my face in water where, only sixty seconds earlier, there had been gas fumes. Therefore, I would strongly prefer to be swimming beside the boat (or outside the wake), not behind the boat.

Vicki's reply, December 19, 2007:

The swimmer swims beside the kayaks or zodiacs. The zodiac or kayak follows the navigational boat from a distance. You should not inhale fumes, and if you find yourself inhaling fumes, you can ask the boats to change formation so you can avoid the fumes.

  Ever since the day I decided I wanted to undertake this crossing, I had assumed that there wasn't any current in Lake Ontario that I couldn't handle; I assumed that Lake Ontario was stagnant save for the flow from Lake Erie through Lake Ontario and into the St. Lawrence River. I had concluded that as long as I didn't get too cold and could keep my head above water, I could make progress and continue to go forward. I was totally unaware of the Humber River, let alone the current that results from its outflow. In addition to the Humber River current, I encountered wind-generated lake circulation currents.

John C. may not have been completely correct when he said it would be "game over" if I didn't complete the crossing within thirty hours but he had a point worth making. I had been swimming for more than thirty hours. Although I still felt like I was swimming at a reasonable pace, was completely comfortable and felt no sign of fatigue, my stroke had slowed to the point where it didn't take much of a back current to halt all progress. For a while, I was even moving backwards. The crew wisely refrained from telling me this fearing I would get too discouraged and quit. For several hours, the Toronto shoreline had not appeared to be getting any closer. I asked whether I was making progress and received an affirmative reply. One time, I asked out loud, "Does this lake even have an 'other side'?"

While I was treading water for a feeding break, Pam told me to turn my back, i.e., face away from my destination; this way, I wouldn't drift backwards as much.

In the afternoon, Marilyn doubted whether I would be able to finish the swim within the planned 36-hour window. She was also worried whether I would finish the swim at all if we were to continue on the route to Marilyn Bell Park. Again, the crew wisely refrained from informing me of the latter doubt.

Marilyn, who had supervised several marathon swims, strongly recommended that the swim be rerouted to land at the Leslie Street Spit. This was primarily because the wind was blowing the flotilla towards the Leslie Street Spit and I was unable to make headway against it. This also shortened the route by five km but still classified as a complete crossing. Marilyn relayed the suggestion to me through Pam and Karen, who were in the Zodiac at the time. I didn't have a strong preference on the finishing location. I'm not sure how sleep-deprivation was affecting me at that point; I trusted the crew's judgment, instinctively agreed to follow the boat, and then resumed stroking.

While my supporters were waiting patiently at Marilyn Bell Park, Pat Probert, whom none of them had ever met before, graciously offered to bring Claire, my mother, Margot (the executive director of Asperger's Society of Ontario), Jens, the media, and a few others on his Margaritaville boat to join the flotilla. Pat met the flotilla a number of miles out and due south of the Leslie Street spit. Pat started running low on fuel as his offer to go out of his way was unexpected. He transferred Claire and my mother to the lead boat in the flotilla. The rest of the visitors traveled back to shore with Pat where he arranged for them to get a ride to join the others. Pat had even arranged some live radio interviews from the boat to encourage people to support my cause. He also provided his boat so the TV crew could do live shots of me swimming with the background of Toronto. During the couple of hours in which Margaritaville was with us, I covered a grand total of four hundred metres. Jens almost cried. Claire joined me as a pacer and told me that she was very proud of me. Although the rules will allow only one pacer in the water at a time, both Karen and Claire paced me at the same time for a while so that I had one pacer on each side. This was very encouraging as I was getting tired.

Meanwhile, Pam told me that Mr. Fulford was waiting for me on shore. I was surprised and delighted as I repeated, "Mr. Fulford!"

At 5:00 p.m., Peter took over kayaking for Rob, who had been paddling since the morning except for a two-hour break. Peter continued kayaking for the remainder of the crossing.

Table 37-1 – schedule of kayakers

10:10am - 3:00pm	Peter
3:00pm - 6:00pm	Rob
6:00pm – 8:30pm	Marilyn
8:30pm - 6:30am	Peter
6:30am - 11:00am	Rob
11:00am - 1:00pm	Peter
1:00pm - 5:00pm	Rob
5:00pm - 3:00am	Peter

As soon it got dark at about 9:00 p.m., Claire came out of the water. Pam attached a glow stick to Karen. The rules say that pacers are not allowed in the water at night but Marilyn told Pam that it was OK. Karen felt cold and had a strong urge to get out. For the sake of supporting me, Karen was committed to keep swimming until she either started shivering or she was asked to come out. Marilyn, who knew as early as that morning that I was unlikely to be finished before sundown, left the Zodiac for only a few minutes to do what she had been prepared to do all along: she put on a wetsuit and got into the water with me. She stayed in the water for the remaining five hours. Marilyn ordered Karen out of the water when Marilyn entered the water shortly after 10:00 p.m. The reason for the "no pacers at night rule" is for safety; keeping track of one swimmer at night is difficult enough. Swim Masters are allowed to use their discretion if they feel the swimmer is at risk. It was actually safer for Marilyn to be in the water with me since she could monitor my condition more closely from the water than from the Zodiac. On account of my slow progress, Marilyn basically treaded water most of the way to stay beside me. Marilyn was getting cold despite wearing a wetsuit. This was the most grueling-paced swim that Marilyn had ever been involved with.

Claire and Karen were told that there was not room for both of them in the Zodiac; Karen let Claire be in the zodiac since Claire had been on shore for most of the swim. Karen was transferred to Precious Lady, the 68-foot lead boat. When I was about 1000ft from shore, Formula One, the 33-foot cigar boat which had been at the tail end of the flotilla, took over for Precious Lady as the lead boat. At that point, Precious Lady left the flotilla and headed to Polson Pier. This meant that Karen and some others were too far away to see the last part of the swim. Karen was content, concluding that she would rather have seen the entire swim except for the last few hours than only have seen the last few hours.

My original estimated time of arrival was 6:00 p.m. and it kept being pushed back by two hours. Needless to say, no one slept from the second afternoon onwards. Everyone was pumped with adrenaline, thinking I'd be touching the shoreline soon and no one wanted to miss the sight.

Experience taught me that the amount of sunlight during a swim makes a big difference in how chilled I feel. This was a positive factor that resulted from moving my swim ahead two weeks, even though the water itself might be warmer in August than in July. Other than a minimal chill the first night, I didn't feel at all cold or drowsy until darkness came the second night. I suddenly felt drowsy and started to feel cold as July 29th crawled towards July 30th. At 9:10 p.m., I had been swimming for 35 hours and awake for 38 hours . I said, "Pull me out. It's taking longer to get there than I thought. I don't know if I can make it. I feel sleepy and I'm starting to get cold." I said this partly because I intuitively knew that, being sleep deprived, I wouldn't be as attentive to the pre hypothermia symptoms but more because I had "had enough".

Pam immediately replied, "You'll be very disappointed if you don't finish."

Without saying another word, I resumed swimming. The nineteen hour swim at Chippego Lake had taught me that it is not wise to tread water for ten minutes while discussing whether or not to continue the swim and then proceed with a colder body. It made much more sense to conserve my body heat – and make distance – than to talk. I didn't necessarily need to come out at that point; I was willing to continue swimming as long as the crew was willing to proceed and continued to encourage me. I was second guessing my ability to finish the swim. I thought, "What's the point?" given that I was no longer comfortable and didn't seem to be making headway. My crew was probably relieved that I was so easily dissuaded from quitting.

Some time later, I said again, "Pull me out."

This time, as instructed, Pam said, "John will say, 'I told you so.'"

Pam actually said "John will say 'I told you so.'" more than once. Although this is the only time I remember Pam saying this, Pam repeated it over and over. (I have difficulty hearing unless I have both ears out of the water at the same time.)

Once again, I immediately continued swimming. I am thankful to have had such a marvelous crew that could be with me in spirit the whole way and demonstrate faith that I could complete the crossing. In February 2008, I wrote Heather a letter to say the following regarding the marathon swim at Chippego Lake:

> *Heather, I truly hope you will be able to be part of the support crew when I swim across Lake Ontario...There are times during the swim in which the swimmer begs to come out...Sometimes, the swimmer needs just a little more encouragement. If anyone can provide the encouragement I need, you can. Before the swim, remind me to promise you that I will let you know before I quit - unless I physically cannot keep my body afloat or doing so is excruciatingly painful - and this is after I have tried every stroke I know including legs-only scissor kick or flutter kick.*

Unfortunately, Heather was unable to be on the support boat. Karen was my next best source of encouragement. Shortly before the crossing, I made it clear to several crew members, "If I'm thinking of quitting, make sure Karen knows." Several weeks after the swim, I asked Karen whether she knew that I had asked to be pulled out. Karen hadn't but she concluded that if I was so easily dissuaded, the crew probably thought they didn't need to get her to come and encourage me.

The water temperature was 73°F the first day and 69°F the second morning. It's not uncommon to hit 55°F water near the Toronto shore since the wind sometimes blows away from the shoreline causing upwelling of the cold deep water. During the last stretch, the surface water was uniformly 70°F but I encountered several patches of colder water two or three feet underneath. I sprinted – and screamed – through each of them. The patches of cold water close to the surface were colder than 60°F and possibly as cold as 55°F. I learned through experience that I can handle 55°F water for one hour in broad daylight when I'm well rested but not for four hours after dark when I'm sleep-deprived and getting depleted.

From 1:00 a.m. onwards, spectators at Vicki Keith Point, who had kept vigil since the evening, could hear cries from the boat: "Follow Marilyn, Jay, follow Marilyn." Eden remarked nearly two hours later, "I think that last kilometer was horrible."

In their Regulations and Information manual, SSO warns that it is very difficult to distinguish between hypothermia and fatigue. By the second night, I was clearly fatigued. I remembered this warning but then I thought to myself, "I can think through this danger; therefore, I'm not in hypothermia – yet." I was so determined to finish that aborting the swim simply to be sure of avoiding hypothermia wasn't an option I wanted to consider. I had done so many training swims, including the nineteen hour swim at Chippego Lake, in which I had to be my own guard against hypothermia. Having Marilyn and Charlene as my guardians allowed me to pour every last ounce of energy into completing the crossing. Besides, I knew that paramedics would be available immediately to give me all the attention I needed when I got to the shoreline at Toronto. I had given Pam and several others a list of questions to help discern whether or not I was in hypothermia. (See Appendix M.) Pam didn't have the list with her and therefore wouldn't have known whether I was answering correctly. Instead, Pam asked me a specific questions that we both knew the answer to: "What's your mother's name?"

Once a swimmer encounters hypothermia, the swimmer's muscles don't move as effectively. This means that the swimmer doesn't generate as much heat and will become even colder resulting in a vicious cycle. In fact, this will happen when the swimmer gets noticeably cold, even before the swimmer becomes hypothermic. When I was marginally close to finishing, I said, "I can't feel my arms and legs. Please pull me out."

My arms were barely leaving the water because my stroke kept "falling apart". The crew counted my strokes out loud. They shouted out the numbers from 1 to 30 in unison at a brisk rhythm and then started counting more slowly from 1 to 30 again. The crew was trying to get me to swim in cycles of thirty strokes in the pattern of sprint – slower stroking – sprint.

Claire remarked after the fact that I was so close to finishing but so slow. The support crew could tell when my legs dropped because the level of the glow stick which was pinned to the back of my bathing suit went down abruptly. Pam kept yelling, "Keep your legs up. Reach down to your toes. Keep your armpits down." I tried and succeeded at keeping my legs closer to the surface after each prompt from Pam. After several minutes, however, I'd get tired of keeping my legs up and they'd drop down again. This sinking and raising created resistance and required more of my energy. Pam, who left the Zodiac only once to go to the washroom during the entire 41 hours, had yelled herself hoarse. She had no voice left by the end of the swim.

Many times my stroke fell apart and many times I almost came to a complete stop. Each time I somehow managed to revive my stroke. Regardless of whether I really wanted to quit when I asked to be pulled out, I had shut out all thoughts of quitting. I was back to the mindset I had clung to all along: I was not going to fail my mission to swim across Lake Ontario because I would give it no less than 100 per cent of my effort and energy. I was going to continue stroking until I reached the other side regardless of how long it took, how tired I was or how much pain I felt.

Marilyn asked me how I felt and I replied, "I'm going to keep swimming until I become unconscious." I have no recollection of having said this. Marilyn knew immediately it was her job to catch me just before that happened. I'm not sure if Marilyn was confident that my body would stay afloat for a few seconds if I passed out. Throughout the training process, I had relaxed my body many times and the top part of my head would stay above the surface. I was fairly confident that this meant that my rescuer would still have time to get to me if I became unconscious.[60]

Meanwhile, the crew was intentionally deceiving me. They told me it was 12:30 a.m. when it was really 1:30 a.m. in order to prevent me from thinking I was moving too slowly.

Hypothermia can usually be avoided if the following three conditions are met:
1. the swimmer knows when to get out of the water;
2. the swimmer is able to get out of the water; and
3. the cold swimmer can get to body-warming resources.

When training, I always knew when I needed to get out of the water. On the crossing, I would have insisted on coming out of the water as soon as I felt the chill come the second night if this had been just another training session. However, I was so determined to finish that I didn't necessarily pay attention to the pre-hypothermia symptoms. I could not have it both ways: avoiding hypothermia at all costs and completing the crossing if all possible.

I encountered moderate hypothermia within one mile of reaching shore. Since I was so close, Marilyn chose not to abort the swim. When I was only 200 metres from finishing, I told Marilyn I was tired and basically stopped moving. Marilyn asked me, "Do you want me to pull you out of the water?" I interpreted Marilyn's question as a threat and immediately took off like a bullet.

Swimmers rarely plan to land at Leslie Street Spit. It is an artificial piece of land which protrudes from the eastern gap entrance to Toronto Harbour. The extreme tip of the spit is used as a dump site for construction debris which makes it difficult to access by land and an unpleasant place to swim. Marilyn had instructed Gord, the Zodiac driver, to find a clear path with no construction debris. Marilyn got a piece of rebar between her legs when she tried to stand up and hold me. Cars are not normally allowed into the park except on weekends and holidays. A special exception was made for my swim landing but only several cars were allowed out on the spit.

As I was slowly approaching the finish line, Peter said, "C'mon Jay. You're not the only one that is hurting."

Suddenly, a wall of rocks appeared in my sight. Cousin Mike said, "Touch the wall."

---

[60] When swimmers are exhausted, they may not float as well because they may not be inflating their lungs as deeply.

At 3:11 a.m., 41 hours after entering the water at Niagara-on-the-Lake, I touched the wall, signifying the completion of my swim across Lake Ontario and fulfilling my dream desire of the last two years.

The spectators on the shore clapped in unison. Cousin Mike shouted, "You did it Jay. You're in Toronto. Your dream has come true!"

Despite the accomplishment, I have no recollection of how I felt. All I wanted to do was sleep, which would have been the case even if I weren't hypothermic.

Chapter 38

Treatment

Q. Why did the swimmer cross Lake Ontario?
A. Because the QEW was too slow.
                              —Source unknown

    As soon as I touched the wall of rocks, I swam back to the Zodiac. Gord and Rob pulled me into the boat. I was positioned in such a way as to be leaning towards Gord. When I got seated, I found my voice through my total exhaustion and asked "Will you hold my head up, please?" Gord passed me to Rob and Rob held my head up while Gord drove the Zodiac towards Formula One.

    I was transferred to Formula One which transported me to Polson Pier where I would receive medical attention. Not only did Formula One leave but so did all the spectators who had kept vigil at Vicki Keith Point for nearly six hours. This meant that the headlights of the spectators' cars no longer lit up the scene. The Zodiacs drove part of the way back but one of them ran out of gas. This left the people in the two Zodiacs and Peter in his kayak struggling to see with minimal light. Luckily, Peter's cell phone had just enough power left to call Karen who was at Polson Pier in Precious Lady on her cell phone. Formula One returned, and then all three boats were placed on top of Formula One and brought to Polson Pier.

    My core temperature was 33.8°F when I finished the swim and then 32.5°F with after drop, leaving me in moderate hypothermia. (See Appendix L for a description of the different levels of hypothermia.)

    En route to Polson Pier in Formula One, when the nurse was with me, I recalled her full name, Charlene Wilhelm, and tried to tell her a joke. Months later, when I told Claire that I had told Eden one joke when she first entered the water with me, Claire replied, "Lucky Eden! She got to hear your only joke during the entire course of the swim." Then Claire suggested that perhaps I went into hypothermia because I was deprived of telling jokes. That was the longest I had ever gone without telling a joke. It was also the longest I had ever stayed awake. I now clearly understand what Vicki meant when she mentioned that a swimmer may be able to answer questions but still be hypothermic. I was clearly in hypothermia even though I was able to recall Charlene's name.

The Ambition of an Aspie

> *excerpt from e-mail message from Jay to Vicki, September 25, 2007:*
>
> *Below is a list of questions which I give to my paddlers; people have found some of them to be funny, although I didn't intend them to be funny. (See Appendix M.)*
>
> *Vicki's reply, September 26, 2007:*
>
> *The questions below are well thought out and could be beneficial. There are so many signs to hypothermia that I don't know that I would wait until the athlete was too confused to answer questions like these. If I see significant, uncontrollable shivering, an inability to follow direction, or bluing around the lips and fingernails I would seriously consider asking the athlete to shorten their training session, or if during the crossing, consider pulling them out unless completion was only a short distance off.*

When I was back on shore and being looked at by the paramedics, one of them said, "We're going to wrap you in blankets. You have a bit of hypothermia."

Sleepy, physically exhausted, and with shivering in my voice, I replied, "But Swim Master Vicki Keith said that hypothermia wasn't going to be a huge i---"[61] Then I lost my voice.

I felt I had balanced my concerns about hypothermia quite well. If I had not been forewarned about the possibility of encountering hypothermia, I wouldn't have done so many cold water swims in order to condition myself. I would have encountered hypothermia earlier in my crossing without this training and Marilyn may have had to abort the swim because of hypothermia. If Vicki hadn't told me to stop focusing on hypothermia as a major concern, I would have kept concentration on that aspect and may not have given other aspects of the swim the focus I needed. I was pleased with how it all worked out in the end. I did get hypothermia, but I managed to get across the lake!

While I was huddled under blankets, Eden called out to me to make sure I was still conscious.

"What's your name?" I asked.

Eden replied, "My name is Eden."

---

[61] I saw myself saying this on video; I have no recollection of saying this at the time.

I replied, "Oh, you're the one who recertified your NLS after so many years and you did it just for me…"

"Yes, it was one of the many gifts you gave me."

"Gifts? I didn't give you anything."

Eden explained, "No, you didn't physically hand me any gifts but just the same you gave me many."

"What were they?"

"Well, I am in the best shape of my life entirely because of you. I recertified my NLS for the first time in 10 years, which I would never have done if it weren't for you, and I swam longer and further than I ever have before. These are just a few things you gave me. Most importantly, I had the privilege of being part of your crew." [*Cantkier, 2008*]

Eden felt that she'd witnessed a miracle first hand as well as had a chance to stand next to "greatness". I was very flattered. Eden thinks that I did her a favour by letting her be part of my crew. I think Eden did me a favour because I wanted to swim across Lake Ontario so badly and I couldn't have done it alone. Besides, Eden re-did her lifeguard certificate even before I was officially sanctioned by SSO. The net result is that Eden and I are in a win-win situation. Eden really enjoyed the experience of watching me fulfill my dream and I was very appreciative of her help.

While the paramedics were looking me over, Karen asked Marilyn, "How do you decide when to pull the plug?"[62]

Marilyn replied, "If I wasn't prepared to get in the water with him, I wouldn't have let him continue into a second night. The second night is too difficult."

I appreciate that making the decision about when to abort a swim is only one of several factors which makes a Swim Master's job complicated. I really respected Marilyn's judgement and am very grateful that she had such faith in me.[63]

I remember touching the wall and hearing the spectators clapping. I don't remember the boat ride. The next thing I remember is being lifted onto one blanket, then being lifted onto another blanket with eight people standing around me, at least one of whom was wearing a paramedic uniform. Other than that, my mind was blacked out until I woke up in the hospital five hours later.

---

[62] "pull the plug" means "abort the swim"

[63] When I returned to work, one of my co-workers later pointed out that I managed to pick the only 41 hour window period since June 1 that didn't have any thunder. It thundered the night before, was supposed to thunder five hours before I finished, and thundered the following evening.

Jay training in Lake Ontario (downtown Kingston in background).

Jay (right) swimming across Navy Bay in November for United Way with two colleagues, accompanied by Jane in kayak.

Alicia kayaking beside Jay during his qualifying trial swim (Amherst Island in background).

After Jay's qualifying trial swim, left to right: Pam (swim coach), Shannon, Kristine, Collin, Jay

Jay with his parents and sister Claire at Queen's Royal Park at Niagara-on-the-Lake prior to the crossing.

Left to right in Zodiac: Marilyn (Swim Master), Andra (Assistant Swim Master) and Pam (Swim coach).

Precious Lady

Zodiac gets a tow from Formula One

Pacers Eden (left) and Karen.

John P. (left) and Rob.

Peter (right) coming off night shift of kayaking, in Zodiac with driver Gavin.

Toronto skyline.

Jay swimming with sister Claire (left).

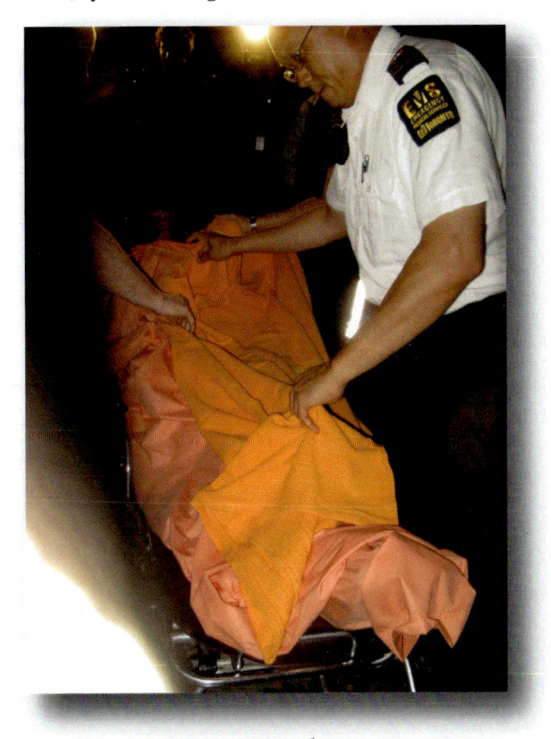

Jay on stretcher.

Jay (left) with swim coach Pam.

Colourful view from Mount Martin on Thanksgiving weekend, town of Deep River in background.

Part Five

After a Dream Comes True

Chapter 39

St. Michael's Hospital

"Our fatigue is often caused not by work, but by worry, frustration and resentment."

—Dale Carnegie

When I arrived at Polson Pier in Formula One, the paramedics quickly looked me over and then lifted me on a stretcher and carried me into the ambulance that had been waiting for me. My mother accompanied me in the ambulance to St. Michael's Hospital. The hospital has three levels of emergency care and I was taken to the highest of the three.

After leaving Leslie Street Spit, my father had driven Claire to her car and made a few more drop-offs before heading to St. Michael's hospital to accompany my mother. My mother and father stayed by the side of my bed so that they would be there when I finally woke up at 8:00 a.m. I got sick to my stomach as soon as I tried to sit up. My throat was so dry that I could only speak in hoarse whispers. My first question for my parents was, "What day is it?"

My mother and father, who during their vigil were reassured by the readouts for my body temperature among other vital signs, especially the temperature, as they could see that it was rising slowly and steadily, were relieved when I woke up. My question reassured them that I was coming back to full consciousness. Then I proceeded to talk about the efforts I had put into the swim and that I didn't think I could do any more – not realizing I had actually completed the crossing. My mother, being hard of hearing, had to keep her ear close to my mouth to make out what I was whispering, and it didn't seem totally coherent.

My body temperature rose by ~$1°C$ per hour and was back up to normal ($37°C$) within five hours. I was actually running a bit of a fever at one point. One of the nurses asked me to take Tylenol to help lower my body temperature to where it was supposed to be. I refused by saying nothing, being a firm believer in natural healing whenever possible and confident that my body temperature would return to normal on its own.

My blood pressure remained at 80/40 for the entire first day. My heart was in dire need of rest. I never would have guessed that my blood pressure was that low because, after I woke up in the hospital, I did not feel weak; just fatigued. When you're sleeping over half of the time, lying down most of the time, and never get out of bed except to go to the washroom, your heart doesn't have to work very hard.

I noted that after the crossing my shoulders felt fine. When I woke up in the hospital, I had other things to worry about and seldom got out of bed for the next two days except to go to the washroom. I was only minimally sunburned and the sunburn was barely noticeable at first. By the time the other factors were under control, the sunburn was negligible and didn't bother me.

I had no idea that people had been posting comments on my website[64] while I was swimming until I started receiving visitors in the hospital. During the crossing, I didn't get much information from the crew because I couldn't hear well; I was wearing earplugs and I never had both ears out of the water at the same time while doing the front crawl. I could hear if the crew yelled really loudly but they eventually lost their voices so they were wisely being selective about what they told me. The only exception was when I was treading water while taking a feeding break. The number of people who followed my swim on the website had grown in the two days of my crossing. Many of them hoped that someone would read their messages to me while I was swimming but there were so many posts that the crew probably couldn't possibly pass them all along. They were much too busy looking after me!

Karen came to visit me wearing the volunteer T-shirt that all crew members had been given. When she walked into the hospital room I didn't initially thank her for coming to visit me or express my gratitude to her for being part of my crew or even say "Hello". The first thing I said was, "Turn around," because I wanted to see the list of sponsors on the back of the shirt. Nonetheless, Karen congratulated me and we both enjoyed the time together, even though I was still tired and wanted to sleep most of the time.

A sense of accomplishment still hadn't sunk in. I knew I had crossed Lake Ontario but I didn't realize it. The fact that I had made my dream come true didn't seem real to me as I lay exhausted in a hospital bed with needles in my hand attached to IV tubes. A lot of my focus was catching up on my lost sleep. I was caught up in the excitement of seeing so many visitors and this distracted me from focusing of the huge feat I had accomplished.

---

[64] http://www.swim4aspergers.wordpress.com/

Meanwhile, Aunt Ileen kept sending me food. The hospital didn't provide me with enough food to replenish all the energy I had burned during my crossing. Hospital food made me think of a story about a friend of mine. This happy-go-lucky friend told me that he wants to go to jail because, according to his wry sense of humour, he wouldn't have to worry about buying groceries, preparing meals or washing dishes. In prison, everything would be planned and provided for him and he would have an easy lifestyle. I warned him that if he had a criminal record, he would lose his freedom. He likes to travel overseas and I pointed out that being a prisoner would make it impossible for him to travel out of the country. He was forced to concede this point and admitted that this factor would deter him from wanting to go to jail. I suggested that he try the hospital instead of jail because that would spare him a criminal record. I'm not sure that qualifying to enter the hospital just to be fed and cared for would really appeal to him much more than becoming a prisoner. Being in jail or the hospital may be free for the offender or patient, but it is not free for the taxpayer. I found out that you have to put up with the quantity and quality of food that is provided for you in the hospital or you need to get someone bring you food. My brief stay in the hospital gave me information that I could pass to my friend who thought it would be fun to have a free ride. My advice to my friend is: Stay out of jails and hospitals! I was really grateful to Aunt Ileen and others who brought me tasty food in enough quantity to satisfy the enormous appetite I had after I finished my swim.

On Wednesday, June 30th, I slept on and off throughout the day. Karen, Claire and my cousin Susan were very thoughtful. They stayed with me while I ate to keep me company but would leave the room when I wanted to sleep. I could not sleep continuously throughout the night because the nurses had to check on me every two hours.

I was moved to the "least urgent" area of emergency on Thursday, July 31st and was given my own room. I might have been moved to the second level of emergency care earlier, but there had not been any available space. Later on Thursday, I was taken off the IV but the needles remained in my hand in case the nurses needed to reattach the tubes.

On Thursday night, the nurses left me alone from 10:00 p.m. to 8:00 a.m. but I had to get up to urinate every two hours.

I was discharged from the hospital at noon on Friday. The person responsible for making the final decision had been unavailable on

Thursday and the staff likely wanted to keep me under their care for at least a few hours after disconnecting the IV.

excerpt from e-mail message from Marilyn to SSO board, August 1, 2008:

Unfortunately, they have kept Jay in hospital until today because he is having trouble taking a deep breath and they can't figure out if it is pneumonia or not. He may have aspirated vomit after the last feed. On a positive note, he is on the 14th floor and can see the Leslie St. Spit landing spot from the window at the end of his hall.

In the discharge report, the doctors recommended that I have a cardiac stress test to make sure that my heart was still functioning properly and hadn't been damaged from the swim.

On Friday, August 1st, after I was officially discharged, Pam, Karen, my parents and I chatted away for close to an hour before I realized that we needed to vacate the room so that it would be available for the next person. Then we went out to the parking lot and said our good-byes.

Chapter 40

Recovery

"He who treads softly goes far"
—Chinese proverb

It was great to be out of the hospital. By the time my parents and I left the hospital and arrived at Uncle Frank and Aunt Ileen's house, we knew that we wouldn't be able to get packed and get out of Toronto before rush hour, especially since it was the start of a long weekend. We stayed overnight with our relatives. On Saturday morning, we left for Deep River. As we were driving along Highway 401, I looked out the window and exclaimed, "There's Lake Ontario!" That was the triggering event; for the first time, I actually realized and felt excited that I had made my dream come true! I had seen Lake Ontario from Highway 401 many times while driving to Toronto. I still remember as a child the very first time my mother said to me, "There's Lake Ontario," when we went to see my cousins. I could now sit back and look at that vast lake knowing that all the painful pushing of my body's limits, the spasms and bone-chilling cold of my long and gruelling training had paid off. I felt very satisfied and accomplished.

I began participating in the Deep River triathlon in 1990. Very seldom had I missed a year since then. In 2008, I had registered for the triathlon but didn't do it since it took place only 48 hours after I had been discharged from the hospital. I hadn't done any physical activity since I had touched the wall of rocks and didn't know how my body would handle two hours of strenuous activity. Instead, I watched the triathlon and shared my story with numerous friends who were at the event. Summerfest, a summer party held bi-annually on the August long weekend which includes music and performances, was also being held. I opted to stay home and sleep rather than attend Summerfest events. Later that weekend, my mother and I swam together in the Ottawa River for about 20 minutes.

On August 4th, the holiday Monday, my parents drove me back to Kingston since they didn't want to leave me to take the bus alone. I slept for 12 hours that night and was back at work the next day. Just as my father had warned me, I didn't get any work done that day because my coworkers wanted to hear my story. Everyone wanted to congratulate me and asked me how it felt to accomplish my dream. I relived the excitement as I recounted the highlights of constant stroking through two cycles and 41 hours of daylight and darkness until I touched the wall of rocks at the Leslie Street Spit in Toronto. As I told the story over and over to my colleagues, I realized again with amazement that I'd really done it! I had successfully achieved my dream desire of swimming across Lake Ontario. Kristine came into my office and hugged me. The whole department had talked about my swim during coffee break on July 28th and 29th, but no one from the department had come to watch me start at Niagara-on-the-Lake or finish in Toronto because of the travelling distance required to watch my swim. They had all eagerly followed the blog on the website. Phil, who is now the acting head of the department of Chemistry and Chemical Engineering at RMC, a position he got after the swim across Navy Bay in 2006, arranged a group coffee break three weeks later, on August 26th, so that everyone could congratulate me as a group[65]. When Phil made the opening announcement, he mentioned, as a joke, that he was worried about me getting injured during the swim across Navy Bay and, by swimming across Lake Ontario, I had gone through great lengths to prove him wrong.

In the evening of Tuesday, August 5th, I attended running club, which was held at a track. Not wanting to do too much exercise too soon, I ran casually for ten minutes while everyone else did the prescribed speed intervals. My sabbatical from running was now officially finished. I had participated in the Around the Bay 30K Road Race in Hamilton in March as I had originally planned, but then put my running on hold until after my Lake Ontario crossing.

I followed my usual cautious routine of doing a small amount of physical activity and paid extra attention to my body's reaction. I waited a few days for a delayed reaction before undertaking more physical activity. I gradually increased the level of activity to what I wanted. Within three weeks, I was back to a decent routine of physical activity.

Despite my gruelling months of training and the taxing ordeal of crossing Lake Ontario, I still wanted to continue open-water swimming for pleasure. It took me a while to get motivated to find the time and coordinate schedules with one of my many paddling volunteers, but about a month after the crossing, I was back into the

---

[65] This date was chosen for the group coffee break because it was after everyone had taken their summer vacations and before people started teaching their classes at RMC in September.

routine of swimming and planning my training swims a few days in advance. I just didn't swim as far or as often as I did while training to cross Lake Ontario.

The excitement stage continued for almost a month because every time I saw people whom I hadn't seen since before the swim, they wanted to congratulate me and hear my story. One month after the crossing, I saw Heather, the organizer of my marathon swim at Chippego Lake. I told her that part of me still regretted quitting the swim at Chippego Lake after 19 hours. Heather replied that maybe it was better that I had quit the swim then. She figured that if I had kept swimming for 24 hours, perhaps I would also have wanted to quit the crossing after 24 hours. Because I had quit a shorter swim, she reasoned, I would know how it felt to have quit. She thought that the memory of having aborted a swim possibly kept me motivated for my actual crossing. Heather's comment reassured me that what might have seemed like a poor decision at one time could have turned out for my benefit.

Before discharging me from the hospital, the nurse referred me for a cardiac stress test to make sure my heart hadn't been damaged by the ordeal of the crossing, but she said there was no urgency to having the test done. First, I had to get an appointment with my family doctor to have the test scheduled. The test occurred in early October, two months after my swim across Lake Ontario. The technician had me run on a treadmill. First, she asked me to remove my shirt and then she put pads on several places on my chest to measure the electrical pulses in my heart. I was instructed to continue running as long as I was able, although not to feel that I had to push myself. Every three minutes, the technician would increase the speed and the grade of incline on the treadmill. Into the fifth three-minute period, I knew that I might possibly be able to continue that pace and grade for a while, but I was quite sure I would have to stop as soon as the next increase occurred. I lasted fifteen minutes total on the treadmill. For a schedule of speeds and grades, see the chart in Figure 40-1. The technician said that was the longest that she had ever seen anyone last on the treadmill; most people don't last longer than six minutes. I felt pretty good about lasting 15 minutes, but then I considered that most people who are asked to do the treadmill test have a heart condition and that is why they are asked to do the test in the first place. It was comforting to know, however, that my heart was still in great shape after my crossing.

Table 40-1 – treadmill test

time frame	speed	grade
0-3 minutes	1.0km/h	10%
3-6 minutes	1.7km/h	12%
6-9 minutes	3.4km/h	14%
9-12 minutes	4.1km/h	16%
12-15 minutes	5.0km/h	18%

Chapter 41

What Next?

"Desire is the most important factor in the success of any athlete."
—Willie Shoemaker

Once I knew for sure that swimming across Lake Ontario was what I wanted to do, my days were filled with either swimming or making arrangements for support for my training. On any given day I would either be psyching myself up and doing a training swim or I would be trying to arrange volunteer paddlers for my next training swim or thinking, planning or organizing other details for the actual crossing. As soon as I woke up every day, I would be focused on ticking off the tasks and doing the training required to make my dream of crossing Lake Ontario come true. Almost nothing else mattered for the entire year and a half before the crossing.

For at least two weeks after the swim, I'd constantly meet friends whom I hadn't seen since before the crossing and they wanted to hear my story. I was very happy to talk about the swim as it kept the details of my accomplishment alive. After the excitement of sharing my story had died down, I felt depressed. I wondered whether it was the norm to feel depressed after completing a marathon swim. The next time I went home, I informed my mother and father of my situation. My mother pointed out that what I felt was not depression, but simply not knowing what to focus on now that the two-year project of swimming across Lake Ontario had been completed. Before long, I decided to pour my energy into a new goal of writing a book about my training and the swim. This gave me another dream to focus on, so the depression I had felt went away.

❧

Now that my swim is past, a logical question to ask is: What is my next physical challenge? I don't see any reason to undertake anything big, at least not right away. The training took its toll on me and it's time to give my body a rest.

At Christmas time in 2007, I was visiting my parents. With the training well underway and with my heart set on swimming across Lake Ontario, my father was watching on television a program about a woman who was climbing Mount Everest. My father called me downstairs, concluding – correctly – that I would be interested in watching the program. My father suggested that I make climbing Mount Everest my next goal. (He was only joking.) Part of me is surprised my father would even mention that given that he is the cautious one in the family whenever there is risk involved.

I knew right from the start that, in order to swim across Lake Ontario, I would have to be able to swim long distances continuously for many hours and swim in rough waves. Living only a five minute walk from Lake Ontario made it feasible to test all of the above without significantly altering my lifestyle; it just took time.

I do not believe in undertaking any big challenge (and certainly not asking others to support me) unless I have reason to believe that I can complete the challenge. Before I have reason to believe that I could climb Mount Everest, I would have to test whether I can handle exercise with low oxygen. Not only am I not in a position to try this out without significantly altering my lifestyle, but I also would not have found it comfortable to do so. The cold temperature would have made it doubly uncomfortable. The narrator of the television program mentioned that the woman who was climbing Mount Everest can run a double marathon at sea level without panting and she was struggling trying to put one foot in front of the other.

I promised Debbie that I would participate in the Swim for the Cure in 2009, partly to assist breast cancer research but more because I like swimming. 2010 will mark its tenth anniversary and, to celebrate this occasion, participants will have the option of doing the usual 13-kilometre route or 26 kilometres, from Swift Rapids to Big Chute and then continuing to the next set of locks at Port Severn. The Swim for the Cure will probably become an annual event for me. A 2-kilometre triathlon swim is too short because it doesn't motivate me to train throughout the winter; a 52-kilometre swim across Lake Ontario is too long because it pushed me to my limit, not only the crossing but the training as well. 13 kilometres is about the right distance.

While I sought people to paddle beside me on my training swims, several people were not only willing but were willing to do so repeatedly. If I find out that someone really wants to paddle beside me, I will make sure that s/he gets at least one chance. The Swim for the Cure only happens once a year so, if more than one person really wants to paddle beside me, who will be the lucky person to get that opportunity?

Participating in the Swim for the Cure every year, training for the Swim for the Cure, cross-country skiing, cycling as a means of transportation plus the occasional bicycle to Gananoque will probably keep me physically fit enough to be happy. I could probably give up running entirely and still be happy, although there is no way to find that out for sure without trying it. It's not that I want to give up running; it's nice to know that I have this option.

I would like to help the Asperger's community but I would also like to maintain a physically active lifestyle. Training for the annual Swim for the Cure provides the ideal opportunity to maintain such a lifestyle.

Although it feels great to be in shape, I would occasionally wonder if I was wasting my life away since I had been performing the same routine day after day and participating in the same races year after year. Eventually I will die, and what will I have accomplished, other than being able to say I maintained a healthy, physically active lifestyle? Part of the reason I took the nineteen month sabbatical from running is that I knew that my life was due for a change.

⁂

Initially, I wanted to swim across Lake Ontario as a personal challenge. When I decided to do it as a fundraiser for Asperger's Syndrome, this led to my ongoing involvement with the Asperger's community. I have been asked to give speeches about Asperger's and my swim for Kerry's Place Autism Services, Asperger's Society of Ontario, Community Living , and several schools. There are many other organizations which are looking for someone to help describe Asperger's Syndrome because they don't know very much about Asperger's Syndrome and want to learn more.

Although it wasn't my intention, the organization required for the swim gave me the opportunity to get involved with KPAS, an organization committed to assisting people with Autism Spectrum Disorder to live with dignity and respect through a variety of personalized supports including consultation, vocational training, respite, and residential supports and more. Because I had already learned to live with Asperger's Syndrome without even knowing I had it, part of me had been dormant for years. This part sprang back to life when I made connections with KPAS, started getting to know the members and began giving speeches for them and for other organizations. Not only do the speeches give me the satisfaction of knowing that I am helping others, but they also help me learn more about myself. Now that I have established these connections and

What Next?

realize how much more benefit can come from my swim, it is time to move on. I became energized after my swim when I realized that the swim wasn't really over. My new dream desire to write this book has been renewed and strengthened every time I think about the good that can continue to flow from my accomplishment of crossing Lake Ontario.

When I reflect on my swim across Lake Ontario, I think that it was like a bridge leading me to Kerry's Place Autism Services. I hadn't heard of KPAS until I sought their help with my training. Before the swim, Kerry's Place Autism Services had me speak six times within one year to groups they organized, and then asked me to be the guest speaker for their Annual General Meeting after the swim. It would have been awkward before the swim for me if I had approached them and said, "My name is Jay. I have Asperger's Syndrome. Is there any way I can help? Would you have any use for me as a speaker?" Besides, I didn't know about their organization or what their needs were. During the training for my swim and after it, I crossed the bridge that separated us from each other. They understood my passion for swimming and were proud that I, as an Aspie, had achieved this remarkable goal. I, in turn, had gotten to know about their organization, appreciated their support during my training and wanted to help them in any way I could. Giving speeches and writing this book to raise money for KPAS and other organizations who support young people with Asperger's has really motivated me and given me a great sense of purpose after making my initial dream come true.

After I had spoken for Kerry's Place Autism Services a few times, they invited me to be part of their Board of Directors, but made it clear that I would be invited after the swim when I would have more time. Since then, I have been officially nominated to be part of the board. My mission to swim across Lake Ontario may be over, but my mission to raise awareness for Asperger's Syndrome has just begun.

Conclusions

"If I had my life to live over... I'd dare to make more mistakes next time." – Nadine Stair

At the end of October 2008, I went to a two-hour lane swim and did front crawl nonstop for the entire two hours, which I had done several times during my training. After half an hour, I got tired and didn't want to go on. The next time I saw Andrew, the coach from KMAC, I asked him how someone who gets tired after half an hour could possibly have swum for 41 hours just 3 months ago. Andrew pointed to his forehead and said, "Mind over matter." Several months before the crossing, I had made up my mind that I was going to "keep stroking" until I reached the other side of Lake Ontario regardless of how long it took.

During the contentious discussions about the timing of my swim at the end of February, 2008, Vicki had remarked that I was mentally ready and she agreed with me that putting the Lake Ontario crossing off for another year would make it very difficult for me to keep up my spirits and my fitness. This was not the only time I had heard the phrase "being mentally ready". Now I know from experience what that really means.

Q. What does "mentally prepared" mean?
A. I'm aware that there will be difficulties and I have the determination to keep pressing on despite the difficulties – which is easier said than done.

excerpt from an email message from Swim Master Colleen Shields, October 30, 2008:

When you have a dream and you really want something – your focus changes and sometimes it is really quite amazing what the body will endure because your mind is set to accomplish your goal.

When undertaking a gargantuan task, an Aspie is less likely than a non-Aspie to undertake the task in the first place, but once the candidate has firmly decided to fulfill a goal, an Aspie is more likely to succeed than a non-Aspie.

The following warning is in order here: having completed a marathon swim in the past gives the candidate a psychological advantage but you still need to be prepared mentally. You can never overestimate the importance of being mentally prepared.

I had never stayed awake for much longer than 24 hours; therefore, I had no idea how I was going to stay awake for 30–36 hours. There was only one way to find out and I wasn't going to give up in advance just because of the possibility that I might not be able to stay awake. I would *not* have believed that I could last over 40 hours. I had simply made a firm resolution not to give up and to keep stroking. That resolution may have been easier said than done, but it certainly helped. In hindsight, staying awake and swimming for more than 24 hours was actually easier than staying awake for the same time without something like my Lake Ontario crossing motivating me. My head would have gone under if I hadn't keep moving, which was an incentive to keep on going. Even with all that motivation and momentum behind me, after swimming for 41 hours, I basically passed out as soon as I entered the zodiac. My body was completely spent and I didn't have a single stroke left in it after I touched the Leslie Street Spit wall at the end of my crossing.

For the sake of being cautious, someone pointed out that I should not have attempted the crossing until I had swum continuously for 24 hours at least once. However, I'm not sure that continuing the swim at Chippego Lake would have made any difference. Too much training can overload your capacity and throw your training out of whack. Even if I had continued the swim at Chippego Lake, I may have encountered hypothermia ten minutes before completing my Lake Ontario crossing and then people might have said that I should have swum for 30 hours in training.

Thanks to warnings, I knew all along that hypothermia was a possibility. For the sake of achieving my dream of a lifetime, however, and the added bonus of swimming to raise awareness of Asperger's Syndrome, I was willing to risk hypothermia just that once.

Since I didn't have a coach, I had to oversee my own safety and therefore quit the Chippego Lake swim prematurely. Should I have put off the swim across Lake Ontario for another year? Should I have put off the swim until I'd found a coach? If I hadn't found a coach, should I have put off the swim indefinitely? I believed it was better to complete the swim as soon as I could. When all was said and done, the only reason I resolved to do the swim in 2008 instead of 2007 is that I didn't have enough information in winter of 2006-07 to decide whether I'd be ready to do the crossing in the summer of 2007, but I knew I'd have more than enough facts and experience if I trained for one more year and did my swim in the summer of 2008.

Over a year before the crossing, when I knew I'd have to find a way to organize the swim but hadn't seriously thought about how to do so, I talked with someone was in a position to offer some good advice. He told me that organizing a marathon swim like I was taking on was a lot of work, and I agreed with him. He went on to say that the organization would be more difficult than the training, and therefore I shouldn't focus on the training until I had the organization in place, in case I went through all the training for nothing. I disagreed with him for three reasons: I enjoy swimming, and, if nothing else, I would benefit from the physical activity; I required more training than most candidates in order to complete the crossing; and my conscience wouldn't allow me to impose on other people to assist with the organization unless I was fairly sure I was going to do the swim, and I wouldn't know if I could complete the feat without starting my training.

~

excerpt from e-mail message from Vicki, August 21, 2008:

I am thrilled that you were able to complete your swim. I always measure the success of a swim by the number of obstacles and challenges the swimmer had to overcome to be successful. By my score, your swim was a huge success. Your determination to continue against the odds shows how big a heart you truly have.

Congratulations again!

Vicki

~

excerpt from e-mail message from Jay to Vicki, August 14, 2008:

I don't want you to feel badly for telling me that hypothermia wasn't going to be huge issue. I think what you had been trying to tell me is that I was already aware of the possibility of encountering hypothermia and that there was nothing more I could do to avoid it that I wasn't doing already – except to give up the idea of swimming across Lake Ontario and you would be the last person to tell me to do that.

Vicki's reply, August 21, 2008:

You are right about my comments about the hypothermia, I just felt that you didn't need to focus on that aspect any longer, as you had already done everything in your power to prove to yourself that you could handle cold temperatures. Everyone will get hypothermic sooner or later; you have the mental capacity to push beyond what most people can face and you proved that during your swim.

  The other thing Vicki had been trying to tell me is that swimming across Lake Ontario is no small feat: there are so many aspects and details to be considered in training for and organizing a swim of this magnitude that a swimmer can't afford to waste too much time and energy focusing on any one issue. Hypothermia was only one of several crucial issues to consider. I'm confident that I would not have become hypothermic if the water temperature had been uniformly 70F.
  It is interesting to think what would have happened if I hadn't taken a sabbatical from running. After Jenna swam across Lake Ontario I still would have wanted to do the crossing, but I would have been torn between running and swimming.
  The MDS Nordion marathon in Ottawa began in 1975. There were about 300 participants that year. Now, over 6,000 people participate and the organizers have recently had to set a limit and turn people down. The organizers of the first marathon are likely surprised that the Ottawa Marathon is an annual event over 30 years later. Since then, several more marathons have been founded and run annually. Obviously, people are becoming more aware of the benefits of physical activity. I predict that within the next 50 years, the percentage of people who swim across a great lake will increase tremendously. Although fitness wasn't my initial reason for making exercise a regular part of my daily routine, I have found that being physically fit has been beneficial to my overall wellbeing.
  If I could only give one piece of advice to someone with Asperger's Syndrome, it would be the following: "Get good at something – ideally physical activity." Being good at a physical activity – or something which will make your classmates/peers/coworkers admire you – will increase your chances of being accepted by people. The net result is that you'll be welcomed into a circle of friends long enough for you to learn by example what types of behaviour are socially acceptable and

under what circumstances those behaviour patterns are socially acceptable. You meet people when you share a common interest and marathon activities are a good place to meet others who are very physically active. Gaining the acceptance of people is poor motivation if you're doing it solely for that reason. It takes time to fit in and feel comfortable with a group of friends, so you might become discouraged if you only focus on being socially accepted. It is far better to become physically active because you want to or because it's good for your health - and let other peoples' approval follow naturally.

People were amazed by my dedication to physical activity – cross-country skiing, long-distance cycling, running marathons, and participating in triathlons – even before I thought of swimming across Lake Ontario. It is certainly not necessary to undertake a feat of that magnitude to earn people's respect; I met people who appreciated me as a friend even before they knew I was physically active.

If you want to run a marathon or become physically active to win friends, it might work, but I really don't recommend this as a sole motivation. A desire to make headlines, become famous, and have people be in awe of your accomplishments is absolutely not sufficient motivation to propel someone across Lake Ontario; a feat that big requires much more determination. You have to be driven to achieve that dream, focus all your energy and attention on that goal, and train relentlessly towards it for many months without any distractions if you want to be successful.

excerpt from e-mail message from Vicki, November 5, 2008:

Motivation is a funny thing. You have to be so passionate about achieving your goal that the motivation comes naturally (not always easily) but it is always a part of who you are and what you know you are going to achieve.

Swimming across Lake Ontario – let alone the required training – was not an option for me in high school or university. My courses were sufficiently demanding that I never had enough time to devote to a physical feat of that magnitude. Similarly, swimming across Lake Ontario was not an option while I was job searching because I take a while to adapt to a new situation and I had to be ready to give any new job all my energy and attention. The only time that swimming across Lake Ontario became an option was after I had settled into a job.

Shortly after I decided to swim Lake Ontario, my mother asked my father, "Which is further: across Lake Ontario or across the English Channel?"

My father replied, "The English Channel is rougher."

At first I thought that my father meant that there is less landmass to shield the waves in the English Channel and, therefore, the waves would be higher. I now understand that my father was also referring to the tide, which is not a consideration in swimming Lake Ontario. After I read *Swimming to Antarctica* by Lynne Cox, what my father meant is now crystal clear. You would have to complete crossing the English Channel before the tide changes; otherwise, the swimmer would be pulled backwards. At my speed, it's highly unlikely that I would succeed in swimming across the English Channel.

Once again, however, my friend Karen has shown exceeding faith in me. After I had completed my swim across Lake Ontario, I asked Karen just for the fun of it, "Do you think I could swim across the English Channel?"

Karen replied, "If you really wanted to do it and if you trained for it, yes."

It's heartening, but also frightening to inspire so much confidence in my friends. The temptation might be to take them up on their implied challenge.

Highlights

When I started organizing my swim across Lake Ontario, I thought the most difficult part of the process would be finding people to paddle beside me on my training swims. This was not the case; I simply spread the word, put up posters and then I had many people who were eager to help me.

While recruiting paddling volunteers, I divided all my potential recruits into the following four groups:
Group 1: I am excited and I can't wait to paddle beside you. I would be disappointed if you never ask me to paddle beside you.
Group 2: I am willing to paddle beside you but I'm equally willing not to do so. I won't be disappointed if you don't ask me.
Group 3: I could paddle beside you but I'd prefer not to. Ask me only if you're stuck.
Group 4: I absolutely will not paddle beside you.

I made sure I really wanted to swim across Lake Ontario and that I had some encouraging support before I told too many people.

I may be easily dissuaded initially, but once I have my mind set on something, it is much harder to deter me from reaching my goal than it would be for the average person. I am very focused.

Do not stand in the way of people with Asperger's Syndrome once they are determined to accomplish something; it would be futile. Aspies can and will find a way to overcome any obstacles you place in their paths.

Because of my difficulty multi-tasking, training for a swim across Lake Ontario was not an option for me during high school, university, while I was unemployed, or while I was trying to get settled into a job. The Lake Ontario crossing only became an option after I was settled into a job and had plenty of time to devote to training.

It's easier to train when you have support and it's easier to get support once people know you're committed to a goal. Therefore, the most difficult part of training is often the initial stage – until you've trained long and hard enough to prove to people that you're completely dedicated to achieving your dream.

Being mentally prepared for a marathon swim is ultra-important – perhaps more important than being physically prepared – even if you've done it before.

Being mentally prepared means having the attitude to continue even when the going gets tough.

The fact that I have stamina is partially an illusion; my determination and perseverance are what helps me build my stamina.

The distance across the English Channel is shorter than the distance across Lake Ontario by the traditional route – Niagara-on-the-Lake to Marilyn Bell Park. However, the English Channel is rougher.

Preparing to swim across Lake Ontario involves swimming long distances, swimming in rough waves, swimming continuously for many hours in daylight as well as at night, and acclimatizing to swimming in cold water. In comparison, preparing to climb Mount Everest would involve adapting to walking with low oxygen, which might not be as straightforward.

I do not believe in undertaking any big challenge – and certainly not asking others to support me – unless I have reason to believe that I can successfully complete the challenge. Before I have reason to believe that I could climb Mount Everest, for example, I would need to make sure I could handle strenuous exercise at high altitudes where there are low oxygen levels.

For the longest time, I thought I was wasting my life by following the same fitness routine day after day and participating in the same running races year after year.

I had a number of reasons for taking a voluntary sabbatical from running, but the main reason was to test myself and see if I could stay in shape without relying on running to stay fit. That opened the way for swimming to become my passion and it proved to me that there are a number of ways to stay in excellent condition as an athlete.

I was 26 when I was diagnosed with Asperger's Syndrome.

I still might not know that I have Asperger's Syndrome if Ron Abarbanel hadn't suggested that I make another attempt to get properly diagnosed.

Sometimes I don't want to talk and want to be left alone.

When dealing with an Aspie, it is far better to ask questions that have a specific answer – such as, "How far did you run?" or "Did you win the chess tournament?" – instead of open-ended questions, such as, "How are you?" or "How was your day at school?"

It is almost always the grey areas in which an Aspie falls apart.

I don't have the people skills to say no in a polite way. Therefore, if the other person won't take 'no' for an answer quickly, I have three choices:
1. I say no in a rude way.
2. I give in to what the other person wants.
3. I leave and avoid having contact with that person or people.

In order to explain something to someone else, I often have to translate my terms into the other person's terms. Often, explaining my reasons is more hassle than it's worth and I'm tempted to "give in" and do things the other person's way because that is less of a disturbance than explaining why I am doing things my way.

Sugar combined with mental stress gives me headaches.

I have often found myself doing things which, unbeknownst to me, are deemed inappropriate by most people.

When I'm not sure whether something is appropriate, my solution is to tread lightly and then pay extra attention to the other person's reaction before proceeding. This is often easier said than done.

An unanswered question is often an albatross around my neck.

With an Aspie, everything is usually fine as long as the communication is smooth, but the Aspie will likely collapse as soon as there is disagreement.

One particular individual wronged me three separate times and is now one of my most valuable sources of advice. This is a typical example indicating that if I can make it through the initial problems that may come up when I'm first getting to know someone, things get easier as we go along; I quickly learn who I can work with and who is unable to work with me because of my Asperger's.

My advice to all young people reading this book is as follows: enjoy your youth while you can.

Just as the number of people who run marathons has increased phenomenally over the last 30 years, I predict that within the next 50 years, the percentage of people who swim across a great lake will also increase tremendously.

If I weren't so resistant to cold water, I would not have made it across Lake Ontario; I would have encountered hypothermia much sooner during the crossing and my Swim Master would have had to pull me out.

The threshold at which it is considered safe to train in open water depends mostly on the water temperature. For me, 55°F seems to be a safe cutoff; however, the usual recommended cutoff is 60°F. Wind conditions, air temperature, and access to hot drinks, warm clothes, and shower facilities should also be considered when swimming in cold water.

I have learned through experience that I can handle 55°F water for one hour in broad daylight when I'm well rested – but not for four hours after dark when I'm sleep-deprived.

When training in open water, whenever there is any doubt, play it safe and stay close to shore –ideally within 100 metres.

Avoiding hypothermia means not only knowing when to get out of the water, but what to do after leaving the water; what to do after you get out of the water is more important for increasing your body temperature.

Hypothermia can usually be avoided if the following three conditions are met:
1. the swimmer knows when to get out of the water;
2. the swimmer is able to get out of the water; and
3. the cold swimmer can get to body-warming resources.

Through practice and acclimatization, the body can increase its resistance to cold water.

Prior to the crossing, I had assumed that there wasn't any current in Lake Ontario that I couldn't handle. I had concluded that as long as I didn't get too cold and could keep my head above water, I could make forward progress. I know better now.

Although it wasn't part of my initial plan, swimming across Lake Ontario provided the framework for getting me involved with Kerry's Place Autism Services. My mission to swim across Lake Ontario may be over but my mission to raise awareness for Asperger's Syndrome has just begun.

Frequently Asked Questions

Q1. My child who has Asperger's Syndrome seems stressed out or reluctant to answer when I ask him/her, "How was your day at school?" What could I do differently?
A1. Ask questions with a more specific answer. In grade three, the teacher gave a flashcard drill every day and when I came home from school, my parents would usually ask me, "How did you make out in flashcards today?" I was able to answer this specific question.[66]

Q2. Do you have trouble figuring out if and when people are joking?
A2. I tend to rely mainly on the context in order to decide whether someone is serious or joking. Many people are able to make jokes with a straight face. I tend to resort mainly to solutions that work in most – if not all – cases. I find that relying on facial expressions is often misleading for me so I don't use that to figure out if or when people are joking.

Q3. What is the biggest challenge you face day to day?
A3. Two issues come to mind:
   1. I have difficulty answering a question without going into too much, and often unnecessary, detail. I have trouble deciding on the spur of the moment how much detail is necessary to answer the question. Even if I initiated the conversation, it is typical for me to stop my sentence midword and then begin a totally different thought. This happens because, while I'm speaking, I realize that the other person will better understand what I'm saying if I explain something else first.

Here is an example: Someone once asked me, "Who is Graham?"
   I replied, "When I was in my 2A term at University of Waterloo, Graham had just finished 1A and was supposed to be on a work term. He didn't find a job, so he spent an extra term at University of Waterloo to take some courses. He was in my house in residence."
   The other person commented, "A more concise way of saying that would be 'Graham is a friend from residence'."

---

[66] Be warned though, that the answer to some questions may not always be as simple as you might think, such as the following question: "How many scones did you bake?" (see page 242)

2. I have trouble multi-tasking.
   a. Multi-tasking is especially burdensome when someone asks me to do something while I am focused on something else. If I don't reply, the other person might think I didn't hear him/her. I could say, "I'll answer that later", but I'm often afraid to say that because it will only work a certain number of times, after which the other person will think I don't want to answer the question and I'm using that as an excuse.

   b. I am focused on a task, and someone, often out of interest, asks me to explain what I'm doing. Answering the question often requires me to drop my focus. First, I have to figure out what the other person already knows and then I usually feel that I have to explain something else first. My way of thinking is that one thing must be understood before it can be used to learn another thing. In a perfect world, I would finish what I was doing and then answer the person's question and this would not be considered rude or unusual. My solution has been to try to explain my situation to people when I'm not focused or in a rush and can therefore give them my undivided attention.[67]

Q4. What is the most difficult challenge of living with Asperger's Syndrome?
A4. In order to communicate my thoughts successfully, I have to translate my terms into their terms. If I'm the person who initiated the conversation, then I am usually prepared to take this extra step. If, however, the other person initiated the conversation, I'm caught off guard and not prepared to take this extra step or make the necessary translations. Often when someone asks me a question – especially a question which doesn't have a specific answer such as "What are you doing?" or "Where are you going?" – I have to drop my focus on whatever I was doing to answer the question.

Q5. What is another tough challenge that you face?
A5. I find "cross-examination" very difficult, i.e., when two or more people with different backgrounds ask me questions – either when I'd

---

[67] This is analogous to fixing a leaky roof. You can't fix a leaky roof while it's raining, but you don't see any need to fix it when it's not raining because it doesn't present any problems. The obvious solution is to fix it anyways when it's not raining in anticipation of a future rainfall.

prefer to be left alone or about a topic that I'm not thrilled to talk about. Sometimes, all it takes to set this chain reaction off is for one person to ask me a question. My answer gives the other person or people who listen to the question the ammunition to ask other questions which they otherwise would never have thought to ask. My answer to those questions, in turn, gives the person who asked that first question the go ahead to ask another question, and this gruelling interrogation session goes on and on.

Q6.   What is the most unusual question asked by neurotypical people?
A6.   People ask, "How are you?", when they really mean it sometimes and other times intend it as a greeting. I think this is wrong. I think people should avoid ambiguity by saying "Hello" as a greeting, and reserve "How are you?" to use only when they really mean it.

Q7.   Should we try to "change" people with Asperger's Syndrome or should we leave them as they are? After all, several people – notably Albert Einstein – with Asperger's Syndrome have grown up to accomplish great things.
A7.   It depends on the circumstances, and also on your motives. Are the people with Asperger's being harmful? offensive? disruptive? If they are alone, perhaps they prefer to be left alone or are not ready to interact socially. People can only handle so much social interaction so perhaps they are over their own personal quota for interactions for the day. You could ask yourself if you are trying to change these people for their benefit or for your benefit and act accordingly.

"It does people good to have to do things they don't like to do – in moderation."
—Lucy Maud Montgomery

Q8.   If you could tell the world only *one* thing about Aspies, what would it be?
A8.   Aspies are different than neurotypical people and this is often difficult to realize because they seem normal on the outside. They handle differently than most people. It will take time to learn how to deal with an Aspie. Do not assume – even subconsciously – that they will understand what you are trying to tell then as quickly as you or the average person would, i.e. do not assume the person is trying to be difficult. Communication with an Aspie can go much smoother if both parties make

small but significant changes. Over time, both parties will learn which small changes are significant. In summary, be patient with them.

Q9. In your opinion, do Aspies have a unique, beneficial gift that makes them special when comparing them to neurotypical people?
A9. I think Aspies are very gifted with an excellent memory. They have other attributes like thoroughness, truthfulness, perseverance, and the quality of being less likely to make assumptions, that make them exceptional. Another gift is the ability to think everything through by relying on intellect instead of intuition. This drains the Aspie's energy. but is less likely to lead to misunderstandings between the Aspie and others. [*Attwood, 2007*]

Q10. When is it appropriate to ask you or another Aspie questions?
A10. I don't mind answering questions when I'm relaxed, but *not* when I'm just coming in the door or when I'm en route from one place to another with my mind focused on something else. When I'm writing a letter or working on the computer – and therefore focused – is also *not* the time to ask me questions[68]. When I'm prepared for the questions – and you know that I'm prepared – Is a good time. However, the other person can seldom be expected to know that I'm prepared.

Q11. Have you had any mentors?
A11. I have one sister, Claire, who is two years older than I am; she very knowledgeable about interpersonal skills. I am a born-again Christian and two older Christians from the church in my hometown have been regular mentors to me over the years.

Q12. What helped you while you were growing up?
A12. My mother was a stay-at-home Mom. I lived close enough to walk to school, so I avoided complications taking the bus with other students. I almost always went home for lunch[69] unless there was some specific reason to stay at the school for lunch.
   "Another reason that children with Asperger's Syndrome are more likely to be the target of bullying acts is that they often actively seek and need quiet solitude in the playground. They may be able to cope

---

[68] When I'm writing a letter, it might be okay to ask me questions which have a specific answer and whose answer cannot wait until later, i.e. okay to convey short/quick pieces of information but not the time for chitchat.
[69] The majority of problems at school for children with Asperger's Syndrome happen in unsupervised settings such as recess and the lunch room.

reasonably well with the social demands of the classroom, but when class is over they are mentally and emotionally exhausted. Their restorative for mental and emotional energy is solitude, in contrast to other typical young children whose emotional restoratives in the playground are being noisy, active and sociable. Unfortunately, one of the prime characteristics of a target for bullying is being alone. When children with Asperger's syndrome re-energize by isolating themselves from their peers, they are placing themselves in circumstances that are more likely to make them potential targets of teasing and bullying." [Attwood, 2007, pg. 99]

It also helped that I lived in the same town all my life until I went to university. This meant that neither my parents nor I had to explain my behaviour to several teachers at once – which is the case for people who move to a new town or switch schools.

Q13. You found out that you have Asperger's Syndrome when you were 26 years old. How has that knowledge affected you?
A13. At first, it didn't affect me at all. Now it helps me understand that I am not necessarily unusual. The process of explaining my differences to other people requires more effort at first, but usually pays off in the long run. At first I was afraid to tell people that I have Asperger's Syndrome because I thought they'd look at Asperger's Syndrome as a handicap. I thought my most promising solution was to bluff. Now I am more open and comfortable telling people I have Asperger's because more people have heard about it. Part of the reason I enjoy giving talks about my swim is to inform people about all the abilities that people with Asperger's possess. I want to spread the word about the positive qualities of Asperger's Syndrome to help children who have the syndrome to adapt and make friends like I have.

Q14. My child/brother/sister/friend has Asperger's Syndrome but refuses to get help or – worse yet – refuses to acknowledge that s/he has Asperger's Syndrome). What can I do?
A14. Establishing trusting relationships with Aspies will usually take longer than establishing a relationship with non-Aspies. However, Aspies tend to be predictable and, over time, you will gradually learn how you can change your behaviour effectively. In any relationship, you can usually make small but significant changes. The key is knowing which small changes are significant.

The Ambition of an Aspie

Offering your assistance will definitely be much easier on both sides if the Aspies want to be helped. In the event that they do not want to be helped or refuse to acknowledge their situation, you can:
- be aware of how they processes information differently;
- be patient with them;
- show them that you care, and be ready to go out of your way to help them if necessary;
- be prepared to wait until trust is established. They will open up their feelings in good time after they've learned to trust you. It may be better to wait until this happens than to try and persuade them to unload their frustrations on you before they're ready. I have a word of warning to offer: it is often difficult to get a person with Asperger's Syndrome to stop talking;
- do not assume that the Aspie knows what you mean. For example, in grade one, at recess time, I went back into the school and told my teacher about something that a bully had done to me. The teacher asked me, "Did you tell the teacher on duty?" I didn't know what was meant by "the teacher on duty". I gave no indication that I didn't know what this means and the teacher would have walked away without the slightest clue that I didn't know what she meant.

Q15. Do swimmers wear a wetsuit when swimming across a great lake?
A15. Solo Swims of Ontario, Inc. will not allow marathon swimmers to wear a wetsuit because it is considered floatational assistance. In addition, over that length of time, a wetsuit will rub a swimmer raw[70] (Pacers, however, are allowed to wear wetsuits.)

Q16. Have you thought about joining a swim team?
A16. No. I'm not fast enough to compete. I swim mainly for enjoyment. The pressure to swim fast would create so much stress that it would take the joy out of swimming. It was my determination to succeed and my perseverance to stick with the training regime that got me across Lake Ontario.

Q17. Have you done – or would you consider doing – an ironman?
A17. I had a bad experience doing a half-ironman several years ago.

---

[70] "rub a swimmer raw" means that the swimmer's skin will chafe to the point where it will break open and bleed.

(See Appendix K for more details.) I might do another half-ironman just to say I've done one but I can't see myself ever doing a full ironman.[71]

Q18. The route you took across Lake Ontario included the stretch of water near Toronto that is almost always colder and you also had to fight the Humber River current swimming the route you did. Why didn't you swim across Lake Ontario in the opposite direction?
A18. Niagara-on-the-Lake to Marilyn Bell Park is the traditional route. Swimming the route in the opposite direction would have left me fighting the Niagara River current. Unfortunately, I could not avoid fighting a current at the end of my swim no matter which direction I crossed the lake.

Q19. Why did you choose a weekday (instead of a weekend) for your lake crossing?
A19. It's easier to get media coverage for a weekday but harder to get boat volunteers.

Q20. How did you feel when you entered the water at Niagara-on-the-Lake and couldn't see the other side?
A20. I felt pumped despite not being able to see the other side. I was mentally ready. The training I had done gave me confidence that I could complete the crossing. The adrenaline, the excitement from the crowd, and the encouragement from the crew made the swim easier.

Q21. What was the most difficult part of the swim?
A21. The chill and discomfort of the second night and the frustration at not making obvious progress during the latter part of the swim.

Q22. Do you wish you had been pulled out of the water during your crossing, or are you glad that you were allowed to continue?
A22. I'm glad I wasn't pulled. Words cannot express the satisfaction I felt after I completed the crossing.

Q23. If you had known both during the training process and the actual swim what you know now, what would you do differently?

---

[71] Since this document was begun, I completed the Canadian Iron 113 (half-ironman distance) triathlon in September 2009, which is part of the annual Somersault series (www.somersault.ca).

A23.
- I would hire someone to transport me in a powerboat to 10 kilometres from Marilyn Bell Park and stay beside me while I swim the last 10 kilometres in order to get an idea of how difficult the last stretch would be. Then again, how would I have knows that 10 killometres was the magic distance at which the combined effects of the Humber River current and the wind-generated lake circulation currents become noticeable? I'm not sure how I could have known that without actually doing the crossing.
- Secondly, I would try sooner and harder during my training to find a pool with longer, more openly-accessible lane swims.
- Finally, I would start doing Vicki's prescribed speed workouts earlier as well as regularly doing them once a week.

Q24. Would you swim across Lake Ontario again?
A24. I can't see that happening. The training took its toll on me. Now that I have demonstrated that Aspies can accomplish large feats if they put their minds to it, doing it again would result in diminishing marginal returns. It's time to help the Asperger's community in other ways.

References

Attwood, Tony. *The Complete Guide to Asperger's Syndrome*. London: Jessica Kingsley Publishers, 2007.

Cantkier, Eden. *In the Wake of Greatness*. "Living with Autism", Kerry's Place Autism Services, Fall 2008.

Cox, Lynne. *Swimming to Antarctica*. Alfred A. Knopf, 2004.

Diamond, Harvey and Marilyn Harvey. *Fit for Life*. Warner Books Inc., 1985.

Forgey, William W., M.D. *Hypothermia – Death by Exposure*. ICS Books, Inc., 1985

Laughlin, Terry. *Total Immersion – The Revolutionary Way to Swim Better, Faster, and Easier*. FIRESIDE, 1996.

Myles, Brenda Smith and Richard L. Simpson. *Asperger Syndrome: a guide for educators and parents*. PRO-ED Inc., 1998.

Pyles, Lise. *Hitchhiking through Asperger Syndrome*. London: Jessica Kingsley Publishers, 2002.

Serdula, Jay. "How to Say No: The Straw that Broke the Camel's Back", unpublished.

Tannen, Deborah. *That's not what I meant*. The Random House Publishing Group, 1986.

http://community. livejournal.com/ask_an_aspie (*website last visited on November 21, 2009)

http:// soloswims.com/sso.htm (*website last visited on November 21, 2009)

http://www.sarbc.org/hypo1.html (*website last visited on November 21, 2009) http:// members. fortunecity.com/fuzzyklik/iqtest.htm (*website last visited on November 21, 2009)

http:// www. swim4aspergers.wordpress.com (*website last visited on November 30, 2009)

http://www.freshpatents.com/-dt20090430ptan20090107491.php (*website last visited on November 21, 2009)

Appendix A

Outline of a Typical Talk Given by Jay

Introduction

Thank you very much for having me. My name is Jay Serdula. I was born in 1972 and I have Asperger's Syndrome.

My education

In 1996, I completed a Bachelor of Applied Mathematics with electrical engineering electives at the University of Waterloo. In 2003, I completed a Masters degree in Physics/Oceanography at the Royal Military College of Canada.

My employment

I am currently employed as a research assistant in the Chemical Engineering Department at the Royal Military College of Canada. I am working as a civilian and I study defective fuel rods in nuclear reactors, doing mostly mathematical analysis and computer programming.

Just like cars need gasoline to run, nuclear reactors need fuel to make them operate. On rare occurrences, a fuel sheath may become defective; this causes coolant to leak into the fuel, making the fuel rod defective. At the same time, radioactive nuclides leak into the coolant. My supervisor and I are working on devising algorithms that will predict the number of defective fuel rods in a reactor based on a measurement of the concentration of radionuclides in the coolant. This knowledge will assist power stations to deal with defective fuel and to decide whether there is a need to shut down a reactor when the fuel fails. If we can find a way to reduce the amount of exposure to station personnel, this will result in a more efficient operation at the station.

How Asperger's Syndrome affects me

Asperger's Syndrome affects me in the following ways[72]:

---

[72] There are other stories which I usually include in my speech but they are omitted because they are found elsewhere in the book.

I take words and phrases literally

When I was eight and my sister was ten, my father broke his leg and was in the hospital for two days. There was a sign in the hospital that said, "Maximum two visitors. Children under 12 are not allowed." Just before we left the house, my mother said to my sister and me, "If there's no nurse nearby, quietly follow me down the hall."

My sister asked, "What if she comes in when we're in there?"

My mother replied, "She'll kick you out."

I thought my mother meant that the nurse would pick up my body and kick it out of the room like a soccer ball.

I am very focused but cannot multitask

I found myself in a difficult situation every day in the first months after taking a job away from home. My landlords asked me, "How was your day, Jay?" as soon as I opened the door to my apartment. Also, the dog would come racing toward me and I was afraid it would jump on me and shred my brand new coat. As soon as the dog got too close for comfort, I would shake one leg rapidly and the dog would immediately turn around and run in the opposite direction, which is precisely what I wanted.

The landlords would say, "Jay, don't shake your leg because it gets the dog all excited."

I didn't have the nerve to be sarcastic and say, "Nice try! How could I be responsible for "getting" the dog excited when it already is excited?"

I tried to take off my coat, answer the question, and ward off the dog all at the same time. And that happened every single day. In hindsight, I wish I'd explained to them when I moved in that I prefer that people don't ask me questions when I'm "in transition", i.e. coming home or leaving for work. I can cope with a specific question that requires a straightforward answer if the question is being asked as a request for exact information, not out of general interest. Transitional times are *not* the times to ask me questions. That's because I'm focused on what I need to do next. I highly recommend to people that they give me a few minutes to get settled or else warn me by asking me if I have a minute to answer a question.

On the contrary, I am able to focus on something and block out all other distractions, once I have my focus. For example, there has been more than one case in which I was playing a chess game in an otherwise social setting. I'd be bent over slightly with both elbows on the table and both hands touching my forehead. One of the spectators commented that I was clearly focused on the chess game and nothing else.

I get "sidetracked" by one sentence

An older Christian mentor at my church knows that it is typical of me to try to understand everything I hear. When he's talking to me, often he'll be able to discern that I'm following what he's saying, and then, all of a sudden, I will look confused. That's almost always because I don't understand one sentence and I'm so focused on trying to understand that particular sentence that I don't pay attention to what he says next. When he notices that I look confused, he will find out which statement he said that confused me, back up, explain that statement and then proceed.

∽

Elementary school

When I was in grade one, my teacher believed – with reason – that I wasn't physically capable of sitting still. She made a written request to the director of the school board that I be taken out of the school board unless I was put on Ritalin.

My father objected and firmly said to the teacher, "No way I am doping my kid for your sake."

"But he can't sit still. He needs Ritalin for his own benefit," the teacher continued.

"He can sit still," my father insisted.

My father agreed to come to the classroom. While he was present, I sat still and behaved just like anyone else in the classroom. This is because I knew I would have been in trouble with my father if I didn't behave. As soon as he left, I was back to my normal behaviour.

My father said to the teacher, "Do I have to come to the classroom every day to make sure he sits still? It's your job to control the students. You haven't got class control."

At the time, I had no idea that there was any communication – let alone disagreement – between my parents and my teacher or principal regarding my behaviour until 11 years later when my parents showed me the movie *Rain Man*; after we watched the movie, they explained that I had a lot of traits similar to those of the main character in the movie. They told me that I might be autistic. Then they told me about what had been going on behind the scenes in Grade 1. That year, I spent a lot of time in the principal's office because the teacher would send me there whenever I misbehaved.

After my father had "proven" to my Grade 1 teacher that I could sit still, the teacher started devising "charts". Each square of the chart represented half-hour blocks and if I was good for the entire half hour, the teacher would give me a sticker to put in that square. If I was bad, the teacher would write an X in the box. If I was good for the first half hour and, less than two minutes later did something naughty, the teacher would say to me, "Jay, you just lost your sticker for hitting your classmate."

At another time, everyone was given a piece of cardboard in the shape of a train with their name on it. The "trains" were connected together along the bottom of the classroom wall so that it looked like a long choo-choo train. Whenever someone did something good, such as helping a classmate get dressed for recess, that person would get a sticker to put on their choo-choo train. At first, it took me a while to get accustomed to the process. Sometimes it takes me a while to catch on to routines, but once I've caught on, I can follow the routine with ease – as long as the idea is reasonably straightforward. Before long, I had more stickers than anyone else.

In Grade 2, I don't remember my regular teacher ever sending me to the principal's office, but I do remember my French teacher sending me to the principal's office twice: once for pushing a girl out of her chair. I didn't mean to hurt her – I just push her too hard – and the second time for emptying the pencil shavings from the sharpener into the same girl's hair. Apparently, the teachers had realized that sending me to the principal's office wasn't "working". I had a social worker spend one-on-one time with me fairly regularly that year.

In Grade 2, there was a table in the classroom where students could do paintings or glue pictures in their spare time. An old tablecloth was spread on top of the table to catch the paint and glue. Using a pair of scissors, I would cut strips in the tablecloth. I pretended that the tablecloth was a road map, and each time I cut a strip, I was making another road. Around that time, we were planning a class trip to the forestry station and some adults were needed to help so my mother volunteered. One day when I was just about to make another "road" in the tablecloth, the teacher said, "Jay, when your Mom comes in for the forestry trip, I'm going to show her that.

I was scared. I dreaded the day of the trip thinking, *I am going to be in T-R-O-U-B-L-E*.

The trip had been scheduled for the afternoon, and immediately before the teacher dismissed the class for lunch, she announced that the forestry trip had been cancelled. It got re-scheduled for another day and my mother couldn't make it that day, so she found someone to replace her. I never cut the tablecloth again after the teacher said she would show it to my mother. My mother never found out what I had done to the tablecloth – until I told her years later and she just laughed.

In Grade 1 and 2, I had a female teacher. In Grade 3, I had a male teacher. I didn't know until my mother pointed it out years later, that having a male teacher really helped me. That's because I was less likely to resist male authority. Every day, students were given a one-hour break for lunch and a fifteen minute recess both in the morning and in the afternoon.

One day between morning recess and lunch time, the teacher said, "You step out of that seat once between now and dinner time and you're in trouble." I thought "dinner time" meant supper time but he probably meant lunch time. Respecting the teacher's authority, I sat still in my chair for the rest of the day, knowing that I was allowed to leave for lunch and afternoon recess. The teacher's reprimand worked better than he thought it would!

My parents got connected with a staff worker at a summer camp for children with behaviour problems. In Grade 3, that staff worker agreed to come to my school to see if the camp would be suitable for me. He observed me in the classroom and the playground. He didn't think there was anything wrong with me so my parents were getting different stories from different people.

The book *Hitchhiking through Asperger Syndrome* by Lise Pyles contains not only an entire chapter on school in general, but another chapter on school specifics. Two of the problems mentioned that I completely identify with are "gotcha" and "the common denominator".

Other students know how to pick on a student with Asperger's Syndrome while staying under the teacher's radar. My classmates would often see a teacher approaching at the other end of the hallway. They would ge*ntly* nudge me and then I'd finally react by hitting one of them. I would get in trouble because the teacher saw what I did, but hadn't seen what the other students did.

There are several other ways in which the classmates picked on me in subtle ways. If I didn't react, that would give the students a license to continue disturbing me, but if I did react, I would get into trouble for the reaction. Either way, the other students had me at a disadvantage, hence Lise Pyles's term, "gotcha".

Students with Asperger's Syndrome are often a target for teasing and bullying since they are different. It is not uncommon for them to be bullied by one classmate on Mondays, a different classmate on Tuesdays and so on. By Friday, the Aspies have been bullied by five different people and teachers assume that the Aspies are the cause of the problem. Just because an Aspie is the "common denominator" to a problem doesn't mean that she or he was the cause of the problem.

For more examples on how people with Asperger's Syndrome are taken advantage of in school see Appendix B.

Finding out about true friends

At one time, I had so few friends that I was lonely. This made me a perfect target for people to be nice to me in order to win my trust, only to take advantage of it later. I learned the hard way that just because people were nice to me didn't mean that they are my "friends". It takes time for people to appreciate and accept me for who I am. Therefore, if they don't accept me right away, that doesn't mean that they won't become my friends once they understand me better. Even a "true" friend may get frustrated with me once in a while – or just need space. In grade school, one friend, Derek, seemed to be the ideal friend. He was a good listener and he always came to my assistance when others tried to take advantage of me. At least two separate times, while Derek and I were out for a leisurely bicycle ride, someone noticed me and said, very slowly, "Jay Serdula" in order to aggravate me. Derek looked straight towards the person and said, "Got a problem, kid?" However, more than once, Derek said, "I'm never speaking to you again." Within a few days, he was nice to me again – but I remember that "a few days" seemed like a long time at that age. Chances are, either something I had done had frustrated him or he needed time away from me in order to "recharge his batteries". Therefore, someone who won't help me isn't necessarily my enemy.

Appendix A

excerpt from Appendix 3 (Social Skills) of Hitchhiking through Asperger Syndrome by Lise Pyles [Pyles, 2002, pg. 257]:

What is a friend?

Do they give things to you? Share with you? Do they take turns with you? Offer to help you? Walk with you?

What is not a friend?

Do they make fun of you? Hurt you? Do they try to make you do bad things? Do they take things from you?

When Dealing with an Aspie

If I could only give one piece of advice to someone dealing with people with Asperger's Syndrome, it would be: "You have be firm with them."

If you tell Aspies that something is not acceptable, they will try it again. Then you tell them – again – that it is not acceptable. After you tell them three or four times, they will get the message that it is not acceptable and will stop doing it.

Another piece of advice I would give is: "Be careful asking questions that don't have specific answers[73] including 'How are you?'"

How are you?

In Canada, the question "How are you?" is, more often than not, intended as a greeting and not for its literal meaning. Many times, someone has asked me "How are you?" when I'm focused on something, under stress or would prefer not to be disturbed. I'd prefer that people say "Hello" instead of "How are you?"

In any event, often I don't know how to answer the question and have been accused of "not talking". Seeing that the other person often wants only a greeting in return, my solution is to "beat" the other person to it and say "hello" first. If s/he replies with "How are you?", I'm allowed to disregard the question because I've already reciprocated the greeting. This works most of the time, but doesn't always work.

---

[73] Some questions may seem to have a specific answer that actually do not, such as "How many scones did you bake?" (see page 242)

It has happened that I say "hello" to people and they reply with "How are you?" not once, but twice. I've explained to them that when they reply to my "hello" with "How are you?" once, that's one thing, but when they say it twice, that sends the message that they're not satisfied with my initial "hello" and they're training me not to say "hello" to them in the first place. The way I see it, I am saddled with the burden of answering a question which I might not have had to answer if I had rudely ignored them. In one case, someone told me I was being silly and had thought I didn't hear her when she repeated "How are you?". I also have to be guarded with my facial expressions in these cases: it's very important that I don't let my facial expression contradict what I'm saying, which is almost impossible to do when I'm under stress.[74]

If this doesn't work, my next line of defense is to say, "This is your last warning. If you reply to my "hello" with "How are you?" twice on one more occasion, I'm going to stop saying "hello" to you." This works effectively if only a few people disregard the warning and only if I remember to whom I've issued the warning. If too many people disregard this warning, the effort required to follow through with the warning will overwhelm me.[75]

Upon hearing my viewpoint, more than one person has told me to lie and say "I'm fine" even if I'm not. Ninety-nine times out of one hundred, this works. However, the one hundredth time, when it doesn't work, is not only going to happen when I least expect it, but also when I'm stressed out and therefore not in a position to comfortably figure out what is required to "shake the other person loose". People ask "How are you?" expecting to hear nothing other than "I'm fine" – sometimes threatening to "blow up" upon hearing any other response. Why ask a question when you already know what the answer is going to be? That doesn't make sense. It's far better to say "hello" and expect a "hi" back.

How many scones did you bake?

I like to bake scones and my father would often walk through the kitchen while I was baking and ask me, "How many scones did you

---

[74] In Sweden, unlike in Canada, "How are you?" is taken for its literal meaning. "You know you've been in Sweden too long when someone asks you "Hi, how are you?" you actually take time out to explain how you are." (http://aussieclouds.appspot.com/sweden/youknow.html) I have jokingly told people that I want to move to Sweden to avoid being saddled with the burden of answering the question "How are you?"

[75] As it turned out, on a later date this person asked me, "How are you?" and then immediately corrected herself by saying, "Hello" – thus acknowledging that she remembered that she wasn't supposed to ask me "How are you?"

make this time?" Not being able to multi-task, I would have to drop everything to be able to focus and answer my father's question. Once, I decided that the next time my father asked that question, I would reply, "Twenty-four" – an approximate number. When that happened, my father replied, "Are you sure it wasn't twenty-five?"

I finally took the time and effort to explain to my father – in a letter – the impact that this question had on me. It was worth the time and effort, but I can't always take the time to use this "brute force" method every time someone says or does something disturbing. I wrote:

> *You have asked me that question so many times that I'm going to ask you some questions:*
> *Why does the exact number of scones matter?*
> *How badly do you want to know the answer to that question?*
> *How urgently do you want to know the answer to that question?*
> *Are you aware that how large/small I cut the scones affects how many scones there are but does not affect the total overall mass or volume of scones?*
> *Are you aware that your question puts me in an awkward situation? (The true answer is "I don't know" but I'm afraid to tell you that because I'm afraid you'll yell at me and say, "If you don't know, who knows? I sure as h*** don't know?")*
> *Do you expect me to count them?*
> *If so, do you expect me to do so before they're finished baking?*
> *If so, do you expect me to take them out of the oven while I count them or leave the oven door open and stick my head in and risk burning myself while I count them?*
>
> *Just in case I haven't made myself clear, I don't want you to ask me that question EVER AGAIN. If you think this is too harsh, then don't ask that question until you have answered all of the above-mentioned questions.*

Questions NOT to ask Jay

The next time I came home, my father had a list on the fridge entitled "Questions NOT to ask Jay":

How many scones did you bake?

Incidentally, my father – like me – also needs, on occasion, to be given specific instructions, but is good at holding steadfast to the instructions once they're stated clearly.

Concluding remarks

My sister, Claire, pointed out that when I tell stories, I often go into too much detail. Often, the people don't really care about the small details. I read in [*Myles and Simpson, 1998*]: "For example, a child may discuss at length a single topic that is of little interest to others." When I mentioned this quote to Claire, she replied sarcastically, "That doesn't sound at all like you!" Claire went on to say that it's interesting that there's actually a name for what I have, but that's good as well as bad. It's good because she can do some reading on the syndrome, but it's bad in that I lose my uniqueness. Claire had always thought of that behaviour as "just Jay". She had seen similar behavioural patterns to a lesser degree in herself and in Mom and Dad. I later thought to myself: *Take heart Claire. There are vast differences among people with Asperger's Syndrome.*

Appendix B

Excerpt From *Hitchhiking Through Asperger Syndrome* by Lise Pyles

excerpt from Chapter 6, *School Specifics* of *Hitchhiking through Asperger Syndrome* by Lise Pyles [Pyles, 2002, pg. 153]

Bullying is More than Hitting

It's not enough to ensure your child doesn't come home with bruises. Here are some of the many ways our kids can be made miserable that I've compiled from a few articles on the topic. These are all types of bullying: hitting, kicking, spreading rumors, threats, rude gestures, pushing, tripping, stalking, excluding, silent treatment, insults, unwanted touching, making fun of, hurtful comments, staring, damage to personal belongings, name calling, encouraging or daring to do something wrong. Only two of these categories would produce a bruise!

One would think that that's a pretty hefty list, but they forgot a few. To give you a more vivid picture, here are some of the things my own son has endured. I hope teachers all over the world are reading this, because every incident happened on school property:

- books, calculator, money, lunch stolen (many episodes)
- repeatedly touched on the back of the neck, causing a startle reflex
- sand poured in his ear
- moths put down his back
- kept from his locker by four kids
- given a 'wedgie'
- soda poured all over him
- mustard packet squished on him
- banana peels and other things thrown at him
- rude caricatures drawn of him
- books pushed to the floor
- lunch box hidden in tree
- dead poisonous snake put in his locker
- ink and paint put on his shirt

Appendix C

Infallible IQ Test

Mix and match the following:

___ 1. That which Noah built.
___ 2. An article for serving ice cream.
___ 3. What a bloodhound does in chasing a woman.
___ 4. An expression to represent the loss of a parrot.
___ 5. An appropriate title for a knight named Koal.
___ 6. A sunburned man.
___ 7. A tall coffee pot perking.
___ 8. What one does when it rains.
___ 9. A dog sitting in a refrigerator.
___ 10. What a boy does on the lake when his motor won't run.
___ 11. What you call a person who writes for an inn.
___ 12. What the captain said when the boat was bombed.
___ 13. What a little acorn says when he grows up.
___ 14. What one does to trees that are in the way.
___ 15. What you do if you have yarn and needles.
___ 16. Can George Washington turn into a country?

  A. hypotenuse   I. circle
  B. polygon   J. axiom
  C. inscribe   K. cone
  D. geometry   L. coincide
  E. unit   M. cosecant
  F. center   N. tangent
  G. decagon   O. hero
  H. arc   P. perpendicular

reference: http://members.fortunecity.com/fuzzyklik/iqtest.htm

Appendix D

Injuries

During my second last semester at the University of Waterloo, I was running from one place to another when my shins started hurting. Having been taught that, the more one can accomplish in a given time period, the better, I lived every single term of my undergraduate degree in the fast lane[76]. I did not enjoy that fast-paced lifestyle, and have no desire to go back to it. The fact that my case of Asperger's Syndrome made it difficult to find a co-op job meant that I had to spend almost all term every term looking for a job in addition to taking courses. This certainly didn't help matters. At the time, it was typical of me to try to save time by running instead of walking. (Since it was winter, riding my bicycle was not an option.)

The shin pain continued for several days. Someone told me that a common cause of this pain is that the shin bones are about to break. In other words, that I was suffering from a stress fracture, which is analogous to breaking a wooden ruler, but not quite separating it into two pieces.

Two weeks after the pain began, I saw a physiotherapist and, luckily, the problem was muscle-related and not bone-related. I had had a paper route ever since grade six, and did not relinquish it until I began attending university, since I was unable to find any other job except for mowing lawns. While delivering papers I was forced to walk on ice so many times that I discovered I could get "better traction" by lifting my entire foot instead of pushing backwards against the ground with my toes. I unknowingly trained myself to continue walking and running in this manner until I encountered the muscular side effects years later. The net result was that my calf muscles were weak from lack of use, while the muscles at the front of my legs below the knee were fatigued from overuse. These muscles got especially fatigued when I was running and more so when I wore winter boots, which are heavier than running shoes. The physiotherapist told me to do calf raises: stand with my toes on the edge of stairs and raise my entire body using only one leg. I also continued to put ice on my shins

---

[76] I take things literally and, to me, "live life in the fast lane" means that every task I undertake must be completed in as little time as possible or, alternatively, I must accomplish as much as possible within any given time period. In this case, I am given so much to do and the deadlines are too tight that I feel forced to complete each task in as little time as possible.

The Ambition of an Aspie

for two years. (I probably could have stopped sooner, but icing became part of my running routine.) Jens commented that, if there were ever a running race on ice, I would win.

I ran my first marathon in Calgary, ran the Around the Bay 30K Road Race in Hamilton and had planned to run another marathon in Ottawa – all within one year and all with the same pair of running shoes – until I encountered knee pain resulting from a tight ilio-tibial band (ITB). The first solution was to buy new running shoes. With a full-time job, I could now easily afford new shoes. But how badly did I want to continue running to the extent that I was running?

The point was that I was either doing too much exercise or not enough stretching. Take your pick. I'm lucky that my muscles complained before my bones did. For years, I had been stretching before and after a workout, but only doing three different types of stretches: two stretches for the quadriceps, and one for the hamstrings. Because of the ITB injury, I added two more stretches: ilio-tibial band and hip flexor.

Every day, I spent thirty minutes doing basic leg exercises and fifteen minutes massaging the ilio-tibial band in addition to icing and stretching. Someone commented that stretching my leg and icing my leg and rubbing my leg was a full-time job. The fact was that running meant a lot to me, and I wanted to get back into running quite badly, so this routine was worth it.

The physiotherapist recommended that I buy a four-pronged massager so that I could massage my leg. When Gunnar and Chantal came to visit me on their way through Kingston, I told Gunnar about my tight ilio-tibial band, showed him the massager and told him that I've been using Johnson's baby lotion on my leg to make the massager glide more smoothly. I went on to say that, without the lotion, the massager won't glide smoothly because of the hair on my leg. Gunnar replied that he has that problem too.

"Oh, you also have a tight ilio-tibial band?"

Gunnar replied, "No, I also have hair on my legs."

◈

In 2001, I had a part-time job as a lab assistant while doing a Masters degree. One morning, I was sitting at my desk marking tests. My car had broken down on my way back to Kingston the day before; hence the time pressure. I was sitting in a certain position for so long that, when I tried to stand up, I had to hunch over for twenty seconds before I could stand. I did not try running for a few weeks.

The following summer, I played on the church baseball league, which I had joined every summer since moving to Kingston. While cycling home from a baseball game, I hurt my back. I'm not sure whether that was from being in a hunched-over position for too long or wearing a backpack that was too heavy. (It's typical of me to carry an unusual amount of luggage. Bicycle rides are no exception since I like to make sure I have lots of food, water and sunscreen.) I resorted to unusual measures including putting a towel in the freezer so that I could "ice" my back by lying on the chilled towel.

My back continued to give me problems on and off for a few years. In April 2005, while visiting my sister in Calgary, I went downhill skiing for a day. One could get a bus from downtown Calgary to Sunshine Village plus a lift ticket for a decent price. I took a taxi from Claire's house to downtown. I didn't want to take public transit lest I risk missing the bus. On the way home, as usual, I tried to save money by taking public transit. I wasn't sure where to catch the bus so I started walking, hoping to locate the bus route, and ended up walking all the way back to Claire's house carrying my ski gear, which took about 45 minutes.

The next morning, when I got out of bed, I couldn't stand up straight for several minutes without pain. For the first time in my life, I took ibuprofen. It took forty-five minutes before I noticed any significant improvement to the pain. Two hours later, the problem returned and I would have taken two more ibuprofen tablets, except that the bottle said to wait four hours. One of Claire's friends told me that one's muscles are typically stiffer when one first gets out of bed. If I had known the truth of this statement then, I wouldn't have taken ibuprofen, but would have tried extra-hard to adjust my lifestyle to reduce the pain without taking medication. For the rest of the week, if I wanted to pick something up, I could not bend over in the usual way; I had to squat and keep my torso vertical.

✥

At Christmas of 2007, while I was visiting my parents, I developed plantar fasciitis in my right foot. This could be because, when I'm visiting my parents, I have more spare time and therefore do a lot of baking, which requires me to stand for long periods of time. Since then, I have been wearing running shoes indoors whenever possible. Nonetheless, with my heart set on swimming across Lake Ontario, I continued to run to the 6:00 a.m. Masters swimming practices – except when I could get a ride – until bicycle season returned.

After the swim, the natural thing to do would be to have some downtime and not do another physical feat too soon. However, every year the Aspergers Society of Ontario (ASO) has a few people participate in the annual Scotiabank Marathon, which involves collecting pledges. ASO asked me to be their ambassador and paid my registration fee, an opportunity I couldn't turn down.

For a week after the marathon, I had plantar fascitis in both feet – until one week after the marathon when my right foot magically healed. Since then, my left foot has bothered me more than my right foot used to. About one month after the marathon, I ran 8 kilometres and found it noticeably painful to stand the next day. This made me think that perhaps I shouldn't press my luck. Perhaps I shouldn't run, but resolve to be happy as long as I can swim, cycle, cross-country ski, stand, and walk. It has been suggested that I "speed up" the healing process by taking ibuprofen but, being a firm disbeliever in taking drugs, I don't want to go that route if I can possibly avoid it. Unlike with the back injury, I am able to perform life's essentials – sleeping, showering, dressing myself, eating, standing, and walking short distances – without any noticeable pain or discomfort.

In high school, not wanting to leave the house without saying where I was going, I would often say to my mother, "I'm going out for a run."

Many times, my mother replied, "You're lucky you can run."

Eventually I made a resolution to reply to that comment each time with, "You're lucky to be born with enough talent to get a job to live this long."

Given that, except for the paper route, I had never been hired on a company payroll outside my family, I had reason to believe that I may never get a job. Therefore, I might not be able to support myself long enough to live to be my mother's current age.

The reason my mother had problems trying to run is that she wasn't stretching. More than a year after the doctor told my mother not to run anymore, my mother was shown some stretches – after which she was able to resume running. People with Asperger's Syndrome require a routine, and I am adamant about following a routine of stretching before and after a workout. Within one year after starting university, I could not run without knee pain unless I did a warm-up run for two or three minutes and then stretched and then did my run. (I was in better shape ten years later, and I'm still in better shape now than I was then.)

This is what you're supposed to do anyway, because you're not supposed to stretch cold muscles. Likewise, after finishing a run, you should stretch and then do a cool-down run. I have been stretching so long that I notice when I try to exercise without stretching first. Stretching before a workout is important; failure to do so results in problems during the workout – these problems are easier to notice and easier to deal with. Stretching after a workout is more important; failure to do so results in problems later on – these are harder to notice and harder to deal with.

Once, while walking to the bus stop, I was in a hurry, so I tried to run part of the way. I had difficulty running for very long at once (not only because of my foot, but I'd also get short of breath earlier than I had before). That day, I made a startling discovery: I'm not young anymore. Then again, perhaps the reason I had to breathe harder was that I hadn't run for a while, so my lungs weren't used to it. Either way, my advice to all the young people reading this is to enjoy your youth while you can.

Appendix E

Letter to Asperger's Society of Ontario

Ms. Margot Nelles
Aspergers Society of Ontario
161 Eglinton Ave. East #401
Toronto, Ontario
M4P 1J5

October 27, 2006

Dear Ms. Nelles:

My name is Jay Serdula. I am a 34-year-old single man with Asperger's Syndrome, living in Kingston, Ontario. I work as a civilian researcher at the Royal Military College of Canada. I am interested in working with the Aspergers Society of Ontario to help raise money for your organization.

I ran my first marathon in the summer of 1999 and have run five more marathons since then. Since 1990, I have competed in one or two triathlons each summer. As a personal challenge, I plan to swim across Lake Ontario in the summer of 2008. This challenge, if fulfilled, will illustrate that people with Asperger's Syndrome can, indeed, live happy and healthy lives. At the same time, I would like to collect pledges to the Asperger's Society of Ontario from family members, friends, co-workers and neighbours. This will raise awareness of Asperger's Syndrome plus support your organization financially.

This marathon swim will require insurance, gasoline for the accompanying vessels, paramedic services and food for the support crew, which could easily bring the cost of the swim to ten thousand dollars ($10,000.00) or more. In anticipation of this cost, I am asking whether I may draw upon your fundraising expertise to help publicize the event to organizations which may be able to assist. This assistance may be accomplished in several ways including but not limited to: contacting various marinas to either donate a support vessel or provide one at a reduced rate, contacting oil and gasoline companies regarding subsidy of gasoline, and contacting grocery stores regarding food supplies. Under affiliation with the Aspergers Society of Ontario, I would be happy to make these contacts if permitted. A complete list of the requirements for the marathon swim can be found at http://soloswims.com/sso.htm and clicking on the link to the PDF file.

In July, Ms. Jenna Lambert, 15, of the greater Kingston area swam across Lake Ontario from Baird's Point, New York to Kingston, Ontario as a fundraiser for the Penguins Swim Club of the local YMCA. The Penguin Swim Club is a club for people with physical disabilities. Ms. Lambert was coached by Swim Master Vicki Keith of the Solo Swims of Ontario. Ms. Lambert has cerebral palsy and swam using only her upper body. She was accompanied by five boats, all of which were donated.

In order for your organization to get to know me better and vice versa, I am available to come to Toronto for an interview at your convenience. I look forward to hearing from you and discussing with you how we may be of mutual assistance with each other.

Sincerely,

Jay Serdula

Appendix F

Letter to Special Olympics Kingston

Mr. XX
Special Olympics Kingston
1412 Princess Street
Kingston, Ontario
K7M 3E5

March 12, 2007

Dear Mr. XX:

My name is Jay Serdula. I am a 34-year-old man with Asperger's Syndrome. For the last seven years, I have lived in Kingston and worked as a civilian research assistant at the Royal Military College. (I am not a member of the military.)

Last summer, I set a goal to swim across Lake Ontario. I plan to do it as a fundraiser for the Asperger's Society of Ontario (ASO) (www.aspergers.ca). My tentative date for the crossing is August 2008. This goal, if fulfilled, will benefit the ASO (as well as the Asperger's community in general) in three ways: (1) it will raise financial support for the ASO; (2) it will raise awareness of the existence of ASO and of Asperger's Syndrome in general; (3) it will demonstrate that people with Asperger's Syndrome are, in fact, capable of unusual feats.

At the end of last August, I swam from HMCS Cataraqui to the ferry dock on Wolfe Island (5.25 kilometres). One of my friends, who is a member of the Cataraqui Canoe Club, paddled his kayak beside me. For the winter, I have joined the Kingston Masters Aquatic Club at Artillery Park. I look forward to being able to train in open water in the spring. My plan is to swim in some of the smaller lakes in May and to be swimming in Lake Ontario by early June.

Unlike training for a running marathon, one cannot train for a swimming marathon alone; one needs to be accompanied by a boat for safety reasons as a swimmer is hardly visible to motorboats and the boat should carry a spare lifejacket in the event that the swimmer gets tired or gets a cramp. It is also helpful for the swimmer to have an accompanying boat in order to help point the swimmer in a straight line and to carry food and water, which are required for long swims.

With my condition of Asperger's Syndrome, it is difficult for me to reach out to people. When I ask people to accompany me on my training swims, I am often unable to discern from their intonation whether they are outright refusing but not wanting to be impolite or only mildly interested. Several people have declined to paddle a canoe or kayak beside me on my training swims on account of family obligations, job obligations plus their own personal life. Most people are uncertain about what is required, with the net result being that few people are willing to volunteer.

Please note that I am referring to finding accompanists on my training swims and not for the actual event. I have several friends from out of town who are willing to be part of the boat crew for the actual event. Solo Swims of Ontario Inc. (soloswims.com/sso.htm) will make sure that I have the necessary equipment and support team. The few local friends I have found who are willing to accompany me on my training swims will not be able to do so all the time. My hope is to find several willing people and rotate among them. This summer and next summer, I plan to do a long swim (~> 4 hours) every weekend plus once during the week. I also hope to do one marathon swim 24 hours long and be accompanied by a relay of kayakers, with two kayakers accompanying me at all times. I own a white-water kayak and have friends who are willing to loan me a canoe for my training swims. Canoes and kayaks are also available for rental at both Trailhead and Ahoy Rentals Ltd. during the summer months.

I am writing to ask whether Special Olympics Kingston has any kayakers or canoers who might accompany me on one or more of my training swims. Or perhaps you could suggest another way your organisation could help me to safely train to swim across Lake Ontario while accomplishing my dream of raising awareness of our abilities and strengths.

This summer, I will put up posters at various places, such as Trailhead, Runner's Choice, Artillery Park, and the YMCA, stating my goal, whom I am fundraising for, and advertising the need for people to accompany me in a canoe or kayak on my training swims.

In summary, I have recovered from the initial handicaps of having Asperger's Syndrome. I feel for the children who are now suffering from what I suffered from as a child. I know that your organization exists in order to help athletes with intellectual disabilities. I reasoned that, with your background, your organization would be aware of Asperger's Syndrome, and would be in the practice of helping people train for athletic events, and may even have workers or volunteers who are willing to accompany me on my training swims.

I would be interested in becoming a volunteer for Special Olympics Kingston. I am available for an interview at your convenience. I look forward to hearing from you and discussing with you how we may be of mutual assistance with each other.

Sincerely,

Jay Serdula

Appendix G

Letter to Lois

Dear Lois: March 25, 2007

I probably put Harley and Mandy in an awkward situation when I informed them about my dream desire to swim across Lake Ontario. One of them asked if there were any way they could help and I immediately mentioned my need for people to accompany me in a canoe or kayak while I train. I can't really say, "I'm sorry" because I'm probably going to do it again. All I can say is that I acknowledge that I may have put them in an awkward situation. When Harley and Mandy offered their help, they were probably referring to the area of advertising and/or organizing the logistics of the actual event.

Now for an explanation on why I said what I said to Harley and Mandy. Regarding my ambition, one question that has arisen is: why am I planning to swim across Lake Ontario in the summer of 2008 and not the summer of 2007. One reason, although not my main reason, is that I like to enjoy my training sessions. If I set the goal for 2007, I will not be able to relax throughout the training process because I will constantly be wondering whether I will be ready by August. Plus, I may be tempted to push myself beyond my comfort level in order to increase my training distance. Another reason is that it may be too much work to organize the training logistics as well as the logistics for the actual event (e.g. fundraising, advertising) - and this is in addition to my job. If I try to do both and it turns out I can't recruit enough training partners, my effort spent on fundraising and advertising will be for naught. In summary, this winter I will focus on recruiting training partners and, next winter, I will focus on fundraising and advertising. (This is assuming that I'm ready to do it in August 2008 and, by the end of swimming season in 2007, I should be able to decide whether I'll be ready.) Perhaps I'll solicit Harley's and Mandy's help next year when I'm in the process of fundraising and advertising.

I recently touched base with Special Olympics Kingston and Kerry's Place Autism Services. They were very helpful and supportive; I am confident that both organizations would be delighted to have my goal fulfilled. I'm about to touch base with Volunteers Kingston, the

Rotary Club of Kingston and possibly the Lions Club of Kingston. My father is a member of the Rotary Club in Deep River and he gave me some contact names of people in Kingston.

On June 12, 2002, I swam from RMC to Cedar Island unaccompanied. Normally, I wait until later in the summer but I was training for my only triathlon that summer which was at the end of June. (I didn't do the Deep River triathlon that year because of my sister's wedding.) On the way back, I got chilled. The words of a friend were echoing in my mind: before cold water physically kills you, it will numb you to the point where you can't move your arms and legs in which case you will sink. A lifejacket will keep you breathing in which case a companion may have time to get to you before you drown. I actually wondered if this might happen. Instead of swimming back to my starting point at RMC, I swam to the nearest shoreline at Fort Henry and then ran around Navy Bay along the grass, barefoot and in my speedo. In hindsight, I'm sure I could have made it to RMC. I didn't know my limitations then as well as I know them now. I knew I was breaking a safety rule by swimming alone but I felt I had no choice because I either couldn't find a swimming companion or someone to paddle a boat beside me or didn't want to go through the effort required to find someone who was willing. I reasoned that I may have had to break one safety rule but I'd follow all the other safety rules as best as I could: I will only swim in broad daylight and I will exit the water at the first sign of getting chilled. I swim partly to train for triathlons but also for enjoyment. When I wonder whether I'm going to complete the swim alive, that takes away the enjoyment. I don't think I've ever swum to Cedar Island without questioning at least once, while swimming in deep water, "Am I going to make it back to the mainland alive?" This should explain why having access to a spare lifejacket while I'm swimming means *everything* to me.

I know you're worrying (and you're not the only one) what will happen if I go into hypothermia. I'm banking on feeling chilled (and in a lot of pain) well before I become hypothermic. The warning signals will (if my understanding is correct) give me enough time to swim to shore before I go into hypothermia. The only way I won't have enough warning is if I'm extremely vulnerable to hypothermia. In this case, I shouldn't even be thinking about swimming across Lake Ontario. I will point out that, in all the swims I have done, I have never even had to resort to my first line of defence which was asking the accompanying paddler to throw me a lifejacket. I have done so many unaccompanied swims where I have had to spot myself that I'm cautious enough to take potential dangers into account, even when accompanied by a canoe or kayak.

Last August, I was riding my bicycle to Camp Iawah. As I was passing through Verona, a man opened the door of his two-door car into my path while I was traveling at about 20 kilometres per hour. I hit the door and fell to the ground. Only minutes earlier, there was a long string of traffic. If there had been another car coming behind me, I would have been dead. The day that I spoke at your school, before I left for work, I prayed that, if God wanted me to speak to your students, that I would get there safely. On the way to work, the driver of a parked car opened the door into my path. Luckily, it was far enough ahead of me that I had time to go around it. On the way from work to your school, the same thing happened. I had to swerve quickly. The driver apologized and said he didn't see me. In both cases, if I had been five seconds quicker and not extremely observant, I would have hit the door. Ten years ago, my cousin got hit by an eighteen wheeler while riding her bicycle. She hasn't ridden a bicycle since then and won't ride a bicycle ever again because she's afraid she'll die. My point is that, yes, I am taking a risk of going into hypothermia and not being able to get out of the water when I swim to Wolfe Island accompanied only by a one-person kayak. But that danger is much smaller than the possibility of me dying riding my bicycle to work.

One characteristic of Asperger's Syndrome is that, once I put my mind on something, I stick with it and don't give up easily. I am fairly determined to accomplish my goal of swimming across Lake Ontario. I know that no one will be willing or able to accompany me on a training swim every week. With any luck, I'll find several people who are willing and rotate. If I can't find enough people to accompany me, I will do some training swims unaccompanied. This may sound like blackmail and I'm using discretion in whom I tell this to. Nine times (or more) out of ten, this argument is not going to sway someone to change his/her mind and accompany me for two reasons: (1) it sends the message that I am irresponsible and thus makes the other person even less likely to accompany me because it's easier to spot a responsible person; (2) if s/he "gives in", that sends the message that I can control him/her.

The divorce rate has skyrocketed in the last fifty years, leaving children to be raised by single parents. Not only have my parents stayed together but my family has vacationed together. My parents own a sailboat and used to take Claire and me to the Thousand Islands, staying overnight at different islands, for one week every summer. For many years, during the March break, we'd go on a downhill ski trip. Once we went to Mexico and once we drove to New Orleans. One Christian said to another Christian (referring to a beggar in downtown Toronto), "There, if it wasn't for the grace of God, stand I." Who knows where I'd be if my parents hadn't been diligent in sticking with me throughout my childhood and adolescent years?

My point is that there are a lot of children (with Asperger's Syndrome and other disabilities) who are less fortunate than I was. By swimming across Lake Ontario, I will not only raise money for the Asperger's Society of Ontario but also raise awareness plus demonstrate that people with Asperger's Syndrome are, in fact, capable of unusual feats. If you don't retain anything else from this letter, please retain this: *I am doing this for the children.* True, I originally planned to swim across Lake Ontario before I knew which charity I'd raise funds for. With all the preparation and training that I've put forth, especially getting up at 5:00 a.m. to go to the early morning swimming practices, I probably would have given up the goal by now if it weren't for the support for ASO. If someone says something which could potentially discourage me from pursuing my dream desire of swimming across Lake Ontario, I might lay a guilt trip on that person and say, "I was thinking of giving up this dream desire."

The goal of swimming across Lake Ontario and raising awareness for Asperger's Syndrome is something which a lot of people would like to see happen (and I'm probably speaking on behalf of several children) but won't happen without a lot of initiative. Unlike a running marathon, one needs accompanists to train for a swimming marathon. This makes training for a swimming marathon more difficult which is one of several reasons why few people attempt to swim across a great lake. In turn, anyone who completes such a swim will receive even more recognition than if these difficulties weren't there.

Tentatively, I plan to start my open water swimming in some of the smaller lakes in May and in Lake Ontario by the first weekend in

June. This may be pushing it but it's certainly worth testing the water. Closer to the date, I plan to put up posters at several places stating my need for canoeists/kayakers, who I'm fundraising for, plus my contact information at various places: Artillery Park, the sports centre across from RMC, Trailhead and Runner's Choice. If it's OK with you and your principal, perhaps I'll put a poster up at your school.

It is possible that I am going overboard in the manner in which I am recruiting people to accompany me on my training swims. You never know whether someone is willing until you ask. I think it would be a shame if this goal didn't get fulfilled because I couldn't train for it because I couldn't find enough people to accompany me. And, I think it would be doubly shameful if there were people who were willing to accompany me but I didn't know of their willingness and they didn't know of my need. It's very possible that people may enjoy spotting me in a canoe/kayak. (If I remember correctly, you told me that John likes doing that.) One must not overlook the fact that anyone who accompanies me - even once - is playing a part in raising awareness of Asperger's Syndrome. This will, hopefully, give the other person a sense of satisfaction and delight.

Your persevering brother in the Lord,

Jay Serdula

Appendix H

Ben Wronged me Three Separate Times

While Ben and I were living in the same house for four months during the Ottawa '97 Navs summer program, Ben told me that one should always communicate directly and never communicate indirectly. I had him read a book that was meaningful to me [*Tannen, 1986*] since, when I tried to explain my viewpoint, I was only translating what the book said. Ben didn't agree with the author's opinions. However, about a year later, he told me he wanted to take back his statement that one should never communicate indirectly.

During the same four-month term, Ben wronged me three separate times:

Wrong #1

Years ago, I was giving Karen and two others a ride to a retreat. I was unsure which road to take so I pulled over to look at the map. In addition, it was winter, it was snowing, and it was pitch dark. With my case of Asperger's Syndrome, I have difficulty focusing on two or more tasks at once (in this case, driving plus trying to figure out where I was). The last thing I needed was another distraction. As I was pulled over, Karen told the following joke:

Q. What does an agnostic, dyslexic, insomniac do?
A. He lies awake all night wondering if there's a dog.

I didn't get the joke (I had never heard the term 'dyslexic') and I made no reply.[77] I told Ben this story, and Ben told me that I was in the wrong for not saying anything. Less than a month before, I had driven off the road with my parents' car, which probably would not have occurred had I been more cautious. There was no damage done to the car, but my father wasn't exactly thrilled at what happened (which, in turn, put pressure on me to be more cautious next time). Furthermore, if I had said, "I don't get it," most people in Karen's situation would interpret that as a request that I want the joke explained

---

[77] One week later, my aunt just happened to explain to me, in passing, what 'dyslexic' meant. All of a sudden, the joke registered. (With my case of Asperger's Syndrome, it is typical for a joke to go over my head, but I'll suddenly get the joke days, sometimes weeks, later.)

to me. I was feeling overloaded enough as it was, and I didn't want the joke explained. Needless to say, I disagreed with Ben, but because I'm not a confrontational person, I would only go so far in voicing my disagreement.

Once, I told Ken Franklin a joke. Ken was silent for a while and then laughed. The pause between my joke and Ken's laughter was so long that I wondered whether it was actually the joke that he was laughing at.

I asked Ken, "Are you laughing at me or the joke?"

Ken replied, "I'm laughing at your response to my lack of response."

One of these days I'm going to tell Ben that I'm interested to know why he bawled me out[78] (for not responding to Karen's joke) but didn't bawl Ken Franklin out (for not responding to my joke).

Wrong #2

As I was eating cereal, I almost finished the first bag of a jumbo box containing two bags. Ben, who doesn't eat cereal, was downright insistent that I finish eating the first bag, claiming that it wasn't fair to the next person to have to unroll the bag just for a small amount of cereal. (There were five other housemates living with Ben and me.) I asked Ben, "Where do you draw the line? How much cereal can you leave, below which you must finish the bag?" Ben replied, "A bowlful." I was full and don't believe in stuffing myself. I am not a confrontational person and didn't have the nerve to tell Ben to shut up or to say, "I am not eating the cereal. End of story." Luckily, I found a mutually agreeable solution: put the nearly-finished bag of cereal in one of my own cereal boxes. In hindsight, I wish I had said, "I disagree." However, I have a restraining bolt that prevents me even from saying, "I disagree," unless I can back up my argument. Preparing a backup argument takes time and time is what I did not have.

Wrong #3

One time, I was wearing pants, a dress shirt and a tie. I was going to an interview with the media on how I conduct a job search. Just as

---

[78] A friend recently explained to me that, if someone tells me in one sentence to do or not do something, that is not "bawling me out". And, if the other person is asking me questions, that also is not bawling me out. To "bawl someone out" usually means to talk – and often yell – for several minutes in accusatory words and intonation. Perhaps "reprimand" is a better term.

I was about to head out the door, Ben insisted that I tell him where I was going. With my case of Asperger's Syndrome, it was too difficult to put my thoughts into words on the spur of the moment. Ben told me afterwards that he asked me where I was going so that he could pray for me, and that it's better if I'm late for the interview than to leave the house without telling him where I'm going and why. Ben told me that he was offended that being on time for the meeting meant more to me than explaining to him where I was going. Ben and I were both attending a work-study programme with the Navigators; participants were expected to either be working full-time or else treating looking for work as their full-time day job. Therefore, it shouldn't have surprised Ben to see me leave the house dressed in such a way as to indicate that I would be meeting someone. How do you argue with someone who firmly insists on a statement that you know isn't true? Putting someone in the position in which he is repeatedly uncomfortable and must decide whether to risk terminating the friendship is one thing. Putting him in the position where he has to argue with you in order not to damage a relationship with someone else is another thing. It doesn't take a rocket scientist to conclude that Ben should not have demanded an explanation on the spot.

In summary, if Ben was firmly insistent that I inform him of every interview and that I not leave small amounts of cereal in the box, he could have made my life simpler by telling me that in advance. Then I would have taken the time to tell him about the interview before I was in a hurry, and wouldn't have eaten that much cereal unless I was sure I could finish the box.

✧

Years later, Ben is one of my most valuable sources of advice. This goes to show that, if I'm patient (and am willing and able to undergo the hardships that sometimes come when getting to know someone), I will eventually find out who my true friends are.

Ben clearly had the best intentions in each of the three above-mentioned situations. It's unfortunate that the immediate outcome wasn't so pleasant. Given that Ben never raised his voice or seemed upset at me ever again, it's very possible that Ben actually felt badly for reacting that way. Another lesson to be learned from this story is that if you can't say something nice and in a nice way, don't say anything, except possibly if the situation is so urgent that an incorrect reaction now is better than a correct reaction later. Asking *one* question might be okay, in order to show interest, but if the other person is in a hurry or seems stressed, perhaps it isn't the best time to talk to him/her. I'm pretty sure Ben realized this after the three above-mentioned situations had occurred.

Appendix I

Help!!

From: Jay Serdula
To: organizational committee for Jay's swim
Sent: Feburary 27, 2008
Subject: HELP!!!!

Last night, someone at the organizational meeting broke the news to me that people have been slow at completing what they said they'd do and that I shouldn't be dependent on everyone else to make this happen. Then she asked me if I'm willing to put off my swim across Lake Ontario until 2009.

Putting off the swim for another year is *not* an option for the following reasons:
1. two of my key players (organizational committee members) may be leaving Kingston in September
2. One more year is not going to change things; people are going to get busy with other things and we will be in exactly the same position at this time of year next year
3. I cannot go on like this even if I wanted to. The training (not to mention communication with all the people on the committee) has been taking its toll on me - to the point where it is interfering with the performance on my job.
4. I am on contract and don't know how much longer my job will continue. The contract ends March 31 but there's a chance of another extension. I get along with my supervisor and, so far, I have been able to manage both the job and the training. There is no way I could start a new full-time job and continue the training. (I am sensitive to distractions, especially when beginning a new job.) If my contract does not get extended, I will either live off EI or work part-time (unless I got offered a job I like at a salary I cannot refuse).

My main reason for not doing the swim in 2007 was that I wasn't sure if I'd be ready. My summer training swims would not have been enjoyable if I were constantly wondering whether I'd be ready by August. Plus, I'd be tempted to push myself beyond my comfort zone.

As soon as the dust settled after I completed my 19-hour swim at Heather's cottage in July, I knew I would have been ready (physically) to complete the crossing last summer.

I would rather pay the cost out of my own pocket to make sure it happens this year instead of taking the risk that it might not happen. If the swim costs me more than an anticipated amount, I will have to decide how badly I want to swim across Lake Ontario.

I have been regularly attending two churches in the Kingston area and I'm about to have it announced at both churches of my need for more volunteers to help organize the event. I'm sure some people would be delighted to help and it certainly won't hurt to ask.

Incidently, one year ago, I thought the most difficult part of the whole process would be finding people to paddle a canoe or kayak beside me on my training swims. I figured I could rent or buy the canoes or kayaks, rent boats for the actual event, hire people to operate them, and I have enough friends from out of town who would be glad to be on the support boat. (This would get expensive but it's doable.) One thing I cannot "buy" is people to paddle the canoes and kayaks for me. I resolved that the only way I will not have enough paddling volunteers is if there aren't people in the Kingston area who are willing. As it turned out, this was NOT a problem; people have been *leaping* at the opportunity to help in this manner and there has been no shortage of paddling volunteers. I successfully recruited (with some help) enough paddling volunteers. I shall do the same thing with volunteers to help plan and organize the event.

It seems that there are people willing to donate a few hours of their time (I just have to find them) but don't have the expertise to "oversee". Forming sub-committees is certainly a step in the right direction. We have one person to be the head of each of the sub-committees; now all we need is volunteers to take on specific tasks. (Or do we need more?)

Today at lunch time, I plan to go to the 90-minute lane swim at the pool across from RMC and do 32x100m intervals (one of the workouts suggested by Swim Master Vicki Keith, to improve my speed) which I would probably have done anyways. I plan to work late tonight and then go to the 8:30-9:30 p.m. Masters swimming practice and then to the 6:00 a.m.-7:00 a.m. practice tomorrow morning. If I'm not going to be able to sleep, I might as well be swimming, until the dust settles and I can figure out how to proceed with the organizational aspect. (Last night, I woke up at 5am and then couldn't get back to sleep on account of the news of the organizational situation, plus thinking about how I was going to word it in my e-mail message to you.)

Now for the joke of the day:

A large crowd was watching a football game at a sports stadium. Just as the fourth quarter was starting, the lights went out. The umpire announced, "Does anyone have any ideas on how we can get the lights back on?"
A Chinese man said, "Everyone, raise your right arm."
So they did.
Then, the Chinese man said, "Everyone, keep your right arm raised and raise your left arm."
So they did.
"Now, wave both arms side to side in synchron."
So they did. Lo and behold, the lights came back on.
The person next to the Chinese man asked him, "How did you know that was going to work?"
"Chinese proverb. Many hands make light work."

Appendix J

I Had a Dream!

On May 8, 2007 I had a dream that I was swimming across Lake Ontario. It was broad daylight, I could see the CN tower, as well as other buildings in Toronto, and I was comfortable – in fact, comfortable enough to willingly do breast stroke or tread water. The Toronto shoreline was close enough that I could be confident that I'd make it, but not so close that I could sprint the rest of the way. This meant that I had made it through the night and wasn't cold, or that I had made it most of the way across before the first night, which is highly unlikely. In real life, on June 23, 2007, I swam for six and a half hours and had originally intended to swim longer but quit because I was getting cold; I couldn't even do breast stroke for ten seconds because I wasn't generating enough heat doing breast stroke and had to switch back to front crawl.

In real life, I watched Samantha Whiteside start her swim across Lake Ontario from Niagara-on-the-Lake in July 2007. I could see the CN tower but only the CN tower. It has been reported that, when swimming across Lake Ontario, the CN tower never seems to get any closer.

I interpreted this dream to mean:
- I would be sanctioned;
- the swim would happen; and
- I would not get discouraged. (Or, if I did get discouraged, I needed to keep swimming anyway and the discouragement would go away.) Any amateur can predict that night swimming is the most difficult part but it's difficult to predict how much more difficult.

In real life, during the attempt to swim for 24 hours at Heather's cottage, I quit after 19 hours, the sole reason being to avoid hypothermia. I felt fine in the daylight but, at 8:00 p.m., as soon as the sun started going down, I felt chilled. My support crew kept expressing their confidence and kept encouraging me to go on even though I kept telling them I was probably going to quit at 1:00 a.m. I kept saying, "The spirit is willing, but the flesh is weak." Each time, Heather corrected me and replied, "The flesh is strong."

In real life, several years ago I had a stressful job and didn't put as much effort into running as I normally do. Mr. Fulford, my high school cross-country running coach, and I ran to Balmer's Bay Gate and back (for a total of 16 kilometres). Shortly after the turnaround point, Mr. Fulford said, "When you make it to the corner, you've got it made." After we made it to the corner, he said, "When you make it to the top of the hill, you've got it made." Once we made it to the top of the hill, he said, "When you make it to the hospital, you've got it made." And then when we made it to the hospital, he said, "When you make it around the next corner, you've got it made."

It may seem like Mr. Fulford was
a. trying to push me past my comfort level; or
b. inconsistent or contradictory because he'd say "You've got it made after this point" and, when "this point" was reached, I still didn't have it made.

In fact, Mr. Fulford was only trying to encourage me to keep going. And, it worked! Mr. Fulford knew that I was a big boy and could make my own decisions. He said those "encouraging" words only after the turnaround point. He knew that I knew that, once I made it to the gate, I had to get back and I should have turned around sooner if I didn't think I could make it.

The SSO Regulations and Information manual comments that there comes a time during almost every marathon swim in which the swimmer begs to come out. The fact is that the swimmer often gets over any feelings of discouragement during the swim and only needs some encouragement. Therefore, it's important that the swimmer has family and friends on the support boat who care about him/her, want what's best for the swimmer and can offer encouragement.

Whoever reads this, please don't be afraid to encourage me by telling me, during the night portion of the swim, "When you make it to daylight, you've got it made."

Appendix K

The Half-Ironman

On Labour Day weekend, in 1996, I participated in a half-ironman triathlon (2-kilometre swim, 90-kilometre cycle, 21-kilometre run) at Wilderness Tours. I had just completed a co-op work term in Ottawa and had driven back to Deep River the day before the race.

One month before the race, I was still unsure whether I would actually do it. The fact is that I enjoy being in water but I don't necessarily enjoy the pressure of having to swim from point A to point B as fast as I can. Nonetheless, while having a picnic with some friends, I went for a leisurely swim and, once again, was reminded that I like swimming and decided to register based on that.

The day before the race, I spent the entire day packing four months of belongings. As a result, I got home late and was in a hurry the next morning. I own two ten-speed bicycles, one that I bought brand new from Canadian Tire ten years earlier, and one that I bought used just over a year before and which is older than I am. For the half-ironman, I used the bicycle I kept at my parents' house, the bicycle I had bought from Canadian Tire, because I was more used to that bicycle. When I switched the water bottle carrier, which is attached to the bicycle frame by two clamps, from the bicycle I used in Ottawa to the other bicycle, I put the clamps over top of the gear cable. This meant I couldn't shift gears for the entire duration of the race. Fortunately, the clamps were on top of only the cable that controls the two gears on the front; the cable that controls the five gears at the back was free. What's more, I realized that I could shift gears despite the clamps; however, it was more hassle than it was worth. The course was so hilly that I forced the bicycle into the low set of gears and left the front (high-low) gearshift lever there for the remainder of the race. Unfortunately, the gears are designed so that that when you shift gears at the back, you have to move the front gearshift lever slightly to avoid a clicking noise. I am someone who, whenever possible, prefers not to fix things but to alter my course of action. In other words, I would rather change my actions than the situation. So even such a slight movement of the front gearshift lever was more hassle than it was worth.

The turnaround point occurred at approximately 40 kilometres, after which participants would cycle back the way they came, as well as cycling an additional 10-kilometre loop. At a certain junction I thought, "This looks like the way I came, but the turnoff isn't marked, so I will continue going straight." I ended up in Westmeath, and the paved road became gravel. I knew I was on the wrong road and turned around, after having cycled an extra 3 kilometres. I carefully retraced my route, unsure whether I'd miss another turn and add on more distance. When I recognized the turnoff for the additional 10-kilometre loop, I omitted it, since the turnaround point wouldn't be marked, and I'd either turn around too early or too late. (I thought I might as well do 10 kilometres less and omit the entire loop.) Therefore, I technically did not complete the half-ironman.

I suspect that after the officials knew everyone (as it turns out, except me) had reached the turnaround point, they drove by in a car, removing the markers on the way. They must have mistaken me for a tourist, because I had dismounted my bicycle for a feeding break (which I had done more than once over the course of the cycle).

At one of the check points on the run, someone gave me a two-litre water bottle, which I carried with me. Some time later, one of the race officials came behind me in a pickup truck. I asked him if he planned to follow me for the remainder of the race. When he replied, "Yes", I asked him to carry the water bottle for me. Every time I merely turned around, he knew immediately what I wanted (and handed me the water bottle).

Despite taking regular drinks, I was dehydrated on completing the event, and probably well before completion. One's body can absorb only so much water in a given time – which is why athletes should take small sips regularly, instead of consuming larger amounts of fluid and thinking that will suffice for a while.

Concerned for my safety, the Wilderness Tours staff would not let me drive home, but insisted that I give them the name and telephone number of someone who could pick up both me and my car. My parents were out of the province, my sister was in Toronto (a five hour drive away) and I didn't have a girlfriend. Therefore, I gave them the name and telephone number of my next-door neighbours. They very kindly came to pick me up, driving from over 100 kilometres away, and drove my car home as well.

Was I responsible for the inconvenience that my next-door neighbours endured? I say no, though not everyone agrees with my point of view. However, if it ever happens again, then I say that I will be responsible. Actions have consequences and one needs to take responsibility for the consequences of one's actions; shifting the blame is a sign of an irresponsible person. Would a reasonable person have been able to foresee that doing a triathlon when I wasn't properly trained would cause my neighbours to be inconvenienced in this manner? That may depend on how one defines a "reasonable person," and also what each of us should be able to expect in advance of a new situation.

Ten years later, when I did another triathlon almost as long as a half-ironman (consisting of a 2-kilometre swim, a 55-kilometre cycle, and a 15-kilometre run), I made sure to explain in detail what happened after the half-ironman to the friends I stayed overnight with and, if the staff asks me to name someone to pick me up, they would be the first people I impose on. I promised to call these friends after the race and let them know how I felt. I did the same when I ran my first marathon.

Basically, I didn't train properly for the half-ironman, didn't prepare properly[79], didn't perform in the race properly, and didn't recover properly. Needless to say, I found the Around the Bay 30K Road Race (in which I participated in five months earlier) much easier than the half-ironman.

Six weeks before the half-ironman, I did a smaller "practice" half-ironman (consisting of a 750-metre swim, a 60-kilometre cycle, and a 16-kilometre run). I did not carry any water with me on the run and stopped at the hospital for a drink of water from the water fountain. If that option failed, I would have stopped at the nearest friend's house. I also undertook a lengthy bicycle ride which I estimated to be roughly 90 kilometres. Being without a car, I had no way of measuring the distance of the bicycle ride; my estimate was almost certainly too high. These were my only two training sessions dedicated solely to the half-ironman. I had also participated in the Deep River triathlon (which I do almost every year), plus the Thousand Islands triathlon in Brockville, for which I would have been training anyway.

In hindsight, was it worth finishing the race? I walked one third of the run and had thus wasted money on shoes, because of the wear caused by walking part of the way. If I wanted to run 21 kilometres, it would have been better to participate in a half-marathon or else run 21 kilometres on my own. Was it worth the extra money spent on shoes just to finish? I was a university student at the time, and therefore had to watch my expenses. Joe told me later that he had calculated that the

---

[79] "train" means the physical preparation within several weeks before; "prepare" in this case means the errands I perform within twenty-four to forty-eight hours before the race - including what I eat, how much sleep I get and other stress factors (such as moving) which could contribute to fatigue.

cost of shoes per mile[80] was greater than the cost of gasoline per mile. This implied that running as a means of transportation is more expensive than driving.

Attempting the half-ironman was clearly premature. Because of the outcome, I didn't exactly make a resolution never to do another half-ironman, but I had no desire to do another one. I have not attempted a half-ironman since then.[81] After a bad experience, sometimes one wants to repeat the experience to show that one has learned from the mistake. At other times, one has no desire to do anything of the sort ever again. For the longest time, I didn't want to think about the half-ironman experience or talk about it.

A few years after I moved to Kingston, during one of my many bicycle rides from Gananoque back to Kingston, I actually thought of doing another half-ironman. I knew that I was clearly in better shape in terms of physical conditioning than during the half-ironman I had done, and therefore I had reason to believe that I could complete a half-ironman. What's more, prior to the half-ironman, I had not done a triathlon longer than the Deep River triathlon (1-kilometre swim, 26.5-kilometre cycle, 8-kilometre run) whereas, now I had done the Olympic distance triathlon in Guelph (1.5-kilometre swim, 43-kilometre cycle, 10-kilometre run) several times, and would almost certainly do either the long course of the Kingston triathlon or the Muskoka triathlon (2-kilometre swim, 55-kilometre cycle, 15-kilometre run) before attempting another half-ironman.

I still don't think I'd have any inclination to attempt another half-ironman if it weren't for Peter. Peter has done the Canadian Iron 113 (half-ironman distance) triathlon – if not the Canadian Iron 226 (iron-distance) triathlon – which is held in Ottawa on Labour Day weekend, every year since 2002 – except for one year when he consented instead to participating in the Canadian Iron 226 (iron-distance) triathlon as a team with Karen and me.

---

[80] It is not recommended to run more than 700 miles (one source recommends 500 miles) in a pair of shoes. The mid-sole of a shoe breaks down first. Therefore, a runner should replace shoes as soon as 700 miles is exceeded or if the runner is experiencing any problems even if the shoes don't look worn. Therefore, at $100.00 for a pair of shoes, running costs $0.15 per mile on shoes. This is comparable to the price of gas. However, gas is only one expense; maintenance, insurance, plus depreciation of the car's value also need to be considered. What's more, after shoes have exceeded the running mileage, the shoes can still be used for walking shorter distances. Therefore, one must deduct the cost that a non-runner would spend on (perhaps cheaper) shoes.

[81] Since this document was begun, I completed the Canadian Iron 113 (half-ironman distance) triathlon in September 2009, which is part of the annual Somersault series (www.somersault.ca).

Appendix K

From 2000 until 2004, the Next church hosted a retreat on Labour Day weekend. And even though I considered doing the Canadian Iron 113 with Peter, attending the retreat meant more to me. In 2005, I volunteered, in large part as a means to view the course and discern whether I could handle it. I was all set to do the Canadian Iron 113 the following year, until I found out that Peter would be doing the Canadian Iron 226. Karen thought I should still do the half-ironman, and asked me why it made a difference whether Peter did the half-ironman or the full ironman. Given that I'm only going to do it once, I don't care in which year I do it, and I won't be disappointed if I never do a half-ironman, it made sense to me to pick a year that Peter was doing the half-ironman. That way, Peter and I could eat breakfast together, travel to the race together, converse at the start line and, even though we probably won't stay together during the race, we will converse after the race, since whoever finishes the race first will stretch, eat and stay at the race site to watch the other person finish. If I do the half-ironman and Peter does the full ironman, he'll leave the house before I get up, and I'll be back at the house sleeping before he finishes. In other words, there would be no socializing between Peter and me that day. What's more, if by chance I have a repeat of my first half-ironman and there's no one around that I know who can help me, I won't be able to say that I didn't know any better.[82]

In summary, the half-ironman was a bad experience that I have not been anxious to repeat. I would consider doing another half-ironman just to say I've done it but I can't see myself ever doing a full ironman.

---

[82] This time, unlike last time, I can't say, "But I didn't know that doing the race would cause this kind of inconvenience to my neighbours."

Appendix L

Hypothermia: Recognition of Signs and Symptoms

Impending Hypothermia:

Due to physiological, medical, environmental, or other factors the person's core temperature has decreased to 36 degrees Celsius. The person will increase activity in an attempt to warm up. The skin may become pale, numb and waxy. Muscles become tense, shivering may begin but can be overcome by activity. Fatigue and signs of weakness begin to show.

Mild Hypothermia:

The person has now become a victim of hypothermia. The core temperature has dropped to 35 - 34 degrees Celsius. Uncontrolled, intense shivering begins. The victim is still alert and able to help self, however movements become less coordinated and the coldness is creating some pain and discomfort.

Moderate Hypothermia:

The victim's core temperature has now dropped to 33 - 31 degrees Celsius. Shivering slows or stops, muscles begin to stiffen and mental confusion and apathy sets in. Speech becomes slow, vague and slurred, breathing becomes slower and shallow, and drowsiness and strange behavior may occur.

Severe Hypothermia:

Core temperature now below 31 degrees Celsius. Skin is cold, may be bluish- gray in color, eyes may be dilated. Victim is very weak, displays a marked lack of coordination, slurred speech, appears exhausted, may appear to be drunk, denies problem and may resist help. There is a gradual loss of consciousness. There may be little or no apparent breathing, victim may be very rigid, unconscious, and may appear dead.

reference: http://www.sarbc.org/hypo1.html

Appendix M

List of Questions (For Rescuer)

Note to rescuer
If you find me unconscious or hypothermic or if you suspect I'm in trouble, ask me the following questions.
I should be able to provide all the answers under normal circumstances.

Q. What is your name?
A. Jay Serdula

Q. When is your birthday?
A. October 22

Q. What type of car did you own?
A. 1989 Pontiac 6000 S/E

Q. What was the car's name?
A. Black Bertha

Q. What incident caused you to dispose of your car?
A. Ruptured brake hose

Q. What date did this incident occur?
A. August 14, 2002

Q. What was the odometer reading of your car when it arrived at the wreckers?
A. 371,966 km

Appendix N

Training History

As the editor of this website I befriended Mr. Serdula as an acquaintance and I must say, I grow more impressed with him by the week. I'm a long-distance runner myself, something Mr. Serdula is also accomplished in, but I am completely ignorant about the training regimens for swimming. It's much more intense than I have ever imagined, and clearly dangerous on some level. Being highly skilled at three very different forms of cardiovascular endurance exercise–biking, running, and swimming–is not something that the average person can attest to, especially considering his duties at the Royal Military College of Canada, so my hat goes off to him. One small note: The italicized portions of this entry are Jay's personal thoughts and feelings of a particular event.

—Eric Weiner

August 26, 2006
Jay swims from HMCS Cataraqui to the summer ferry dock on Wolfe Island in 2:34. (Approximate distance: 5.25 km) This is Jay's first big training swim. (Jay's previous longest swim was on the order of 2.5 km.)

September 4, 2006
Jay swims for three hours, almost halfway to Simcoe Island, back to the shoreline west of the starting point and then back to the starting point.

September 10, 2006
Jay swims for close to three hours, making three laps around Cedar Island.

September 17, 2006
Jay swims for close to three hours, from Everitt Point to Lemoine's Point and back.

October 9, 2006
Jay swims for seventy-five minutes in the Ottawa River. Water temperature not known.

October 31, 2006
Jay joins the Kingston Masters Aquatic Club where he will receive coaching and advice on speed and technique from two certified coaches.

November 2006
Having only breathed on his right side for several years, Jay finally learns to breathe on his left side and after a few more practices learns to breathe bilaterally.

December 20, 2006
Jay swims front crawl nonstop at the KMCSC swimming pool, covering 3.8 km in 85 minutes. This is by far the longest Jay has maintained the front crawl stroke.

March 29, 2007
The ice has disappeared from the shoreline along the RMC peninsula. Jay takes his first open-water plunge of the season, only long enough to get his whole body wet.

April 10, 2007
While visiting his sister in Calgary, Jay is delighted to learn that the SAIT pool has a lane swim for two and a half hours. Jay swims front crawl for the entire lane swim, covering approximately 6.5 km.

May 6, 2007
Jay swims for twenty minutes in Pearkes Lake. With the water temperature at 17°C(63°F), Jay is actually comfortable.

May 9, 2007
Jay swims at Progress Fitness Centre for four and a half hours, with limited breaks. Although curious to know how long he could swim, Jay had, by this time, resigned himself to two-hour lane swims at Artillery Park since this was the longest lane swim in Kingston which Jay knew about. He subsequently learns that Progress Fitness Centre has at least two lanes open for swimming at all times.

May 24, 2007
Anxious to jump-start his open-water training swims, Jay swims for 65 minutes in Lake Ontario along the shoreline of the RMC peninsula

on a sunny day. Water temperature ranges from 10-12°C(50-54°F). Air temperature is 22°C. Within minutes after coming out of the water, Jay starts shivering quite violently but is nonetheless far from hypothermia. A warm meal and a warm beverage, plus the usual routine of drying off and putting on warm clothes, is enough to suppress the shivering. (Jay's open-water swims in the smaller lakes are already in full-swing.)

May 29, 2007
Jay swims at Progress Fitness Centre for five and a half hours, again with limited breaks.

June 2, 2007
Jay cycles to Dog Lake and swims back and forth between the dock and floatation markers, covering 13 km in 5:41. It's a sunny day. Jay feels no chill and experiences no shivering. His shoulders and upper back are somewhat red, despite having put on sunscreen. In contrast to the sunny day, Jay encounters a downpour on his bicycle ride back to Kingston and stops for shelter under a tree for an hour.

June 3, 2007
Jay swims in Lake Ontario for 1:50. Jay is shivering noticeably after completing the swim but, as always, a warm shower and warm clothes were sufficient to cure the shivering.

June 5, 2007
Jay borrows a friend's canoe, paddles the canoe solo in Lake Ontario from Reddendale to Murney Tower (~7 km) to meet two volunteer paddlers whom he had never met before and who graciously volunteered their time to meet Jay on a rainy day with waves on the order of 0.6m (which luckily didn't get big until later on Jay's solo canoe ride). Jay swims for close to two hours, starting at Murney Tower, swimming across the Cataraqui River and then back and forth along the RMC peninsula. At the end of the work day, Jay tries to be a hero and attempts to paddle the canoe solo from RMC back to Reddendale, despite the rough water. An inexperienced solo canoeist, Jay paddles more than one hundred strokes on the same side and keeps the canoe in one direction (not the direction Jay wanted to travel). Several times, Jay was closer to Garden Island than the mainland. Jay was one happy camper to get the canoe anywhere along the shoreline (not to mention not having capsized the canoe). Jay telephoned a close

friend (thank goodness for cellphones) who graciously drove his van to meet him and drive him with the canoe back home. Of course, by the time Jay's friend arrived half an hour later, the lake had calmed down. By this time, Jay decided that, on future swims, he would rather rent a canoe than paddle a canoe solo from Reddendale to downtown and back.

June 10, 2007
Jay swims from the shoreline of Lake Ontario towards Simcoe Island but turns around when in sight of Snake Island, in order to give his paddler, who is visiting from out of town, a view of the island. By this time, Jay is noticeably chilled and swims straight back to Dupont where he terminates his swim. Jay was in the water for two and a half hours. For the first time in his life, Jay shivers while in the water. Jay paddles his kayak back to his starting point, thus generating enough heat to offset the chill, while his paddler runs along the shoreline.

June 15-16, 2007
Jay swims from 11:30 p.m. until 3:00 a.m., starting and ending at HMCS Cataraqui, and going past Cedar Island. This is Jay's first night swim. Jay wanted to know how he handled night swimming when well-rested before attempting a twenty-four hour swim. Jay handled it quite well, although the illumination from the streetlights of downtown Kingston may have provided an inaccurate depiction of swimming in total darkness.

June 23, 2007
Jay has a new idea: a point-to-point swim from Faircrest Blvd (about 4 km east of RMC) to Amherstview. (Estimated distance: 24 km) Jay aborts the swim after six and a half hours due to coldness. Water temperature is approximately 19°C(66°F). Estimated distance covered is thirteen kilometres.

July 7, 2007
Jay makes another attempt at his point-to-point swim from Faircrest Blvd to Amherstview. Jay sets up four shifts of paddlers. The waves get noticeably rough at Portsmouth Olympic Harbour but the second shift of paddlers handle it fine. At the Kingston Psychiatric Hospital, when the third shift of paddlers take over, the swim is immediately aborted due to an inability of the paddlers to control the canoe.

July 13-14, 2007
Jay swims from 10:15 a.m. until 12:30 a.m. at Wolfe Lake. Camp Iawah has graciously given Jay permission to use a canoe, paddles, and lifejackets. The intent was to swim for twenty-four hours but the swim was aborted after 14 hours for safety reasons, plus concerns of liability and hypothermia. Although Jay had goosebumps, Jay did not feel any chill while in the water. Jay was shivering mildly after coming out of the water. Somewhat disappointed at not being allowed to continue, Jay is happy to have more than doubled his previous longest swim plus done some night swimming. In addition, Jay has the psychological benefit of knowing that he could have swum longer.

July 21-22, 2007
Jay travels to a friend's cottage at Chippego Lake and makes another attempt to swim for twenty-four hours starting at 6:00 a.m. At 1:00 a.m., Jay firmly announces that he is quitting despite encouragement from his support crew to continue. Without adequate medical personnel, save one lifeguard, plus being far from a hospital, Jay virtually made the decision at 8:00 p.m., when he first felt chilled and could still think clearly, that he would quit the swim at 1:00 a.m. Jay knew that, once in hypothermia, he would not have the discernment to know when to quit. By the end of the swim, Jay is swimming for twenty-five minutes and then eating for five minutes. Jay shivered for at least twenty minutes after coming out of the water. Jay's crew wrapped Jay in blankets and encouraged him to keep moving so Jay continued walking laps around the kitchen table while one crew member continued walking backwards around the table in order to look at Jay and keep him company. A warm meal suppressed the shivering.

July 28, 2007
Jay participates in the annual Swim for the Cure in Severn River, covering the complete distance of 12.8 km in 5:53. The swim is a fundraiser for breast cancer but from Jay's point of view it is more a training session for the big swim across Lake Ontario.

August 1, 2007
The RMC sea cadets, who have already accompanied Jay on two previous training swims, accompanied Jay in a canoe from the RMC boathouse to the Wolfe Island summer ferry dock, to the winter ferry dock, to Knapp Point and back to RMC for a total of eight and a half

hours. Swimming from the boathouse to the summer ferry dock (slightly more than 5 km) took Jay exactly two hours.

August 8, 2007
Jay's final swim with the RMC sea cadets. Jay swims in the opposite direction this time, from the boathouse, past Cedar Island, to Milton Island, across to Knapp Point on Wolfe Island, and then parallel to the Wolfe Island shoreline towards Garden Island. At 2:30pm, before reaching Garden Island, Jay estimates it will take him an hour and a half to swim back to the boathouse and realizes that he must head back immediately since he told the sea cadets they'd be back by 4pm. On account of rough waves (and possibly fatigue as well), it takes Jay two and a half hours to get back. The sea cadets have graciously accompanied Jay on four of his training swims during their six-week stay at RMC.

September 1, 2007
Jay travels to Ottawa and competes as part of a team in the Iron-Distance Triathlon in Mooney's Bay, swimming 3.8 km in 79 minutes.

September 22, 2007
Jay makes a third and final attempt at his point-to-point swim from Faircrest Blvd to Amherstview. Jay sets up three shifts of paddlers. Jay starts the swim at 7:15 a.m. despite waves more than one metre in height. Who knew how big the waves would be further along the swim where the lake is wider and at a time of day when the waves are usually bigger? After one hour, Jay's paddlers head for shore after concluding that they are unable to keep the canoe near Jay which all but defeats the purpose of having a canoe. Submerged from the neck down, Jay is unable to see how much water is in the canoe. As soon as he gets to shore and sees how much water there is he becomes surprised that his paddlers didn't abort the swim sooner. Jay learns later that his paddler in the bow had only ever been in a canoe once, during Jay's twenty-four hour swim at Chippego Lake. What adventurous spirit! Nonetheless, Jay's chauffeur transports him, the canoe and the others to the PUC dock to meet the second shift of paddlers. This time, the paddlers manage to control the canoe and keep it near Jay for three hours despite the four foot waves (Good job! I'll hire you any day) before aborting the swim. Jay is not shivering but gets vaseline on his windbreaker (an old one) after getting dressed. Jay liberally coated his

body with vaseline before the swim in anticipation of swimming for eleven hours.

September 29, 2007
Having learned of the unwritten guideline that candidates should be able to complete the 16 km open-water trial swim in six hours, Jay gets curious to know how close he is to meeting the guideline. Once again he cycles to Dog Lake and swims 13 km in 5:41. As the homeowners point out, the water level is lower in the fall plus the weeds have time to grow. Consequently, Jay kept getting disturbed by the weeds.

October 16, 2007
Jay swims for an hour and twenty minutes. Having come down with a cold three days ago, Jay is debating not swimming, even at the last minute after two of his paddling volunteers have graciously volunteered their time and kept their word to meet Jay. By now, Jay thinks that each open-water swim is going to be his last.

October 21, 2007
Jay swims for twenty-five minutes in 16°C(61°F) water without shivering. The only reason the swim was aborted was that the wave height was on the order of three or four metres and Jay's paddler, who paddled Jay's seventeen foot kayak, often could not reach the water with the paddle.

October 29, 2007
Jay swims for an hour and five minutes in Lake Ontario. Water temperature is approximately 12°C(54°F) although may have varied from one point to another. This time, running three minutes to get home, a warm shower and warm clothes still are not enough to completely suppress the shivering.

November 2, 2007
At noon, Jay and six of his RMC colleagues swim across Navy Bay, from Fort Henry to RMC (250m) as a fundraising incentive for United Way. A sunny day with little wind, and with the bay flat calm, the conditions could not have been better. The water temperature is 13°C(55°F). Jay discerns with his sense of touch that the water is cold but his body doesn't feel cold. Jay completes the swim without shivering.

November 5, 2007
Jay's final open-water swim of the season. For three weeks, he thought that each open-water swim would be his last swim. His plan was to continue the swims as long as he was able to withstand the water for one hour. After 53 minutes in the water the discomfort is too great to stay in any longer. Water temperature is 12°C(54°F).

November 26, 2007
Jay swims front crawl nonstop for three hours at Progress Fitness Centre, covering 8.375 km.

December 6, 2007
Jay has informed marathon swimmer and Swim Master Vicki Keith about his concern of "failing" the 16 km open water trial swim in anticipation of not meeting the unwritten guideline of completing the trial swim in six hours. Vicki has advised Jay to work on his speed and suggested the following workouts:

8×400m on 8 minutes
16×200m on 4 minutes
32×100m on 2 minutes

Jay completes seven sets of 400m intervals on 8 ½ minutes:

7:20, 7:31, 7:41, 7:36, 7:53, 8:01, 8:18

December 15, 2007
Jay attempts to swim 16 km at Progress Fitness Centre but quits after covering 9.1 km in 3:41, on account of pain in the triceps.

December 24, 2007
While visiting his parents for the holidays, Jay visits the local pool and swims 200m intervals, with warm-up and cool-down. He is unable to do a complete workout since the duration of the lane swim is only one hour. After having done two days of cross-country skiing upon his arrival home, freezing rain ruins the skiing conditions for a few days. But swimming is an excellent alternative.

December 28, 2007
Jay returns to the local swimming pool and swims 100m intervals, with warm-up and cool-down.

January 5, 2008
Jay swims 16 km at Progress Fitness Centre in 6:31.
Progress Fitness Centre has agreed to give Jay complimentary usage of their facilities in exchange for being named as a sponsor.

January 14, 2008
Jay swims 4.525 km in eighty-nine minutes, one and a half minutes faster than his targeted pace of 3 km/h (=30sec/25m)

January 18, 2008
At Masters swimming practice, Jay completes the following:
- five sets of 100m with 20 seconds rest: 1:45, 1:50, 1:48, 1:48, 1:52
- five sets of 75m with 15 seconds rest: 1:22, 1:22, 1:25, 1:20, 1:25
- five sets of 50m with 15 seconds rest: 0:53, 0:53, 0:48, 0:50, 0:52?
- five sets of 25m with 15 seconds rest: 0:24, 0:26, 0:25, 0:25, 0:24?

January 23, 2008
Jay completes eight sets of 400m intervals on 8 minutes:
7:09, 7:28, 7:26, 7:33, 7:43, 7:52*, 8:05, 8:18
*on 8 ½ minutes from here on

January 30, 2008
Jay swims at Progress Fitness Centre for four hours. The original plan was to take only one feeding break (liquid only) at the half-way point. At 1:42, a muscle seizure in the right calf forces Jay to stand and gave him an incentive to take a feeding break early, in addition to another feeding break later in the workout. The muscle pain quickly disappears, enabling Jay to continue swimming. Jay is not concerned about safety because if this were to happen in open water he would, in the worst case scenario, resort to travel stroke (three drown proofs followed by a kick and a pull) until his paddler could throw him a lifejacket. Travel stroke was not an option at Progress Fitness Centre where the swimming pool is 1.35m deep at its deepest point, just barely deep enough for Jay to tread water without touching his foot to the ground.

February 6, 2008
Jay completes fifteen sets of 200m intervals on 4 minutes:
3:38, 3:43, 3:43, 3:48, 3:43, 3:44, 3:53*, 3:55,
3:53, 3:53, 3:55, 3:58, 3:58, 3:55, 3:55
*on 4:15 from here on

February 16-17, 2008
Jay participates in the annual Gatineau loppet, completing both the 53 km race on Saturday (classic style) as well as another 53 km race on Sunday (ski-skating style). For many years, cross-country skiing has, by far, been Jay's favourite winter sport. This winter, Jay is torn between enjoying his favourite winter sport versus swimming in order to train for the big event.

February 24, 2008
Jay swims 16 km at Progress Fitness Centre in 6:51. Having already completed one 16 km pool swim, plus being in the recovery process from the double ski race the weekend before, Jay is not worried about being slower than on his previous 16 km swim. His main motivation was to maintain endurance.

February 27, 2008
Jay completes thirty-two sets of 100m intervals on 2 minutes:

1:43, 1:42, 1:39, 1:38, 1:43, 1:43, 1:43, 1:45?,
1:??, 1:46, 1:45, 1:46, 1:47, 1:46, 1:46, 1:51,
1:52, 1:53, 1:53, 1:53, 1:56*, 1:53, 1:53, 1:52,
1:52, 1:53, 1:54, 1:53, 1:54, 1:53, 1:53, 1:52
*on 2:05 from here on

March 2, 2008
Jay swims at Progress Fitness Centre for four hours and fifteen minutes, doing front crawl the entire time save two feeding breaks (liquid only) at the two-hour and four-hour mark. At four hours, Jay has covered 11.075 km with only one feeding break. Then Jay covers another 550m in fifteen minutes.

March 7, 2008
Jay completes eight sets of 400m on 8 minutes:

7:13, 7:23, 7:30, 7:40, 7:40, 7:38, 7:43, 7:47

March 9, 2008
With the attendance at Masters swimming practice low (presumably because of the snowstorm), Jay has an entire lane to himself and opts for 200m intervals in lieu of the prescribed workout.
The duration of the practice is one hour and Jay squeezes in ten intervals in addition to warm-up and cool-down.

10×200m on 4 minutes
3:40, 3:42, 3:45, 3:44, 3:44
3:43, 3:43, 3:43, 3:47, 3:50

March 12, 2008
Jay completes thirty-two sets of 100m intervals on 2 minutes:

1:37, 1:39, 1:41, 1:42, 1:42, 1:45, 1:45, 1:44
1:44, 1:45, 1:46, 1:46, 1:47, 1:46, 1:45, 1:45
1:45, 1:43, 1:44, 1:45, 1:46, 1:45, 1:47, 1:46?
1:47, 1:49, 1:47, 1:48, 1:48, 1:48, 1:47, 1:47

For the second half of the workout, one of Jay's co-workers who is noticeably faster than him graciously joined him and swam behind him during each interval, usually doing either front crawl at a relaxed pace or back crawl. This motivated Jay to swim faster. A big thank-you to Jay's co-worker, not only on Jay's behalf but also on behalf of all the people with Asperger's Syndrome who will benefit from the increased awareness resulting from his swim.

March 18, 2008
Jay completes eight sets of 400m intervals on 8 minutes:

7:16, 7:23, 7:30, 7:30, 7:47, 7:49*, 8:04, 8:14
*on 8:15 from here on

March 26, 2008
Jay completes sixteen sets of 200m intervals on 4 minutes:

3:32, 3:35, 3:38, 3:42, 3:42, 3:43, 3:43, 3:46
3:48, 3:52*, 3:50, 3:55, 3:56, 3:49, 3:55, 3:59
*on 4:05 from here on

Once again, Jay's co-worker, Catriona, joined him and swam behind him for most of the intervals.

April 2, 2008
Jay completes thirty sets of 100m intervals on 2:05:

1:43, 1:48, 1:44, 1:45, 1:45, 1:47, 1:44, 1:45
1:47, 1:44, 1:46, 1:45, 1:46, 1:49*, 1:46, 1:47
1:48, 1:46, 1:47, 1:47, 1:48, 1:48, 1:46, 1:49
1:50, 1:49, 1:50, 1:??, 1:??, 1:50**
*this interval was started five seconds too early **on 2:10

Dedicated to helping Jay achieve his ambition in whatever way she can, Catriona has agreed to accompany Jay on his speed workouts every Wednesday, whenever possible. This time, Jay accepted Catriona's offer that she swim 10 seconds ahead of him to help him maintain a consistent pace. In addition, Catriona has given Jay several pieces of invaluable advice including:
- swim at a relaxed pace on the first interval (gliding more and focusing on making his stroke feel smooth and effortless) as Jay has been swimming the first interval way too fast
- a consistent pace is more important than the amount of rest (hence the extra rest time)
The intent for today was to swim every interval on 1:45

April 6, 2008
Jay swims for three and a half hours at Progress Fitness Centre. His goal was to swim for five hours with only two feeding breaks in order to help condition himself to complete swim 16 km with limited feeding breaks in order to "save time". Just before the three hour mark, Jay's calf muscle suddenly seized up without warning, probably because of a lack of fluid/nourishment. So much for saving time. Jay rests for ten minutes and then swims for another half hour before calling it quits.

April 8, 2008
Jay takes his first open water swim of the season and stays in for forty-five seconds. The cold water inflicts physical pain. Thanks to the sunny day with little wind, Jay warms up quickly - although he must keep moving for at least twenty seconds to counter the agony. After warming up, Jay goes back into the water for another forty-five seconds.

April 9, 2008
Jay completes eight sets of 400m intervals on 8:20

    7:35, 7:34, 7:32, 7:34, 7:35, 7:32, 7:38, 7:36

The goal was initially to do every interval on 7:40 but was changed to 7:35 after the second interval.

April 14, 2008
Catriona shows Jay some swimming drills from the book "Total Immersion" by Terry Laughlin. Catriona informs Jay that he is to rotate his body to the side with each stroke. Front crawl is essentially

performed on one's side and not on one's front as many amateur swimmers assume. Later in the day, Jay takes another short swim in Lake Ontario near downtown Kingston and is photographed for a front-page picture in tomorrow's local newspaper.

April 16, 2008
Jay completes sixteen sets of 200m intervals on 4:10:

3:42, 3:37, 3:40, 3:44, 3:42, 3:45, 3:46, 3:46
3:48, 3:47, 3:50, 3:52, 3:51, 3:55, 3:46, 3:46

Once again, the goal was to keep every interval at a constant pace. 3:45 was the desired pace.

April 20, 2008
Jay swims 16 km in 6:19 at Progress Fitness Centre, taking only four short feeding breaks. Near the end of this arduous swim, Jay manages to sprint 500m in 11:03

April 22, 2008
At the end of the workout with the Masters swimming club, before the cool-down, Jay swims eight sets of 50m on 1:00

0:47, 0:50, 0:50, 0:52, 0:50, 0:50, 0:50, 0:51

April 23, 2008
Jay completes twenty-seven sets of 100m on 2:05

1:48, 1:47, 1:46, 1:46, 1:44, 1:46, 1:46, 1:46
1:45, 1:47, 1:47, 1:50, 1:47, 1:50, 1:48, 1:47
1:50*, 1:54, 1:51, 1:51, 1:54, 1:54, 1:55, 1:55**
1:48, 1:51, 1:51

*on 2:10 from here on **on 2:30 from here on

April 27, 2008
Jay swims for four hours and ten minutes at Progress Fitness Centre, taking only one short feeding break. Distance covered is 11.075 km. Near the end of the workout, Jay sprints 725m in 15:37

April 28, 2008
Jay plans to swim twelve sets of 400m but calls it quits after the second interval, concluding that there is no point in continuing the workout.

8:12, 7:57

Jay has never been this slow; he guesses and hopes that his body is calling for rest after the four hour swim yesterday. Any other reason for his slowness spells trouble. Determined to salvage something from his visit to the pool, Jay swims four sets of 25m with 10 seconds rest:

    0:24, 0:25, 0:26, 0:25

April 30, 2008
Jay swims front crawl nonstop for 87 minutes, covering 4.15 km. Near the end of the workout, Jay sprints 400m in 8:00

May 4, 2008
Frontenac Outfitters holds their annual open house and blow-out sale. Thanks to Frontenac Outfitters' generous donation of canoes and kayaks for free test paddling, Jay swims for 65 minutes in Pearkes Lake (his first open-water training swim of the season) while two of his volunteer paddlers kayak beside him. Water temperature is 57°F (14°C). Pearkes Lake is seventy feet deep at its maximum depth and therefore warms up quite quickly in the spring. Within the first two mintues, Jay wonders if he will be able to withstand the water. Less than ten minutes later, in a sunny area, Jay was much more comfortable.

May 6, 2008
Jay completes seven sets of 400m on 8:15:

    7:33, 7:40, 7:46, 7:53*, 8:03, 8:06, 8:31
    *on 8:30 from here on

May 7, 2008
Catriona graciously gives Jay one hour of one-on-one attention as she walks Jay through some drills, helping Jay to focus on his form. Drills consisted of distance per stroke, body rotation, and kicking on one's side with head lead and hand lead. Later in the day, Jay swims in Navy Bay (part of Lake Ontario) for ten minutes. Water temperature is 53.5°F (12°C). Jay originally thought he would be calling it quits within five minutes and had told his spotters that ten minutes would be the absolute longest. Experience has shown that, unless Jay is in so much pain that he wants out of the water within five minutes, his heat-generating mechanisms have time to register in which case he can withstand the water for one hour.

May 9, 2008
Jay swims front crawl nonstop for three hours and ten minutes at Progress Fitness Centre. Distance covered is 8.225 km.

May 11, 2008
Jay undertakes his second open-water training swim of the season, swimming for one hour and twenty-five minutes in Gould Lake. Water temperature is 59°F (15°C).

May 14, 2008
Jay completes fifteen sets of 200m on 4:10

    3:46, 3:47, 3:43, 3:45, 3:47, 3:53, 3:53, 3:53
    3:56*, 4:57**, 3:58, 4:01, 4:01, 3:46, 3:46
    *on 4:20 from here on **250m

Later that afternoon, Jay undertakes his first training swim in Lake Ontario this season, swimming for one hour and twenty-one minutes along the shoreline of the RMC peninsula. Surprisingly, Jay is comfortable some of the time but nonetheless chilled most of the time. Water temperature is 58°F (14°C) at the starting and finishing point but may vary by a few degrees over the course of the swim.

May 17, 2008
Jay undertakes his second training swim in Lake Ontario. Jay swims for 1:15 and would have preferred to continue swimming for as long as two hours but his kayaker was ready to call it quits. Water temperature is 56°F (13°C).

May 19, 2008
Jay returns to Dog Lake for a timed 16 km swim, swimming from his friend's dock to the 500m floatation marker and back 16 times, taking only five short feeding breaks. Jay completes the first kilometer in 21 minutes. At the end, Jay has slowed down to 28 or 29 minutes per kilometer. Jay sprints the last kilometer in 23 minutes. Total time was 6:51. Water temperature is approximately 61°F (16°C).

May 21, 2008
Jay completes thirty-one sets of 100m on 2:10:

1:55, 1:58, 1:55, 1:52, 1:52, 1:54, 1:55, 1:55

Appendix N

1:55, 1:54, 1:55, 1:54, 1:54, 1:55, 1:54, 1:57
1:57, 1:56, 1:56, 2:00, 2:01*, 2:01, 1:57, 1:00**
2:04, 2:05, 1:57, 1:57, 2:03?, 1:54, 1:58?, 2:02
*on 2:20 from here on **sudden calf muscle seizure at 50m; Jay rests for 20 seconds before beginning the next interval

Originally, Jay had planned to swim forty-eight sets. Operating on the belief that one key part of the workout is to sprint the last three sets, Jay decides throughout the workout to swim only twenty-eight sets, swimming the twenty-fifth set easy and sprinting the next three. After twenty-eight sets, Jay decides he has enough energy to swim one more set. During that set, he decides he'll do yet another set providing he completes that set within two minutes.

May 23, 2008
Jay swims along the shoreline of the RMC peninsula. The water temperature has dropped to 50°F (10°C), presumably on account of yesterday's rainfall. Jay exits the water after forty minutes for obvious reasons.

May 25, 2008
Jay swims for one hour in Lake Ontario by downtown Kingston. Water temperature is estimated to be 52°F (11°C). Although it takes a few minutes before Jay starts shivering, his friends are concerned for him. One of Jay's friends graciously turns on his car heater after which Jay sits in the car for fifteen minutes until he feels warm. The car feels like a sauna to everyone else while Jay is still shivering.

May 26, 2008
Jay completes twelve sets of 400m on 9:00

8:13, 8:20, 8:26, 8:28*, 8:25*, 8:32, 8:33, 8:33
8:45**, 9:14, 8:13, 8:17
*distances may not be accurate **30 seconds rest from here on

May 28, 2008
Jay completes fifteen sets of 200m on 4:15

3:55, 3:51, 3:51, 3:55, 3:53, 3:52, 3:53, 3:51
2:53*, 3:54, 3:55, 4:00, 3:48, 3:49, 3:52
*150m

June 1, 2008

Pam Haldane, a Total Immersion coach, has agreed to be Jay's coach for the big swim. Spending an entire day with Jay, Pam walks Jay through the total immersion drills, videotapes his swimming and tells him where he can improve. One of Pam's many suggestions is to glide more and thus gain more distance per stroke. With Pam's help, Jay swims 25m with only eighteen strokes where, previously, Jay averaged thirty strokes per 25m. This improvement, if continued, will reduce immensely the number of strokes required to swim across Lake Ontario.

June 4, 2008

While Pam was coaching Jay, one of Jay's friends, whom he met at an earlier training session at Progress Fitness Centre, introduced Jay to Jean who also likes to enforce a longer stroke. Jean walks Jay through front crawl drills after which Jay completes forty-seven sets of 100m:

    1:50, 1:53, 1:55, 1:57, 1:55, 1:56
    2:01, 1:56, 2:00, 2:04, 2:03, 2:04
    2:01, 2:05, 2:01, 1:58*, 1:07, 1:06
    2:05, 2:09, 2:09, 2:08, 2:05*, 2:12
    2:13, 2:14, 2:14, 2:14+, 2:12, 2:10
    2:06*, 2:08, 2:18, 2:14?, 2:10, 2:11
    2:10, 2:14?, 2:17?, 2:??, 2:16, 2:02
    2:05, 2:05, 2:07, 2:07, 2:03

    *at Jean's suggestion, Jay swims the last 25m fast
    +at Jean's suggestion, Jay swims head-up front crawl on the last lap

At the end of the workout, Jean comments that the workout is symbiotic since Jean had not swum that far in some time.

June 7, 2008

Jay's friend Jens comes to Kingston to visit him. Partly for a variety in swimming and partly because Jens enjoys ferry rides, Jay suggests that he paddle his kayak to Amherst Island while Jens drives his car to the island. Once on the island, Jens paddles beside Jay while Jay swims along the shoreline. Jens and Jay stay close to shore, so close that the waves are breaking and pushing Jay towards shore. At least twice, Jay brushes against the bottom of the lake and asks Jens to move further from shore. Jay swims west, against the current, for two hours and ten minutes until the turnaround point and then swims back to the starting point in an hour and a half. This is Jay's longest swim in Lake Ontario this season. Water temperature was 58°F (14°C) most of the time but 54°C(12°C) in a few places. Jens was unable to keep his hand in the water with the thermometer for even 7 minutes without it aching from the cold. While Jay is paddling the kayak back to the shoreline, Jens measures the road distance one way to be 3.4 km, although the shoreline distance may be slightly longer. Once back on the mainland, Jay and Jens have supper at an all-you-can-eat place, which Jay has worked up an appetite for, with two of Jay's other volunteer paddlers.

June 8, 2008
Jay swims in Lake Ontario, further east this time. Jay starts at HMCS Cataraqui and swims around the point of Cedar Island and then swims back. Jay is in the water for two and a half hours, his first time in Lake Ontario this season without feeling chilled.

June 10, 2008
Jay paddles his kayak to work in the morning. After work, Jay's co-worker paddles the kayak while Jay swims home. The swim commences at 5:00p.m. At 9:00p.m., with only two km remaining, both Jay and his paddler decide that it is too dark to continue the swim so they adventurously tow the kayak through DuPont property and then along the road back to Jay's house.

June 11, 2008
Once again, Jean meets Jay at Progress Fitness Centre to accompany him on his final set of speed intervals before the trial swim. Jay completes five sets of 100m as a warm-up:

    2:07, 2:07, 2:16?, 2:09?, 2:11?

Then Jay completes ten sets of 400m intervals:

    9:00, 9:05, 9:07, 8:51, 9:11
    9:19, 9:01, 8:54, 8:40, 8:33
    Rest period is usually 45-60 seconds

June 13, 2008
Jay travels to Hamilton to meet Pam for another day of coaching. Marilyn, Jay's Swim Master and secretary of Solo Swims of Ontario, stops at the pool for a few minutes to meet both Jay and Pam for the

first time and exchange a few words. Later, Jay and Marilyn get together to discuss the logistics of the trial swim including location.

June 22, 2008
Swim Master Marilyn and coach Pam, along with a few other support boaters and paddlers, meet Jay at Loyalist Cove Marina in Bath for Jay's 16 km trial swim. Loyalist Cove Marina has graciously agreed to sponsor Jay by allowing the use of their facilities. Jay is accompanied by a 20-foot power boat plus three kayaks. At three hours and fifteen minutes, Jay is informed that he has swum 8 km and is instructed to turn around. After five hours and forty-one minutes, Jay arrives back at the marina. The power boat encountered engine problems and finally broke down on the return trip. This affected the GPS readings since the GPS was tracking every zigzag. Somehow, Jay knew he had not covered the full 16 km, since Jay had never been that fast even in a swimming pool and the current certainly didn't help matters. Water temperature is 62°F (16°C) and the waves were one to two feet high. Jay starts shivering slightly several minutes after completing the swim. A warm shower and warm clothes suppressed the shivering completely. Marilyn informs Jay after the fact that he had only swum 12km. All said and done, the distance doesn't really matter; what matters is that Jay is now sanctioned.

July 1, 2008
Pam returns to Kingston to give Jay another day of coaching.

July 5, 2008
Jay swims for just over five hours, from the marina at Deadman's Bay to Milton Island and back.

July 6, 2008
Jay undertakes his peak training swim of the season. Jay starts swimming at Faircrest Blvd and swims upriver. Jay had planned to make it to Amherstview. After three unsuccessful attempts last summer, Jay makes it further than ever before. On account of a mix-up with the volunteer paddlers, Jay makes it to Bayridge Drive and then turns around and conveniently ends the swim at his house. Jay had been in the water for ten hours and covered an estimated twenty kilometres. The water is calm for almost all of the swim. There is not a cloud in the sky; Jay does not feel the slightest chill but is quite sunburned

despite having applied sunscreen before entering the water, sunburned enough to notice as soon as he tries to dry his upper back.

July 13, 2008
Now tapering, Jay swims for seven hours and fifteen minutes while accompanied by a powerboat with two RMC sea cadets with rescue training. Partway through the swim, Jay swims back to the boathouse so that the boaters can have lunch, during which time Jay takes a feeding break, treads water, and swims back and forth between two docks.

July 20, 2008
Jay swims for six hours and twenty minutes, accompanied once again by two RMC sea cadets in a powerboat.

July 22, 2008
Jay swims for four hours, starting at the RMC boathouse and swimming almost all the way to Milton Island and back, accompanied in a canoe by three sea cadets who remember Jay from last year.

July 24, 2008
Jay completes his final training swim before the big event, swimming for two hours and twenty minutes in Lake Ontario despite thunderstorm warnings. Jay's paddler keeps the kayak close to shore, almost always within ten metres, ready to abort at any time. Now that the training is complete, there is nothing more to do - except tackle the lake.

Appendix O

Speed Interval Times

December 6, 2007
Jay completes seven sets of 400m intervals on 8 ½ minutes:
    7:20, 7:31, 7:41, 7:36, 7:53, 8:01, 8:18

December 24, 2007
200m intervals plus warm-up and cool-down
pool only open for one hour
times not recorded

December 28, 2007
100m intervals plus warm-up and cool-down
pool only open for one hour
times not recorded

January 23, 2008
Jay completes eight sets of 400m intervals on 8 minutes:
    7:09, 7:28, 7:26, 7:33, 7:43, 7:52*, 8:05, 8:18
    *on 8 ½ minutes from here on

February 6, 2008
Jay completes fifteen sets of 200m intervals on 4 minutes:
    3:38, 3:43, 3:43, 3:48, 3:43, 3:44, 3:53*, 3:55,
    3:53, 3:53, 3:55, 3:58, 3:58, 3:55, 3:55
    *on 4:15 from here on

February 27, 2008
Jay completes thirty-two sets of 100m intervals on 2 minutes:
    1:43, 1:42, 1:39, 1:38, 1:43, 1:43, 1:43, 1:45?,
    1:??, 1:46, 1:45, 1:46, 1:47, 1:46, 1:46, 1:51,
    1:52, 1:53, 1:53, 1:53, 1:56*, 1:53, 1:53, 1:52,
    1:52, 1:53, 1:54, 1:53, 1:54, 1:53, 1:53, 1:52
    *on 2:05 from here on

March 7, 2008
Jay completes eight sets of 400m on 8 minutes:

    7:13, 7:23, 7:30, 7:40, 7:40, 7:38, 7:43, 7:47

March 9, 2008
10×200m on 4 minutes (at KMAC in lieu of prescribed workout; hence fewer sets)

    3:40, 3:42, 3:45, 3:44, 3:44
    3:43, 3:43, 3:43, 3:47, 3:50

March 12, 2008
Jay completes thirty-two sets of 100m intervals on 2 minutes:

    1:37, 1:39, 1:41, 1:42, 1:42, 1:45, 1:45, 1:44
    1:44, 1:45, 1:46, 1:46, 1:47, 1:46, 1:45, 1:45
    1:45, 1:43, 1:44, 1:45, 1:46, 1:45, 1:47, 1:46?
    1:47, 1:49, 1:47, 1:48, 1:48, 1:48, 1:47, 1:47

March 18, 2008
Jay completes eight sets of 400m intervals on 8 minutes:

    7:16, 7:23, 7:30, 7:30, 7:47, 7:49*, 8:04, 8:14
    *on 8:15 from here on

March 26, 2008
Jay completes sixteen sets of 200m intervals on 4 minutes:

    3:32, 3:35, 3:38, 3:42, 3:42, 3:43, 3:43, 3:46
    3:48, 3:52*, 3:50, 3:55, 3:56, 3:49, 3:55, 3:59
    *on 4:05 from here on

April 2, 2008
Jay completes thirty sets of 100m intervals on 2:05:

    1:43, 1:48, 1:44, 1:45, 1:45, 1:47, 1:44, 1:45
    1:47, 1:44, 1:46, 1:45, 1:46, 1:49*, 1:46, 1:47
    1:48, 1:46, 1:47, 1:47, 1:48, 1:48, 1:46, 1:49
    1:50, 1:49, 1:50, 1:??, 1:??, 1:50**
    *this interval was started five seconds too early **on 2:10

Prior to the workout, Catriona gave Jay the following advice

- swim at a relaxed pace on the first interval (gliding more and focusing on making his stroke feel smooth and effortless) as Jay has been swimming the first interval way too fast
- a consistent pace is more important than the amount of rest (hence the extra rest time)

The intent for today was to swim every interval on 1:45

April 9, 2008
Jay completes eight sets of 400m intervals on 8:20

    7:35, 7:34, 7:32, 7:34, 7:35, 7:32, 7:38, 7:36

The goal was initially to do every interval on 7:40 but was changed to 7:35 after the second interval.

April 16, 2008
Jay completes sixteen sets of 200m intervals on 4:10

    3:42, 3:37, 3:40, 3:44, 3:42, 3:45, 3:46, 3:46
    3:48, 3:47, 3:50, 3:52, 3:51, 3:55, 3:46, 3:46

Once again, the goal was to keep every interval at a constant pace. 3:45 was the desired pace.
Jay sprinted the last two intervals.
Jay tried (unsuccessfully) to maintain a steady pace and form on the third last interval.

April 23, 2008
Jay completes twenty-seven sets of 100m on 2:05

    1:48, 1:47, 1:46, 1:46, 1:44, 1:46, 1:46, 1:46
    1:45, 1:47, 1:47, 1:50, 1:47, 1:50, 1:48, 1:47
    1:50*, 1:54, 1:51, 1:51, 1:54, 1:54, 1:55, 1:55**
    1:48, 1:51, 1:51
    *on 2:10 from here on **on 2:30 from here on

April 28, 2008
Jay plans to swim twelve sets of 400m but calls it quits after the second interval.

    8:12, 7:57

Appendix O

May 6, 2008
Jay completes seven sets of 400m on 8:15:
> 7:33, 7:40, 7:46, 7:53*, 8:03, 8:06, 8:31
> *on 8:30 from here on

May 14, 2008
Jay completes fifteen sets of 200m on 4:10
> 3:46, 3:47, 3:43, 3:45, 3:47, 3:53, 3:53, 3:53
> 3:56*, 4:57**, 3:58, 4:01, 4:01, 3:46, 3:46
> *on 4:20 from here on **250m

May 21, 2008
Jay completes thirty-one sets of 100m on 2:10:
> 1:55, 1:58, 1:55, 1:52, 1:52, 1:54, 1:55, 1:55
> 1:55, 1:54, 1:55, 1:54, 1:54, 1:55, 1:54, 1:57
> 1:57, 1:56, 1:56, 2:00, 2:01*, 2:01, 1:57, 1:00**
> 2:04, 2:05, 1:57, 1:57, 2:03?, 1:54, 1:58?, 2:02
> *on 2:20 from here on **sudden calf muscle seizure at 50m; Jay rests for 20 seconds before beginning the next interval

Originally, Jay had planned to swim forty-eight sets. Operating on the belief that one key part of the workout is to sprint the last three sets, Jay decides throughout the workout to swim only twenty-eight sets, swimming the twenty-fifth set easy and sprinting the next three. After twenty-eight sets, Jay decides he has enough energy to swim one more set. During that set, he decides he'll do yet another set providing he completes that set within two minutes.

May 26, 2008
Jay completes twelve sets of 400m on 9:00
> 8:13, 8:20, 8:26, 8:28*, 8:25*, 8:32, 8:33, 8:33
> 8:45**, 9:14, 8:13, 8:17
> *distances may not be accurate **30 seconds rest from here on

May 28, 2008
Jay completes fifteen sets of 200m on 4:15
> 3:55, 3:51, 3:51, 3:55, 3:53, 3:52, 3:53, 3:51
> 2:53*, 3:54, 3:55, 4:00, 3:48, 3:49, 3:52
> *150m

301

June 4, 2008
Jay completes forty-seven sets of 100m with Jean:

    1:50, 1:53, 1:55, 1:57, 1:55, 1:56
    2:01, 1:56, 2:00, 2:04, 2:03, 2:04
    2:01, 2:05, 2:01, 1:58*, 1:07, 1:06
    2:05, 2:09, 2:09, 2:08, 2:05*, 2:12
    2:13, 2:14, 2:14, 2:14+, 2:12, 2:10
    2:06*, 2:08, 2:18, 2:14?, 2:10, 2:11
    2:10, 2:14?, 2:17?, 2:??, 2:16, 2:02
    2:05, 2:05, 2:07, 2:07, 2:03
      *at Jean's suggestion, Jay swims the last 25m fast
      +at Jean's suggestion, Jay swims head-up front crawl on the last lap

June 11, 2008
Jay completes five sets of 100m as a warm-up:

    2:07, 2:07, 2:16?, 2:09?, 2:11?

Then Jay completes ten sets of 400m intervals:

    9:00, 9:05, 9:07, 8:51, 9:11
    9:19, 9:01, 8:54, 8:40, 8:33
      Rest period is usually 45-60 seconds

Appendix P
The Big Day

Today is the big day!

Jay spent the night at the Comfort Inn in St. Catherines to get a good rest last night.

Some of the crew took the Precious Lady from Toronto to Niagara-on-the-Lake yesterday and took several water temperature readings along the way. The water temperature ranged from 62 to 70 degrees!

Jay will be at the Queen's Royal Park by 9:30 to be ready for a 10 am start! We hope there is a big crowd to cheer him on. Expect periodic updates today.

10:30 am

Jay left Queen's Royal Park at Niagara-on-the-Lake at 10:10am. The weather was great for those of us on shore but will create one metre high waves for Jay and may blow him off course. A small crowd cheered him on. One well wisher was a man who has a son with autism who understands why Jay would want to educate others about autism spectrum disorders. Thanks to the Niagara-on-the-Lake Sailing Club for providing us with two berths last night.

12:38 pm

Jay is maintaining a pace of 3.2 km per hour, faster than we anticipated! The Kingston media have been fantastic. Jim Elyot from The Drive will be interviewing Jay's parents today. 96.3 FM spoke with the Program Supervisor from the Ministry of Children and Youth Services who is responsible on matters pertaining to autism and who is a pacer for Jay.

5:00 pm

Jay is keeping up a better than anticipated pace in waves ranging from 0.3 to 0.4 metres. Initially we thought that Jay was swimming quickly because of the calm waters for the first stretch but it appears that his training at Progress Fitness is the reason he is doing so well! Thankfully the crew is not adversely affected by high waves as has been the case for other marathon swimmers and have been able to enjoy the food donated by The Vegetable Fix.

10:00 pm

Jay is doing well and eating in the water has not created a problem for him. He had a bit of a lag as his arms were sore for a while but he is doing well again. Two of his volunteers have been in the water swimming alongside Jay. Eden has encouraged Jay for two 45 minute periods. Andra swam with Jay for 1.5 hours tonight. Jay is in good spirits and in great form. The night swim is a dangerous time and there are several safety measures in place to ensure that Jay remains safe. Two zodiaks are keeping close to him with flashlights donated by the Cataraqui Canadian Tire. Thanks to Bay Port Yachting Centre for making the zodiaks available. Jay's crew enjoyed watching the stunning sunset while watching Jay swim.

Overnight

The crew enjoyed their evening cruise under tons of stars as they proudly watched Jay conquer what is likely to be the hardest part of his swim. Pam, Jay's volunteer coach, did a really good job of talking him through a second period of experiencing pain in his arms. The guys from Gavercon and Hometech have been a great help operating the zodiaks. We want to thank both Gavercon and Hometech for their generous financial contribution even though we made a mistake with your logo on the event T-Shirts (SORRY)!

July 29th 6:15am

Everything is going well and we expect Jay to arrive at Marilyn Bell Park between 7 p.m. and midnight. As we have planned a fun day in support of Jay's efforts to raise awareness of Asperger's Syndrome, we hope that there will be a lot of people at the park to cheer him into shore. Come and enjoy the activities that start at 2 p.m. and the free live entertainment that begins at 3 p.m. at Marilyn Bell Park. The water has been calm and there was no boat traffic last night, but as they get closer to Toronto this morning they are expecting more traffic. Jay has been drinking and eating hourly based on the very detailed and personalized meal plan that Dr. Vogt volunteered her time to provide. Understandably, Jay is slowing down so he is now accompanied by two pacers to try and give him another boost to help bring him out of the difficult time he had last night. Jay typically swims at 2 km per hour but has slowed to 1/2 km per hour; it is expected that he will pick up the pace again.

8:00 am

Jay could see the Toronto sky line lit up overnight, and now as it gets lighter he can still see Ontario Place - right beside where he is planning to come to shore at Marilyn Bell Park. Jay is currently 11 km from shore and is getting close to the Humber River current which he will have to work against. He is encouraged by everyone's support. Jay's friend Peter kayaked beside him all night and the crew is loudly cheering him on. Please keep sending your comments on Jay's website as we are sending them to the crew to be read to him during his feeding breaks. The Kingston community has been a great support for Jay from the time that he started training. Jay's volunteers marvel at the fact that as we promoted Jay Serdula's Swim for Asperger's we were continually told, "Oh, I know Jay" and were told another great story about Jay. When Jay made a purchase at Wool-Tyme very early on in the planning of the marathon swim, they promised a sponsorship and delivered on that promise. The Kingston media promised to support Jay's swim and have been fantastic in pursuing up to date information on how Jay is doing. We are getting messages that people have heard about Jay on FLY FM and 96.3 FM and read about him in the Whig. As we are in Toronto, please send comments on Jay's websites so we can tell his fans what radio stations to listen to and what television stations to watch and what papers to read for news about Jay. We can't forget about Jay's hometown Deep River! Ever since Jay was sanctioned by Solo Swims of Ontario, there has been a generous flow of donations from people who have known Jay for a long time. Let's hope the Toronto community catches the spirit and joins us today at Marilyn Bell Park. The Toronto Sun ran a story about Jay this morning and the Toronto Star has expressed interest in being at the shoreline when Jay gets to Toronto! There is another big community that can help Jay - the Autism Spectrum Disorder community. Yes, Jay is looking for donations to help fund support for people who also have Asperger's Syndrome, but his other goal is to raise awareness. Jay wishes that he had been diagnosed earlier so that his teachers would have understood why he had trouble with communication (such as taking the words literally and not understanding what was meant to be communicated), why he didn't always react as expected in particular social situations and why he had trouble accepting change. There are many children who have a diagnosis of Asperger's Syndrome who wish that people still understood these very same things. Let's help Jay and others who have Asperger's to break down the barriers they face by telling people about Jay Serdula's Swim for Asperger's and provide information about the syndrome.

9:15 am

Once the sun came out and the pacers got in the water, Jay's pace improved again.

11:00 am

Jay is going a bit faster now, and is averaging 2 kph. One of the zodiacs is coming into Marilyn Bell Park to get supplies and more gas; we should have another update then. Thanks to Merry PAWppins Pet Care Services for relaying updates to our volunteer webmaster Eric today.

2:45 pm

Apparently someone spotted white caps on the Lake Ontario shore. As someone not personally vested in swimming I concede to not knowing what that means. However, I expect to receive an update on this from the boat very soon.

3:00 pm

Jay continues to keep up a reasonable pace, though is experiencing resistance from the Humber River basin as he gets closer to the Toronto shoreline. As a result of the strong currents, Jay and the crew have decided to alter the point of landing to the Leslie St. Spit (Vicki Keith Point). This will reduce his swimming time by an anticipated 3 hours. At present, Jay is expected to arrive between 7 and 11 pm. The reception has started at Marilyn Bell Park, and will continue there. People are encouraged to stay at Marilyn Bell Park until Jay's arrival. We will keep people updated regularly, via this site.

3:45 pm

We have confirmed Jay's impending arrival at the Leslie Street Spit with Toronto Port Authority. We would like to thank Michael at the TPA for accommodating this last minute change and for arranging

Appendix P

security. Vehicle access will be restricted. For those at Marilyn Bell Park, please contact Laura regarding vehicle access for those designated as cleared. The press are asked to continue to contact Chris, at the number that has been provided. Jay's anticipated arrival remains 8:00 pm. Individuals are welcome to walk to the lakeshore at the spit, although they should be aware that it is a 5 km hike from the parking lot. The reception party will continue at Marilyn Bell Park. Jay continues to be successful in his efforts to cross Lake Ontario.

6:30 pm

Jay is 2.9 miles from shore. He has changed direction and is heading for the Leslie Street Spit. He has been struggling against the current and as a result it is anticipated that he will not reach shore until approximately 10:00 pm. We would like to thank the media for supporting Jay during the swim, and agreeing to meet him at the Leslie Street Spit. A special thanks to Angela at the Whig Standard, Bryn at the Toronto Sun, and Megan at the Toronto Star.

9:00 pm

Jay is struggling against the current, finding it difficult to make headway, however his spirits and determination remain high. He is presently 2.3 miles from shore. At this rate, it is anticipated it will take another 4 hours to complete the crossing. We are concerned about a potential storm that is developing and could arrive in the area as early as 10:00pm. Jay's crew remain diligent in maintaining his safety at all times. The media attention has been exceptional and clearly Jay has already achieved his goal of raising awareness regarding Asperger's Syndrome.

9:40 pm

Jay's sister has joined him in the water to support him on the last stretch. This has given Jay lots of motivation and energy. His family has also joined him on an adjacent boat. It's been a long swim, but he's almost there.

10:30 pm

Jay's friends and family have been shuttled from the shore at the Leslie Street Spit out to the 68 foot lead boat Precious Lady and the 33 foot formula boat. The weather looks more favourable and Jay continues to push for the shore. He is anticipated to arrive around 1:00 am.

3:10 am

Jay was successful, as he successfully swam across Lake Ontario as promised. He arrived at 3:11am; the swim took a total of 41 hours and 1 minute. Congratulations Jay!

8:45 am

Jay is recovering in hospital, where he is getting some well deserved sleep and is under observation. The family really appreciates all of the support, especially that of the volunteers and those on the boats.

We are very excited and grateful for all of the media attention. All of Jay's training and perseverance yesterday has led to the outcome that Jay had hoped for: people are talking about Asperger's Syndrome. At present, Jay has no voice and therefore is not available for interviews. When Jay finished his swim he had moderate hypothermia; his body temperature dropped to 32.5 degrees Celsius but was back up within a few hours. Jay is recovering in the hospital and our primary concern is his return to full health. Unfortunately, we are not sure how long he will require to recover until he is reassessed by a doctor.

Source: http://swim4aspergers.wordpress.com/

Appendix Q

Swim Master's Report[83]

SOLO SWIMS of ONTARIO
Established 1976
"Promoting safety in marathon swimming"

SWIM MASTER'S REPORT

NAME OF SWIMMER:	Jay Serdula
AGE OF SWIMMER:	35
DATE OF SWIM:	July 28 – 30, 2008
SWIM START LOCATION:	Niagara-on-the-Lake 43°15.471N; 079°04.085W
SWIM START TIME:	10:10:23 am
SWIM FINISH LOCATION:	Leslie St. Spit, Toronto 43°36.5N; 79°20.4W (estimate)
SWIM FINISH TIME:	3:11:35 a.m.
TOTAL SWIM TIME:	41 hours 1 minute
DISTANCE SWUM:	52 kilometers
COACH:	Pam Haldane
SWIM MASTER:	Marilyn Korzekwa
BOAT # 1:	"Precious Lady"; 68 foot twin diesel motor; John Crawford
BOAT # 2:	"Formula 33"; 33 foot twin gas motor; Dave Keates

---

[83] This report is the property of Solo Swims of Ontario, Inc.

Solo Swims of Ontario

Swim Master's Report
Narrative

Jay Serdula is a 35 year old man with Asperger's syndrome from Kingston whose goal was to swim Lake Ontario to raise awareness and money for Asperger's syndrome. He was not diagnosed until in his 20's and hoped that by raising awareness of the syndrome, other children would not be misunderstood like he was.

The trial swim was held on June 22, 08 heading west from Loyalist Cove Marine in Bath Ontario. The plan was to head west for 8 km and return. Unfortunately, the 20 foot powerboat developed motor problems, needing to be towed to shore halfway back. This caused a zigzag course for the powerboat and confusion with the GPS, resulting in our turning around just short of the 6 km mark. Fortunately there were also 3 kayaks in the flotilla to accompany Jay, so he could complete the swim. The water temperature was 62°F for the majority of the swim. On the outbound leg, the wind was blowing at 5-10 knots from the SW, and the breaking waves were 0.4-0.7 m. The wind died down on the return leg. On the return leg, Jay swam strongly, not appearing unduly fatigued. Jay shivered very briefly at the end. His time for the 11.7 km was 5 h 41 min, an average of 2.1 km per hour. Taking the wind conditions into account, a 16 km swim was estimated at 7 h 25 minutes. The trial swim was passed because he appeared to be able to swim at least another 6 hours at this speed, he has a marathon running background, he handled the waves and the cold without difficulty, and he appeared to be maturely determined to complete Lake Ontario.

A preswim meeting was held on July 16, 08 with the large boat captains and their assistants, the inflatable boat organizer, the swim manager and several other crew. During a conversation after the meeting, Andra Jones, whose husband crewed on the Lambert swim, immediately impressed me as a potential swim master. She drives boats, has Power Squadron, swims recreationally regularly, and was very enthusiastic about the swim.

The weather forecast for July 28: Sunny with cloudy periods, High 28. Wind west 10 knots continuing from the night before.

Appendix Q

July 29: A mix of sun and clouds with 40 % chance of showers. Low 16, high 28. Wind west 15 knots. (The showers were of the "pop-up variety", and not described as thundershowers).
July 30: Cloudy with 60% chance of showers. Low 18, high 24. (This appeared to be a front moving in.)

Since the swim was estimated at 28-36 hours, the plan was to start in the morning on the 28th and aim to finish before dark on the 29th.

We met for inflatable boat assembly and training on the evening of July 27 in Niagara-on-the-Lake. Two brand new red 14 foot Mercury inflatables were assembled from their boxes. The motors were borrowed from crew: 2 x 15hp and one 9.9, all 2 stroke. We discussed having at least 4 tanks of premixed fuel with compatible fixtures. Safety equipment was new and in order. The 68 foot diesel and 33 foot cigar boat were already docked and ready. Four drivers practiced, mainly in the one meter waves of the Niagara sandbar. We determined the course had to be set 150m from shore to avoid the unusually high waves. Duties and positions for the morning start were reviewed with crew.

Jay entered the water at 10:10 a.m., wearing a skimpy Speedo racing suit, a bit of Vaseline and thin lycra cap. He stroked at 60 spm the first hour and then settled into a rate in the 50's.

The Niagara's current and its temperature 74-76°F was felt out to the 5 hour mark. The temperature was generally around 71°F except colder at the end. The wind blew from the west to northwest most of the swim, generally in the vicinity of 5-10 knots. The first afternoon the wind was light from the west with waves less than ½ foot. Overnight it increased to 5 knots with one foot rollers.

The second day, the wind picked up from the NW with waves 1-2 feet. Jay appeared to be keeping a fairly steady 1 km per hour against this wind; however, between 9 a.m. and 2:50, he was unable to follow the NNW heading into Marilyn Bell Park, bearing instead almost due north for Vicki Keith Point of the Leslie St. Spit. This was quite striking as the lead boat was pointing towards Oakville and the flotilla was floating in a straight line for the spit. The forecast did not call for a wind change until later in the evening, so we presented the facts to Jay and he agreed with the destination change to VK Point. We also hoped to avoid a second night by shortening the swim. However, shortly after this we appeared to be in the Humber River current, flowing SE, at its worst from 5-7 km out from VK Point. According to the handheld GPS in the Zodiac, he was pushed backwards (south) by the current twice. From 15:40 to 17:40 he progressed only 0.36 km closer to Toronto. Fortunately he broke through it by 18:10 hours, but only made slow (0.3 km per hour) straight line progress (see discrepancy in distance from NOTL and distance swum in each leg readings) for another 3 hours before he could get back on pace and course. During these 3 hours the wind was actually from the SE, neutralizing the current for the boats. By this point, a NNW course towards VK Point was required because of the easterly drift. Fortunately, the wind and waves had died down, but it was dark. We debated going into a second night. Jay's stroke still appeared reasonable, the weather was excellent and he was now making progress. There were only 4 km (2.5 miles) left.

Details of the last 3 km are sketchy as the Swim Master got in the water at 22:07 in order to observe the swimmer's condition closely and for lifesaving purposes. He swam steadily, at a close to 1 km per hour pace until after 23:00. For the next 2 hours he began having periods where he would slow noticeably, but he would respond to specific coaching instructions and pick up his stroke. The last 2 hours he started slurring his speech and his stroke fell apart to the point where his feet were low and his arms did not completely clear the surface on the recovery (churning through the water). He, however, continued to respond to cheerleading and coaching instructions. He was able to focus on the glow-stick in the pacer's cap and follow her to the finish. He seemed lucid until the very end because he argued about distance report discrepancies and was able to appreciate how close he was at 200m. At the very end he seemed confused about where to touch and whether he could stand. He did see the 20-30 people on shore who had lit up the shoreline with numerous bright lights. He was transferred by Zodiac to the evacuation boat, wrapped in 3 sleeping bags and 5 hot packs at the key arterial points, and driven to meet the ambulance in Toronto harbour. His core temperature was 33.8 rectally when first taken but 32.6°C with after-drop when taken a few minutes later. He recalled the nurse's full name (Charlene Wilhelm) and was attempting to tell her a joke enroute to the dock. The family reports he warmed up quickly but was admitted to hospital due to dehydration and difficulty taking a deep breath.

In terms of safety issues, we almost ran out of Zodiac gas in appropriate fixture containers during the second afternoon and we ran out of large flashlight batteries the first night, therefore, the speed boat went in to port for 2 hours to resupply. Fortunately there was no boat traffic while the boat was gone. The walkie-talkies could not be recharged fast enough to be of use in the last 8 hours. Also, the 2 Zodiacs were left "stranded" at the end. The biggest safety issue was the second night. If Jay had to swim 400 m further he would likely have been in a life threatening condition. Even with the colder water near Toronto, he likely would not have gotten hypothermia if it were sunny. The second night would not have been possible without adequate lighting and an accomplished marathon swimmer comfortable in the dark and familiar with hypothermia swimming an arm's length from him. The biggest reason we headed into a second night was that Jay was just not fast enough to combat the elements in time: the waves that were against him most of the swim and the Humber River current. He swam a total of 49.6 km over a 45.3 km course. In retrospect, I would not have passed the trial swim. A swimmer has to have a certain minimum speed to fight the wind and currents to complete the lake in one night and 2 days. The 6 hour cut off seems fairly accurate in ensuring that speed.

This swim was partly a success due to 'above the call of duty' endurance, patience, and enthusiasm from the crew. Special mention: the navigator, John Crawford, knew the waters, currents and shoreline exceptionally well; the coach, Pam Haldane, yelled herself hoarse into the megaphone the last 4 hours with amazingly inspirational cheerleading; the 2 pacers, Karen and Eden paced a total of 16 hours between them; Peter Wong kayaked "right beside" Jay both nights and ½ of both days; and finally the manager, Christine Johnson, pulled it all together. Andra Jones, as assistant Swim Master, is knowledgeable about boating but needs another 1 or 2 swims to learn more about marathon swimming and managing crew.

Jay is an inspiration to all athletes, both disabled and able. He pushed himself further than I have ever seen a human being push themselves. He never asked to come out. He regrouped and revived his stroke countless times in the last 2 hours displaying immense courage every time.

Respectfully submitted,
Marilyn Korzekwa
August 4, 2008

The Ambition of an Aspie

Actual time	Coordinates	Distance from start (km)	Distance between legs (km)	Water temp. (°F)	Air temp. (°F)	Wind direction; speed (knots); wave height	Comments
Jul 28 10:10	43°15.471N 79°04.085W	-		76	82	W; 8-10; <0.3m	
11:10	43°16.681N 79°05.633W	3.0	3.0	76		0.3-0.5m, white caps	
12:10	43°18.158N 79°06.919W	6.3	3.3	76	82	WNW; <5; rollers	
13:10	43°19.081N 79°07.816W	8.4	2.1	73	89	No wind; Flat	
14:10	19.722N 08.692W	10.0	1.7	74			
15:10	20.663N 09.646W	12.2	2.2	73	83		
15:47						W; light	New goggles
16:10	21.451N 10.489W	14.0	1.8	73		0.1-0.2m	
17:10	22.290N 11.190W	15.8	1.8		80	W; light; 0.1m	17:35 pacer in
18:10	23.134N 11.751W	17.6	1.7				
19:10	23.776N 12.222W	18.9	1.4				
20:10							20:43 sunset; pacer out
21:10							
22:10	25.192N 13.603W	22.1	3.2	71	68		
23:10	25.439N 14.107W	22.9	0.8				

Appendix Q

Actual time	Coordinates	Distance from start (km)	Distance between legs (km)	Water temp. (°F)	Air temp. (°F)	Wind direction; speed (knots); wave height	Comments
Jul 29 00:10	25.702N 14.580N	23.6	0.8				
01:10	25.781N 14.951W	24.1	0.5			W to NW; 5; 0.3 m rollers	
02:10	26.449N 15.785W	25.7	1.7		66		
03:10	26.893N 16.313W	26.8	1.1	68	64		
04:10	27.303N 17.194W	28.1	1.4				Quadriceps cramps
05:10	43° 27.517N 79°17.535W	28.7	0.6				6:04 sunrise
06:10	27.799N 17.944W	29.5	0.8	68	64		
07:10	28.284N 18.589W	30.7	1.3				Pacers on & off all day
08:10					69		
09:10	29.361N 19.431W	33.0	2.3				Pushed east by west wind
10:10	29.954N 19.584W	34.0	1.1				Facing west, tracking for V. Keith Pt (VKP)
11:10				70	73		
12:10						W; 5-10; 0.3-0.6m	
13:10	32.021N 19.897W	37.3	3.9	71	82		
14:10	32.631N 19.861W	38.2	1.1				

315

The Ambition of an Aspie

Actual time	Coordinates	Distance from start (km)	Distance between legs (km)	Water temp. (°F)	Air temp. (°F)	Wind direction; speed (knots); wave height	Comments
14:55							5.5 hours tracking north for VKP, Destination changed
15:10							
15:40	33.119N 19.530W	38.7	1.0			SW; 5-10;	
0.6m	Easterly current						
6:10	33.673N 19.497W	39.6	1.0	71	76	S-SW; 0.6m	
17:10	33.683N 19.516W	39.6	0.03				Northeasterly current
17:40	33.306N 19.605W	39.1	-0.7			SSE; <5; 0.3m	Pushed back by current
18:10	34.157N 19.228W	40.2	1.7	71	71		
18:40						SE; <5; 0.1-0.2m	Tracking NE, off course
19:20	34.498N 18.909W	40.5	0.7				
20:10	34.751N 18.764W	40.8	0.5				20:43 sunset
21:10	35.049N 18.894W	41.4	0.6	71		Almost flat; gentle rollers	Out of current, back on course
22:10		About 42.2					Marilyn paces
23:10							

Appendix Q

Actual time	Coordinates	Distance from start (km)	Distance between legs (km)	Water temp. (°F)	Air temp. (°F)	Wind direction; speed (knots); wave height	Comments
Jul 30 00:10		About 43.8		Spots 57-65			Stops frequently
01:10				"			Stroke failing; slurred speech
02:10				"			
03:11	43°36.5N; 79°20.4W (estimate)	45.3					

317

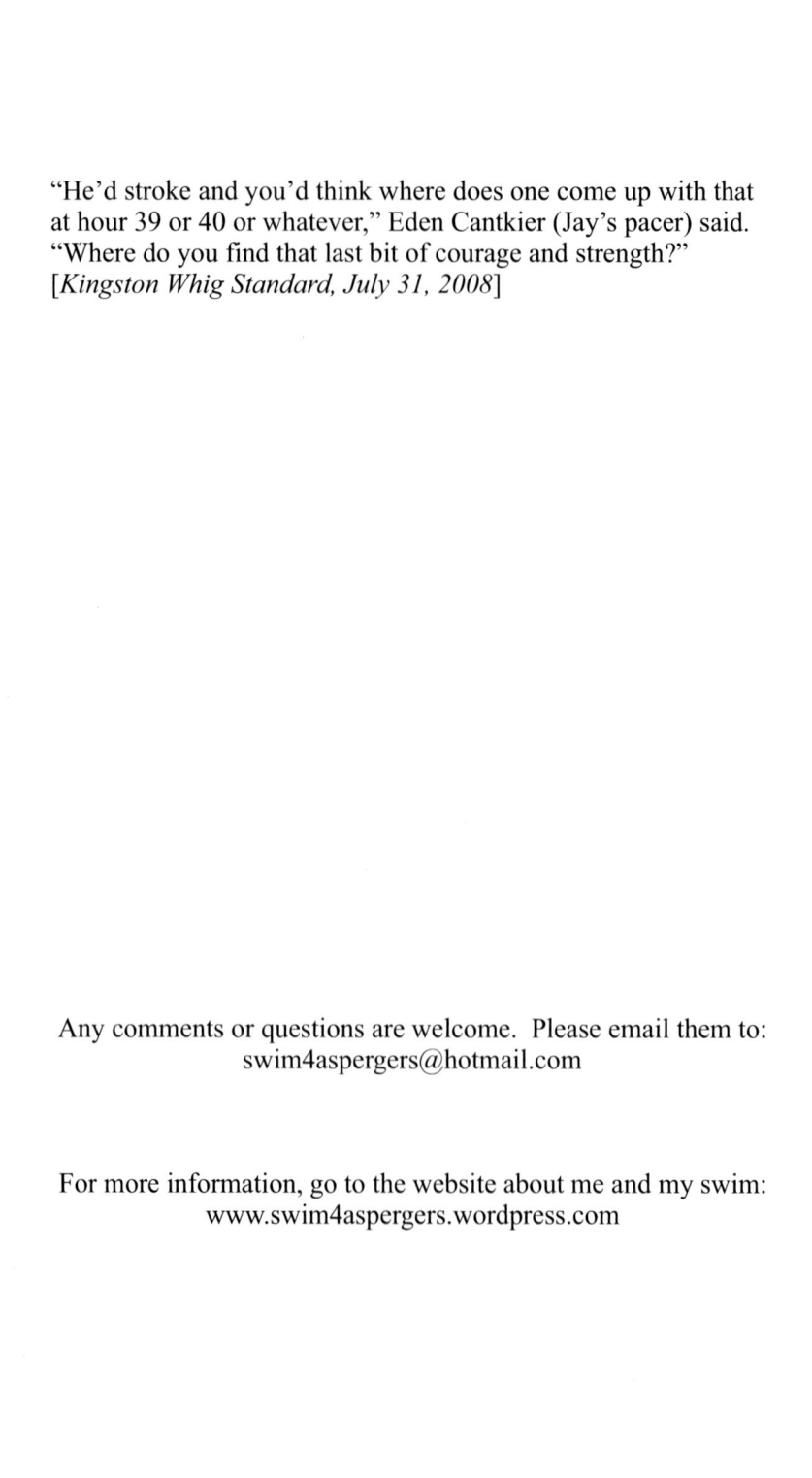

"He'd stroke and you'd think where does one come up with that at hour 39 or 40 or whatever," Eden Cantkier (Jay's pacer) said. "Where do you find that last bit of courage and strength?"
[*Kingston Whig Standard, July 31, 2008*]

Any comments or questions are welcome. Please email them to:
swim4aspergers@hotmail.com

For more information, go to the website about me and my swim:
www.swim4aspergers.wordpress.com